Make It Profitable!

Make It Profitable!

How to Make Your Art, Craft, Design, Writing, or Publishing Business More Efficient, More Satisfying, and MORE PROFITABLE

Barbara Brabec

M. Evans and Company, Inc.

New York

M. Evans and Company, Inc.
216 East 49th Street
New York, New York 10017

Library of Congress Cataloging-in-Publication Data

Brabec, Barbara.
    Make it profitable! : how to make your art, craft, design, writing, or
publishing business more efficient, more satisfying, and more profitable / by Barbara Brabec
        p.   cm.
    ISBN 0-87131-902-0 — ISBN 0-87131-903-9 (trade paper)
    1. Home-based businesses—United States—Management. I. Title.

HD2336.U5 B73 2000
658.02'2—dc21   99-049966

Book design by Rik Lain Schell

Printed in the United States of America

9 8 7 6 5 4 3 2 1

Special Acknowledgments

This book is dedicated to the eighty professionals in the art/crafts community, listed at the end of Chapter One, whose insightful comments and business tips brighten every page of this book.

I am deeply indebted to each of them for the time they gave me over a period of five months, particularly because I know that some of them work as many as eighty hours a week on their individual businesses. That they would take the time to answer my probing questions when they were so busy—and often exhausted from overwork—is proof of how much they care about their fellow artisans. So often they would say, "I hope this information will help someone else."

My name is on this book as the author but, in truth, I've written less than half of it. The rest was written by a wonderful group of men and women who now seem like family to me. All I did was figure out how to present the incredible wealth of information and advice they so generously shared with me. Thank you, everyone!

Contents

||||||||||||||||||||||||||||||||||||||||||||||||||||

Chapter One

Technology
to the Rescue

||||||||||||||||||||||||||||||||||||||||||||||||||||

*The Internet has been both a boon and a bane to the
professional crafter, but the networking it offers is
unparalleled.*

—SUSAN GEARING, SUSIE'S CRAFTS

Back in 1994, crafts event publisher Bill Ronay showed keen
insight when he predicted that the arts and crafts industries
would experience a renaissance and surge of growth as a
direct result of the electronic Information Highway. "The marketing
of individual events, products, and services will take on an entirely
new dimension and concept," he said. How right he was!

Unlike my earlier books, this one places heavy emphasis on the
topic of computer technology and how creative people are using it to
save time, cut costs, improve efficiency, and increase profits in a business at home. If you are not yet using a computer in your home-
based business, this book will encourage and guide you into an exciting new world by showing you how you might use computer technology to make more money (and real profit) from your business.

Success in business isn't entirely dependent on having and efficiently using a computer, of course. More often than not, success is
dependent on picking the right kind of product or service for the
times and knowing how to price it and where to sell it. Your ability
to wear a dozen different business hats and juggle a host of family
and business responsibilities has much to do with the degree of
success you can achieve in a business based at home. Success or
failure may also depend on your attitude and whether you have a
real need for money or not.

Some businesses fail because their owners are poor time or
money managers or are simply too disorganized to get their work

done efficiently. Sometimes, a business fails to make a good profit because its owner is reluctant to make changes. If you are already established in business, this book will awaken you to the need to constantly reanalyze your business in light of our quickly-changing times, technology, and marketplace. In so doing, you are apt to find many areas where some part of your business either needs to be tweaked to perfection or completely changed to maximize both sales and profits.

HOW THIS BOOK WAS WRITTEN

For the record, I hate to make changes as much as anyone. The biggest problem I—and perhaps you, too—have with technology is that it gives us no choices. We simply have to accept all the new stuff or else. I am uniquely qualified to write this book because in my industry (home-based businesses), I have always been one of the last to accept the newest technology. Most of my competitors were using computers five years before I was, and most were on the Internet a couple of years before I fully grasped its importance to my life and work. So I completely understand those of you who may feel somewhat like the little kid who stomps his foot and says, "I don't *want* to go to school!" I, too have stomped my foot and moaned, "I don't *want* to learn this stuff; I don't *need* to learn this stuff; I'm *too old* to learn this stuff!" I will never have the time or inclination to get deeply involved in some of the high-tech computer stuff I've written about in this book, but I have been computer literate for many years and continue to learn more each day.

I wrote my first two books on an electric typewriter and, looking back, I wonder now how I ever did it. My next two books (self-published) were written on one of the early mid-eighties computers. Compared to my electric typewriter, that simple computer was a miracle to me . . . until I bought a 486 machine that gave me more power than I would ever need for writing and keeping my mailing lists up-to-date. State-of-the-art only a short while ago, my beloved 486 is now viewed as a dinosaur alongside the new Pentiums with their Windows environment, but it is perfect for my simple needs as a writer.

Although I have always been slow to grasp the latest technology, each time I have forced myself to accept something new, it has been a blessing to me. Take the fax machine, for example. Whereas for earlier books I gathered information mostly by mail or telephone, I couldn't have written recent books so quickly without a fax machine to communicate with my editors, publishers, and book contributors. For this book, my method of working has changed once again. Only a short while ago, I vowed I would never have an e-mail address or be on the Internet. But now that I've had a Web site since mid-'98 and have discovered the advantages of e-mail communication, I'm hooked.

To gather all the enticing and helpful information contained in this book, I first set up a large e-mail database of art/crafts professionals in my home-business network. Then, periodically, I would send them probing questions and wait for their interesting feedback. It was like having regular business meetings with a wonderful group of successful people who, collectively, have more than 1,200 years of experience as business owners. (The majority of them have been in business for ten to twenty years.)

Make It Profitable! is, thus, the first book of its kind in the crafts or home-business community—a printed collection of five months' worth of e-mail messages from eighty art/crafts professionals who gave me invaluable input on the various topics covered in this book. Added to their great tips, business observations, and marketing insight, you'll find my own tips and advice gained from nearly thirty years of experience as a home-based writer, speaker, publisher, and book seller.

To make the reading fun, some of the book's information is shared in the form of unique Networking Sessions. As you "sit in" on these very personal and revealing conversations—edited to make it seem that all the individuals were in my living room discussing this or that topic—you'll feel like you're right there with them. Other information is presented in the form of tips lists, sidebars, and "reminder checklists." Illustrations and photographs enliven the book.

Because so many people are quoted throughout this book and lengthy descriptions of who they are and what they do couldn't be included with every quote, I have included a complete list of all book contributors at the end of this chapter. Here, you'll find each individual's name and business name, along with their Web site address if they have one. Any time you want to know more about a particular person who is "speaking" in the book, you can flip back to this section.

TIPS FOR BEGINNERS IN BUSINESS

Although business beginners will certainly benefit from this book, it is primarily directed to individuals already in business who are actively striving to increase both sales and profits. Designed as a companion to my other three business books for creative people (*Handmade for Profit, The Crafts Business Answer Book,* and *Creative Cash*), this book does assume some business knowledge on the part of the reader. If you're a complete beginner who needs general business start-up information or answers to questions about taxes, laws, regulations, banking, insurance, copyrights, etc., check your library or bookstore for some of the home-business books listed as follows. Meanwhile, I offer these general "Brabec Rules" for building a successful business at home:

▸ First and foremost, get the cooperation of your family and—in particular your spouse. There is enough stress created by a home-based business without the added stress of family problems. If you have children, plan to get them involved in the business, and reward them accordingly with payment. (Talk to your accountant about the tax advantages related to such business expenses.)

▸ Establish a special area in your home for the operation of the business. This is important not only from the standpoint of tax deductions related to your workplace, but essential for the smooth operation of family life around the business. There will always be something more to do on the business, but it helps to be able to close the door on it when you need to escape. (See Chapter Eight.)

➤ Contact the appropriate local, state, and federal authorities to make sure you're on safe ground where your home-based business is concerned. If you plan to break a law, be prepared to pay the penalty if you're caught. Be especially careful if/when you hire outside help. (See Chapter Ten.)

➤ When making plans, always build in extra time (from 20 to 50 percent more) when figuring completion dates on any job or project. In a home-based business, everything takes longer than anticipated, simply because it's more difficult to control interruptions related to home and family. (See Chapter Five.)

➤ Accept the fact that you will always have the feeling there isn't time enough for everything. This comes with the territory when you work at home. So make a list of all the things you're willing to give up to get extra time for your business, like dinner parties, vacations, and sleep. Plan how you're going to tell family, friends, and neighbors that you may have to limit future get-togethers and surprise drop-in visits. (See Chapter Thirteen.)

➤ Plan where you'll obtain extra cash for your business when you need it in a hurry because no bank will loan money to a fledgling home-based business. Some people borrow from savings, life insurance, or family members, while others simply fall back on cash advances against personal credit cards. But be careful; this can be a dangerous financial pitfall if you are not absolutely certain you'll be able to repay it from business profits. If you borrow heavily to launch a business, you risk losing it all if the business fails. It is far better to start slowly and build your business one small step at a time, borrowing only when you find yourself in a temporary cash-flow crunch. (See Chapter Five.)

➤ Keep careful records, making sure your business income and expenses are never mixed with personal income and expenses. This means having a separate checking account for your business and appropriate books that will satisfy the IRS. (If you fail to do this, the IRS may disallow your home-business deductions, deeming your endeavor a hobby instead of a legitimate business.)

▸▸ Take careful stock of your insurance situation. Home-based businesses are not covered under regular homeowner's or renter's policies. You'll need a special rider or insurance policy to protect business assets. Depending on the nature of your business and its products or services, you may need personal or product liability insurance as well. Several organizations now offer affordable comprehensive insurance plans for home-business owners that include liability insurance.

▸▸ Pay particular attention to your professional image. Home-business owners who find resistance from buyers because they're home-based probably need better printed materials, a more appropriate business name, or more professional marketing strategies. If you have a professional business image, no one will care where your office is located. (See Chapter Thirteen.)

▸▸ Build a support network as soon as possible. Many who work at home suffer from feelings of isolation, and the best medicine for that kind of loneliness is networking with other business owners—in person, by phone, or through e-mail. One of the best things going on the Internet are the many special-interest discussion groups and chat rooms where folks can exchange information and ideas relative to their field. (See Chapter Seven.)

RECOMMENDED CRAFT BUSINESS BOOKS

Crafting as a Business (2nd ed.), Wendy Rosen (The Rosen Group).
Crafting for Dollars, Sylvia Landman (Prima).
The Crafts Business Answer Book, Barbara Brabec (M. Evans).
Creative Cash, 6th ed., Barbara Brabec (Prima).
Handmade for Profit, Barbara Brabec (M. Evans).
Homemade Money, (6 ed., rev.,) Barbara Brabec (Betterway Books).
How to Survive & Prosper as an Artist, Caroll Michels (Owl Books).

DIRECTORY OF BOOK CONTRIBUTORS

The following individuals have contributed to this book. As busy professionals, they do not have time to answer questions from art/crafts beginners, but if you wish to contact anyone mentioned in the book for *business purposes* (*i.e.*, networking, ordering products, etc.) first look for their Web site on the Internet if an address is included with their name. Also use a search engine to locate other businesses listed here, since they may set up Web sites after this book is published.

▸▸ **Charlene Anderson-Shea,** *Anderson-Shea, Inc.*, fiber artist
  ⌐ http://www.andersonshea.com
▸▸ **Derek Andrews,** *Sunrise Woodcrafts*, woodturner
  ⌐ http://www.sunrisewoodcrafts.ns.ca
▸▸ **Steve Appel,** *Appel's Bolt People*, craftsman
  ⌐ http://www.boltpeople.com
▸▸ **Barbara Arena,** *National Craft Association*, Managing Director
  ⌐ http://www.craftassoc.com
▸▸ **Rochelle Beach,** *Cinna-Minnies Collectibles*, professional crafter
▸▸ **Ginger Kean Berk,** designer
▸▸ **Steve and Jean Belknap,** *The Country Spirit*, professional crafter
▸▸ **Joyce Birchler,** *A Glass Act*, glass artisan
  ⌐ http://www.aglassact.com
▸▸ **Elizabeth Bishop,** *Seams Sew Creative Patterns*, fiber artist and designer
▸▸ **Barbara Brabec,** *Barbara Brabec Productions*, author and columnist
  ⌐ http://www.BarbaraBrabec.com
▸▸ **Howard and Ruthann Broman,** *Real Rose Jewelry*, production artisans
  ⌐ http://www.rosejewelry.com
▸▸ **Sue Brown,** *Wood Cellar Graphics*, rubber stamp designer
  ⌐ http://www.woodcellargraphics.com
▸▸ **Carol Carlson,** *Kimmeric Studio*, artist
  ⌐ http://www.kimmericstudio.com

▸▸ **Maureen and Dan Carlson,** *Wee Folk Creations,* polymer clay artist and designer
  ⌂ http://www.weefolk.com

▸▸ **Renee Chase,** *Crafter.Com,* Webmaster
  ⌂ http://www.crafter.com

▸▸ **Bobbi Chukran,** *Wildest Dreams Designs,* artist, freelance writer, pattern designer
  ⌂ http://www.limestoneledge.com

▸▸ **Betty Chypre,** *Choices for Craftsmen and Artists,* periodical publisher and metalsmith
  ⌂ http://www.choices.cc and www.smartfrogs.com

▸▸ **Kathy Cisneros,** *The Bottle Cap Lady,* author, songwriter, columnist
  ⌂ http://www.rainfall.com/caplady

▸▸ **Sue Cloutman,** *The Sewing Room,* toy manufacturer
  ⌂ http://www.colormecreations.com

▸▸ **Karen Combs,** quilt seminar presenter and author
  ⌂ http://www.karencombs.com

▸▸ **Eleena Danielson,** *E&S Creations and Cranberry Junction,* doll pattern designer
  ⌂ http://www.cranberryjunction.com

▸▸ **Cheryl Eaton,** *Cheryl Eaton Art & Design,* artist
  ⌂ E-Mail: cheryleaton@mindframe.com

▸▸ **Dodie Eisenhauer,** *Village Designs,* designer/gift manufacturer
  ⌂ http://www.villagedesigns.com

▸▸ **Pat Endicott,** *House of Threads & Wood, Inc.,* crafts producer
  ⌂ http://www.houseofthreadsandwood.com

▸▸ **Dan Engle,** *Arts 'n Crafts ShowGuide,* Magazine publisher
  ⌂ http://www.acnshowguide.com

▸▸ **Jacquelyn Fox,** *Waxing Moon Designs,* needlework designer

▸▸ **Jana Gallagher,** *Jana's Craft Connection,* professional crafter and instructor
  ⌂ http://www.wyomingcompanion.com/janacraft

▸▸ **Susan Gearing,** *Susie's Crafts,* production artisan

▸▸ **Bob & Carol Gerdts,** *Bob & Carol's Egg-Art, Ltd.,* artisans
  ⌂ http://www.egg-art.com

» **Morna McEver Golletz,** *The Professional Quilter,* publisher and quilter
  ✒ http://www.professionalquilter.com
» **Chris Gustin,** *Homestead Handweaving Studio,* weaver and shop owner
  ✒ http://www.homesteadweaver.com
» **Tabitha Haggie,** *Bunny Hutch Handcrafts,* professional crafter
» **Joann Haglund,** *Painted Babies Originals,* American tole artist
  ✒ http://www.angelfire.com/biz2/TOLEART
» **Kate Harper,** *Kate Harper Designs,* greeting card designer/publisher
» **Eileen Heifner,** *Create-an-Heirloom Doll Kit Co.,* doll artist and designer
  ✒ http://www.createanheirloom.com
» **LaVerne Herren,** *Arts & Crafts Show Business,* newsletter publisher and artist
  ✒ http://www.jacksonville.net/~artcraft
» **Tori Hoggard,** *Harmony Artworks,* artist and teacher
  ✒ http://www.freeyellow.com/members6/harmony88/index.html
» **Geoffrey Harris,** *Harris Collectibles,* artist
» **Myra Hopkins,** *Brush & Needle,* doll pattern designer
  ✒ http://www.crafter.com/syrupbottledolls
» **Robert Houghtaling,** *Sculpture and Design,* sculptor and designer
  ✒ http://www.silcom.com/~rhought and www.frogart.com
» **Linda Beattie Inlow,** *Hidden Meadows,* publisher, soapmaker
  ✒ http://www.galaxymail.com/books/kalama
» **Bobbie Irwin,** Writer, weaver and teacher
» **Nancy Jaekel,** *Anything Doughs LLC,* dough artist
  ✒ http://www.anythingdoughs.com
  ✒ http://www.candlecupboard.com
» **Jacqueline Janes,** *Arizona Bead Co. and Eggplant,* polymer clay artist and bead business owner
  ✒ http://www.arizonabeadcompany.com
» **Sue Johnson,** *Gramma's Graphics, Inc.,* author, crafts business owner
  ✒ http://www.frontiernet.net/~bubblink/donnelly
  ✒ http://www.grandloving.com

- **Carol Krob,** *Carol's Creations,* needlework designer
- **Patricia Kutza,** *Whatknots,* neckwear and home decorative accessories designer/writer
  - http://www.geocities.com/fashionAvenue/2318
- **Phillippa K. Lack,** *Custom Couture,* silk artist
  - http://www.silkbyphil.com
- **Sylvia Landman,** *Sylvia's Studio,* author, teacher, and Certified Craft Designer
  - http://www.crl.com/~studio
- **Annie Lang,** *Annie Things Possible,* designer and author
  - http://www.easlpublications.com
- **Susie Little,** *So Susie Spins,* spinner
  - http://sosusiespins.8m.com
- **Karen Lyons,** K.J. Lyons Design Studio, artist and designer
- **Shirley MacNulty,** *Bay Country Boutique,* knitwear designer and newsletter publisher
  - http://www.craftassoc.com/knitting.html
- **Chris Maher,** *Selling Your Art Online,* artist and Webmaster
  - http://www.1x.com/advisor
- **Kim Marie,** *Kim Marie Fine Pottery,* potter
  - http://www.kimmariefinepottery.com
- **Bill Mason,** *Mystic Merchant,* contemporary metaphysical jewelry artist
  - http://www.MysticMerchant.com
- **Jan McClellan,** *Heirloom Jewelry,* jewelry designer
  - http://www.designjewel.com
- **Anita Means,** *Cottage Crafts,* craft show promoter
  - http://www.monmouth.com/~cottagecraft
- **Mary Mulari,** *Mary's Productions,* author, teacher, and designer
  - http://www.marymulari.com
- **Liz Murad,** *Calligraphy, Ink,* calligrapher and artist
  - http://www.inkybiz.com
- **Chris Noah-Cooper,** *Paperways,* printmaker
- **Michael Noyes,** *Calligraphy by Michael Noyes,* calligrapher
  - http://www. michaelnoyes.com
- **Rita O'Hara,** *Stonewares,* designer and gift producer

▸ **Deb Otto,** *Henri's,* folk artist
  ⌖ http://www.handofhannah.com
▸ **Emily Pearlman,** *Pottery,* potter
  ⌖ http://www.humanarts.com/pearlman
▸ **Leila Peltosaari,** *Tikka Books,* book publisher
  ⌖ http://www.tikkabooks.qc.ca
▸ **Gail Platts,** *InCalico,* cloth doll designer
  ⌖ http://www.incalico.com
▸ **Marsha Reed,** *Craftmaster News,* periodical publisher
  ⌖ http://www.craftmasternews.com
▸ **Joyce Roark,** *Loving Thoughts,* jewelry designer and instructor
▸ **Bill and Camille Ronay,** *A Step Ahead, Ltd., Publishers,*
  industry researchers/consultants
  ⌖ http://www.events2000.com
▸ **John Schulte,** *National Mail Order Association,* Chairman
  ⌖ http://www.nmoa.org
▸ **Lynn Smythe,** *Dolphin Crafts,* bead and fiber artist
  ⌖ http://members.aol.com/dlphcrft/index.htm
▸ **Pamela Spinazzola,** *Pamela's Studio One,* artist
▸ **Rita Stone-Conwell,** *Crafts Remembered,* newsletter publisher and crafter
  ⌖ http://www.taconic.net/crn
▸ **Meg Sullivan,** *Aunt Meg Creations,* needlework business owner and crafter
  ⌖ http://www.auntmegcreations.com
▸ **Vicky Stozich,** *Personal Designs,* pattern designer
  ⌖ http://members.aol.com/VStozich
▸ **Michelle Temares,** *Product Development and Design,* freelance artist
▸ **Wendy Van Camp,** *IndigoSkye Bead Fashions,* bead jewelry artist and videographer
  ⌖ http://www.indigoskyebead.com
▸ **Kathy Wirth,** *Kathy Wirth Design Services,* freelance crafts designer
▸ **Susan Young,** *Peach Kitty Studio,* designer, artist, and author
  ⌖ http://www.craftmallweb.com/peachkitty

Chapter Two

Getting a Handle on Profit

|||||||||||||||||||||||||||||||||||||||||||||||||||||

How can you ensure profit from your popular crafts? Simply receive more than you spend. I know it sounds too simple, but it's the first rule of business. Since profit is the difference between what you receive and what you spend, increasing sales or decreasing expenses increases profits.

—DAN RAMSEY, *The Crafter's Guide to Pricing Your Work*

T here is a big difference between a business that makes "good money" and one that generates a true *profit* for all the time and effort expended. Almost anyone can start a business at home today and make at least *some* money, but on the whole, few artists and craftspeople who are currently selling what they make can live on their earnings.

While I realize that not everyone wants or needs to earn a living from their creative activity, everyone who gets into this kind of business certainly hopes to make a profit. But this is always harder to do than first imagined because profits are eaten up in so many different ways. Profit is most commonly lost when a business is being poorly managed. It diminishes when sales volume drops due to ineffective marketing. Sometimes, selling opportunities disappear if one does not stay up on the latest technology—the Internet being a perfect example. Failure to set selling prices high enough to cover all costs of producing goods is the biggest profit-eater of all. Or, as Bill Mason of Mystic Merchant puts it, "Profit is the value over and above the actual cost of the item and the expense to inventory and sell it. This is the territory where I like to be. It's a challenge to find this fabled land and stay there . . . but worth it."

Profit (or loss thereof) is also related to such things as:

Length of Time in Business. Freelance crafts designer Kathy Wirth says her business is more profitable now than in recent years. "I attribute some of this to having finally attained a level of recognition with editors. It takes a few years to establish oneself in this business. It was surprising to me that my profits were up last year because the industry, especially needlework, is so soft. Historically, when the economy is good, the craft industry is down. However, people tend to place a higher value on handcrafted items in the face of increased reliance on technology."

Market Conditions/Consumer Buying Habits. "My business is much more profitable than it was in the past, with a 17-percent increase in profits last year," says needlework crafter Meg Sullivan. "About 65 to 70 percent of our products are baby and children's handcrafted gifts (cross-stitch, knit, crochet, and sewn items). Thank goodness, people still have babies. They just don't go out of style."

Conversely, Dodie Eisenhauer, a manufacturer/wholesaler of handmade gift items, is seeing sales-slump problems as she continues to compete with imports. "Everything from American quilts to all sorts of American style crafts are being made for a lot less in other countries," she notes. "We continue to show at the national markets and hope for the best."

Business Diversification or Changes in Marketing Strategies. "My business doubled in the past year," says weaver and shop owner Chris Gustin. "And about 90 percent of the increase was due to out-of-state sales from the Internet, specifically eBay auctions and residual business."

Fiber artist Charlene Anderson-Shea also reported an increase in profits. "My business became more profitable when I moved out of retail sales to concentrate on writing and teaching, both of which have few out-of-pocket expenses."

Many long-established business owners who earn a living from their work see the importance of making changes. As author,teacher, designer Mary Mulari puts it, "I now earn my living from book sales, royalties, and teaching, but my industry is changing. I see my income level maintaining for at least a couple more years, but I don't see my income growing without some kind of business or product diversification."

NETWORKING SESSION # 1: IT'S ALL ABOUT CHOICE

The primary goal of this book is to help established business owners figure out how to increase both sales and profits to the point where they could live on those earnings if they had to. And *choice* is a key word here. Some individuals haven't yet figured out how to earn a living wage, while others know how but choose not to.

In this regard, writers and craftspeople have much in common. Only a handful of all the freelance writers today can actually live on

Defining "Profit"

"Profit" is a good work for you to define as you develop your mindset for success. It is not always synonymous with cash. New businesses can lose money for several years in a row and yet still be extremely profitable to their owners. For instance, a profitable year might mean valuable business contacts, acquired knowledge and experience, a new understanding of your strengths and weaknesses, or the discovery of a new marketing channel that will pay off big the following year. It can also mean you have made money, but you put it into a retirement plan or simply reinvested every dime into the business, perhaps in the form of equipment, larger inventories, new employees, a computer, and so on.

Even a failed sideline venture can be profitable if it points the way to a better idea that will work, or if it reveals something important in your character that encourages you to go forth in a new direction. Again, failure has its redeeming qualities, and you will always learn something from it.

Excerpted from the revised fifth edition of Homemade Money— How to Select, Start, Manage, Market and Multiply the Profits of a Business at Home, Barbara Brabec (Betterway Books).

their earnings from writing and I'm grateful to be one of them. But if I didn't have to earn a living, I'd be working on the story of my life, my first novel, or a book about how my husband Harry and I learned to communicate with our dog. Some day, maybe.

One of the first things I learned as a beginning writer was that I had to write for my market and not merely write about things that pleased me. Likewise, artists and craftspeople who create what they want to make—with little regard for what people want to buy—may have a tough time living on their earnings. But for many creative people today, having the freedom to be able to create and sell products they love to make is what a crafts business is all about. As the following discussion proves, some things are simply more important than money. All of the individuals quoted earn supplemental income at present, but some could make a living at their work if they chose to. (My questions and comments are in boldface type.)

Are you earning enough from your business to live on?

Chris Noah (Paperways): "I work full-time, but my income must be considered supplemental. Nevertheless, it has made a significant difference to our family lifestyle."

Wendy Van Camp (IndigoSkye Bead Fashions) "Same here. I work full-time, but I'm not rich by any stretch. Still, I make enough to pay all my bills and have a little extra income."

Derek Andrews (Sunrise Woodcrafts): "At present, income is minimal. It increases each year, but I don't see myself getting rich without some changes."

Karen Combs (quilt seminar presenter and author): "I would find it difficult to live off my income if I was the sole support of my family; however, it is a very nice second income, and I see it increasing in the future as I write more books."

Charlene Anderson-Shea (Anderson-Shea, Inc.): "I am fortunate to be married to a patron of the arts who can support us both, so I travel a lot and am abroad two or three months a year. My income is supplemental, but if I really had to, I think I could make a living at this."

Charlene has just hit the matter on the head. "If I really had to" are key words. People who do not *have to* earn a living from their work have an entirely different attitude about their business than those who must "bring home the bacon." But knowing you *could* do this if it were necessary is like having money in the bank, isn't it?

Sue Johnson (Gramma's Graphics, Inc.): "That's right. I'm not earning enough to support our family to continue to live as we now do, but if I were single I could live on what I make. And that's a comforting thought as our kids become independent and Rick and I grow older."

Jan McClellan (Heirloom Jewelry): "I could not live on what I am netting from my business, but if I had to, I would have to do business in a more careful way, economizing more on my supplies and making more widgets instead of my one-of-a-kind pieces. Since I do have other income, it frees me to do what I want and I realize I am very fortunate in that way. I don't enjoy making widgets—I love making unique pieces. I love being able to buy interesting stones when I find them, even if I have an oversupply already."

Susan Gearing (Susie's Crafts): "Whether you work part-time or full-time depends on your goals. My goal is to provide my household with a good part-time supplemental income. If I wanted to turn this into full-time income, I could do it, but I would then have the problems of all small business persons—having to work around the clock to do it."

It is nice to have choices, isn't it?

Gail Platts (InCalico): "You bet! Being an artisan is a way of life for me. I feel that it has chosen me perhaps more than I have chosen it. You are right when you say it takes a lot of hard work and focus to bring it from a money-making hobby to an income-earning job. I make enough to support myself, but not my three kids and two dogs. It would be a different lifestyle than it is now with my husband's income. Being a full-time artisan may mean less money than an 8-to-5 job, but it's what I want to do, and I've adjusted my lifestyle to fit the income it brings me."

Jan McClellan: "One advantage of being over sixty is that I can make choices. My jewelry income pays for my car, for new tools, more stones, and it supports several charities—plus my kids and grandkids sometimes (charity begins at home)."

Nancy Jaekel (Anything Doughs LLC): "In looking back, I see that I could have done things differently, but one of the reasons I started doing what I do was to be able to stay home and raise our family and still bring in an income. If I had the information back then that I have today, I could have started out making more money right away, but that would have defeated my goal to be a stay-at-home mom."

Obviously, money is not the only consideration in deciding whether to keep one's business part-time.

Vicky Stozich (Personal Designs): "Right! My profit provides a supplemental income. However, some of the benefits of my business are worth more than money. I work when I want to. I have two children at home, and I'm here when they get on and off the bus. They are very involved in school activities and sports, and I'm happy I'm free to take them to practices, games and such. I used to work full time outside the home, so I have dealt with baby sitters and daycare centers. With all the expenses related to working outside the home, my full time income wasn't that much more than I'm making now, but now I have the freedom I didn't have before. Believe me, that's worth a lot."

Gail Platts: "At one point, I thought about taking a 'real job' to make up for the income I lost by moving across the country and losing my retail shows, but I really didn't want to be employed outside. I'm home for my kids, can volunteer at school, and have control over my life and with what I do each day. Employers would expect me to work every day during the hours they say—expect me to work full days in the summer! And they're not too keen about me showing up to work in my pajamas. The important aspect of being successful is to view the business as a business and work toward its success every day."

Who is striving to increase income to the point where it will provide a living, and how do you plan to do this?

Chris Gustin (Homestead Handweaving Studio): "Last year I worked full-time at a newspaper job and sold my crafts and supplies in my spare time. This year I'm not working at the paper and will be expanding my business. I expect to gross $50,000 or more in sales this year."

Robert Houghtaling (Sculpture and Design): "My wife works in the 'real world,' and we seem to each make about the same income each year. Our goal is to increase my income so she can be home working with me in the future."

Meg Sullivan (Aunt Meg Creations): "I'm between the proverbial rock and a hard place. If I could work full time on the business, it would support me. However, I'm not quite brave enough to make the leap just yet. The business does support itself, with a little profit for my partners (my parents). So while I continue to find new ways to increase sales, I continue to toil at a full-time job as well. I'm banking as much as I can and when I have six months' living expenses in the bank, I will be leaping!"

Meg offers a good example of why so many art and crafts businesses are still part-time activities. Lack of courage—the unwillingness to leap into unknown territory or make changes—is a big hurdle to get over, and this is the topic of the following chapter.

A CLOSER LOOK AT PROFIT

Because literally *anything* and *everything* can impact the profits of a small business, it's necessary to step back from time to time and take a close look at your business and ask yourself if it is truly profitable. After querying my book contributors on this question, many reported that their gross income and profits were increasing each year, but few could say that their income was commensurate with the amount of time they were spending on their business.

"My business is more profitable now than ever, but being 'more profitable' is not to say profitable enough," says Kathy Wirth. "I still do not feel I earn enough commensurate with my education, ability, and experience. This is a notoriously low-paying field. Along with many other designers, I am constantly exploring other avenues of marketing my skills. Licensing designs, hardcover books, demonstrating/teaching, and Web-marketing patterns to consumers are all possibilities I've considered. I would love to make my business yield a living wage."

Gross Income vs. Profit. Can you actually earn a living from an art or crafts business? Oh, yes! Yes, indeed. But it's not easy. Although no one has done any formal research on this topic, my contact with craftspeople over the past thirty years tells me that most of them work at their art or craft on a part-time basis, earning supplemental income as a result. (Some work full-time and still make only supplemental income.) About half the people quoted in this book, however, do earn a living from their work, which offers encouraging proof for skeptics who say it can't be done.

When I asked my book contributors whether their business was more or less profitable now than in recent years, some told me business was down last year for reasons they couldn't quite figure out. Yet others reported growth way beyond original expectations. Wherein lies the difference, I wondered.

"If you can figure that one out, you'll be a millionaire," quips cloth doll designer Gail Platts. "I think it's just market flux. The only thing predictable about this business is its unpredictability—which is why it is so hard to make a living. It's a crap shoot, not a steady

40-hour-a-week paycheck."

Tabitha Haggie, a professional crafter in business for three years, thinks long time crafters who sell at fairs may get a little stagnant, or pigeon hole themselves into too small a market. "If you tend to do the same shows year after year, you need to freshen up your booth and products each year so people don't get used to seeing the same old thing to the point where you are no longer noticed. I have a line of primitive woodcrafts, and I have a handful of items I have made for some time, but other than that, I change the items each year. I have profited tremendously from repeat business, and you can't do that by offering the same products all the time. I even hold back a few lines so I have new things to introduce each month. My clients follow me from show to show just to see what's new. I also arrange my booth a bit differently every year."

"I believe my business is becoming more profitable because I have embraced the new technology that can make any small home-based business a global company," reasons bead jewelry artist and videographer Wendy Van Camp. "All it takes is a little elbow grease and arming yourself with knowledge."

Printmaker Chris Noah says her profits for the last three years have been higher than previous years. "We reached a turning point when our special analysis of cost and profit versus volume of sales showed that I would never show much of a profit, if any, doing the paper lampshades and related papercraft items I'd been trying to market. On the other hand, our analysis of small framed pictures showed potential for a profit. The eternal, classic problem is always how to get enough pieces to justify the amount of time used in making them. Shortcuts can result in inferior art, and customers see the difference."

Earlier I mentioned the importance of setting a selling price high enough to cover all costs. Although calligrapher Michael Noyes stimulated his sales and increased his name recognition when he reduced his prices 20 percent, he ran into problems when he did his first wholesale show. "I had to adjust my prices back where they were originally to accurately reflect my costs," he said. "If I hadn't done this, I would have lost money on every order."

To summarize, business owners often increase sales and profits by (1) embracing technology; (2) regularly introducing new products to their line; (3) switching their sales focus to the most profitable items in their line; (4) exploring new markets; and (5) making price adjustments where necessary. These are by no means the only ways to increase sales and profits, however.

Hours Worked vs. Profit. To people who sell art or handmade products, profit is directly related to the amount of time they spend producing goods for sale. They logically conclude that the more hours they work, the more money they will make. To some degree this is true, but as you will learn in various chapters throughout this book, you do not necessarily have to work longer hours to increase bottom-line profits.

Few would disagree that running an art or crafts business is hard work. Creative people can relate to the old joke, "Entrepreneurs are people who are willing to work for themselves twelve hours a day to avoid working eight hours for someone else."

In the crafts industry, however, those hours sometimes extend to eighteen per day! In a survey of businesses featured in this book, I got a good picture of both the way in which creative people work and the number of hours they put in each week. I've always known that craftspople were among the hardest-working people in the home-business industry, but even I was surprised by the long hours my contributors reported. On average, the part-time business owners featured in this book work twenty-six to thirty hours a week, while those who work full-time put in at least fifty-three hours a week. In their busiest selling seasons (or when they're trying to meet a deadline), eighty to ninety hour-weeks are common.

Now think about this for a minute. There are 168 hours in a week. Theoretically, "normal" people work eight hours a day, have eight hours of leisure time, and sleep the other eight, but it doesn't work that way in the crafts community. Craftspeople either sleep less than the average person, have little or no leisure time, or both. As you sit in on the following networking session, you'll get a better idea of what it really means to run your own business at home. But remember . . . these people are working this hard by choice, not because anyone is forcing them to do so. They love their work so much that's all most of them want to do.

NETWORKING SESSION #2: HOME BUSINESS HOURS

Tell me about the hours you work.

Carol Krob (Carol's Creations): "My life and my business are so thoroughly integrated that it is difficult to estimate the exact number of hours in an average workday. Suffice it to say that I live and love the career I created for myself."

Wendy Van Camp (IndigoSkye Bead Fashions): "I work sixty-five to seventy hours a week, fifty-two weeks a year—day and night—and it feels pretty seamless to me. My work *is* my life, but I still have time to get out to the driving range and golf course on a regular basis and feel that working at home has set me totally free."

Sylvia Landman (Sylvia's Studio): "I work fifty to sixty hours a week, which doesn't count all the reading and research I do for teaching and writing, nor the time I am tired and watch TV, but I am never empty-handed as I am always making a project for a class or a column."

Betty Chypre (*Choices for Craftsmen and Artists*): "My weeks run forty to sixty hours. Not bad for a part-time business—at least that's what I intended it to be."

Jacquelyn Fox (Waxing Moon Designs): "As a mother of three, I don't work any set hours. I just grab any time I can when I can get it, usually twenty to twenty-five hours a week."

Dodie Eisenhauer (Village Designs): "I work an average of fifty to sixty hours a week. One way I get extra things done is to work after everyone goes to bed. It's peaceful and the phone doesn't ring, and I can do e-mail or the Internet then. The mornings come too quickly, however, if I do this several nights in a row."

Lynn Smythe (Dolphin Crafts): "My hours average sixty a week. I'd like to get a studio or store away from the house; that way, I could just work certain hours. Because I am home and the work is always here, I now work seven days a week."

Although some of you work "normal hours" part of the year, heavy schedules at others times of the year—such as when you're doing craft shows—may cause you to nearly double the hours you put it on business, right?

Gail Platts: "That's true. Normally I work between thirty to sixty hours a week, but sometimes during the holiday season I put in as much as eighty-four hours."

Leila Peltosaari (Tikka Books): "I may work twenty to thirty hours in a normal week, but when I'm putting together a new book, it's common for me to work up to seventy hours a week."

Jacqueline Janes (Arizona Bead Company): "I work in long stretches with long breaks. For the past six months, I've worked fifteen to eighteen hours a day. We allow ourselves small breaks when we can, like dinner out or a movie, but it always seems like crunch time around here."

Kim Marie (Kim Marie Fine Pottery): "I spend forty hours a week in the studio and twenty-five hours a week on other business-related work. If you count going to shows on weekends, I don't even want to think about the total hours I spend working."

Joann Haglund (Painted Babies Originals): "Although I work around forty-five hours a week, I lose far too much time to mismanagement and general dawdling. I work no set hours, and holidays and Sundays don't exist when I'm doing commission work or need to get inventory ready for a show."

Has anyone done a serious study of how they actually spend their time?

Joyce Roark (Loving Thoughts): "When I tried to keep a log for my own information, I found I was spending an average of ninety hours per week on my business."

Liz Murad (Calligraphy, Ink): "I've been keeping track of how I spend my time on various aspects of my business. I find that, on average, I work thirty-five to forty-five hours a week, devoting seven to ten hours a week to my art, eight to ten hours to the Internet, four hours to reading, half an hour to paperwork, and fifteen to twenty hours planning and dreaming."

Annie Lang (Annie Things Possible): "I kept careful records for a whole year and found that I worked seven days a week averaging seventy-three hours a week. My time off from business was twenty-one days (504 hours). Currently, using a day planner, I keep track of phone calls, car travel, and hours spent working on various projects. I spend much of my leisure time going through magazines, reading business or work-related books, doodling out ideas, etc., as my work is also my hobby. I bring sketchbooks, journals, and often my laptop with me on business trips so as not to waste the many hours spent waiting at the airport."

Pat Endicott (House of Threads & Wood, Inc.): "One should keep better track of hours. I thought I worked all the time, but after doing a daily journal for a month, I was surprised to see how many errands took me away for half the day."

Kathy Wirth (Kathy Wirth Design Services): "I know what you mean. I work between forty to fifty hours a week. I often feel like I work all the time, too, but in keeping track of time for awhile, I was surprised to see how many things intrude—appointments, grocery shopping, and just plain life."

How much time do you figure you lose a year, on average, to illness, vacations, personal time out, or unexpected family situations? (Few of you get sick, it seems, perhaps because you feel you can't afford to be ill.)

Karen Combs: "I don't stop working when I'm sick; I just work slower. If something unexpected comes up, I make up the time later."

Eileen Heifner (Create-an-Heirloom Doll Kit Co.): "Unless I'm sick enough to stay in bed, which doesn't happen often, I work. I am now trying to take a week or two of vacation time each year, but I can do this only because I have a plan in place that will allow me to delegate a part of my work, for a brief period, to someone I have trained in advance for that purpose."

Gail Platts: "I don't know how many hours I lose to illness or childrens' illnesses, or car breakdowns and doctor appointments, etc., but I do take four weeks' vacation with my family each year."

Kate Harper (Kate Harper Designs): "Since I love what I do, it's hard to see it as work, and I never feel like I need to get away. But I generally take two or three trips a year to visit friends. December is always dead in my business, so it's a good time to go away. If I leave for a week, the business can wait, but if I leave for a month, I need someone to run the business while I'm away."

LaVerne Herren (*Arts & Crafts Show Business*): "I love what I do so much I can't imagine doing something else for fun. Vacation consists of occasionally taking off a day and working in our very large yard when my husband is off for a holiday. With five dogs of assorted sizes and ages, we do not travel."

Joyce Birchler (A Glass Act): "We very rarely take vacations, and I usually miss only a couple of days a year to illness. I take one day off a month to visit with a great group of crafter women friends to have fun and discuss business sometimes. Vacations with my husband are when we go off to do shows together."

Wendy Van Camp: "I do go on vacations occasionally, but they are usually more of the three-day weekend variety."

Betty Chypre: "Do I lose time to vacations, you ask? Surely you jest. I haven't had a vacation for over five years."

Even when you're not actually in your office or studio, many of you are still "working," right?

Joyce Roark: "True. I take vacations, but don't lose time from my business when I do. For example, when I went to Japan, I wrote the outline for my book, sketched the projects that would be included, made contacts for a better price on the gold that I use to make the jewelry and contacts for some interesting new items (like meteorites) to use in my jewelry. When I spent a month in Belgium, I worked making Temari eggs for a store and learned to make lace to incorporate into my jewelry. I spent three weeks that year in New Zealand, during which I learned to carve bone and jade. While I was in Antarctica that same year, I learned to do scrimshaw. I think vacations should always be a time to find new things to add to your business."

Annie Lang: "My last family vacation was five years ago when we toured the western states for eight days. I'll be taking our next family vacation for five days to Orlando, but plan to take a sketchpad and do plenty of marketing research during my visit. I just can't seem to leave my brain at home or shut it off at 5 o'clock."

Michael Noyes: "Even when I'm sleeping, I'm dreaming up new designs. Is this healthy?"

WARNING: BUSINESS CAN BE ADDICTIVE!

Consultant Paul Orman says that an entrepreneurial characteristic is to think about your business 100 percent of the time. "Entrepreneurs even dream and think about their business during non-waking hours and often wake up during the night to jot down a flash of inspiration," he says. "Holidays just mess things up."

Michael Noyes asks if this is healthy. Yes and no. There's nothing wrong with letting your subconscious mind help you dream up new ideas, but there comes a point when we all have to pull back from our work and take a breather or pay a penalty—a topic discussed in the last chapter of this book.

As stated earlier, working for yourself in a business at home is all about choice. I've enjoyed the highs and suffered the lows of self-employment in the past thirty years, and the highs have always outweighed the lows. But there have been many times of personal illness and family situations when I would have given almost anything to be out from under the responsibilities that come with self-employment and the commitment to business I've always had. Holidays are often the worst of all, for we home business owners usually work right up to the bloody end and are then too tired to enjoy the holiday itself.

On the other hand, a few years ago when Harry had a heart attack and had to have bypass surgery for the second time, I was never more grateful to be self-employed. Harry needed plenty of moral support during the nine days he was in the hospital and a lot of my time for six weeks afterward since he couldn't drive himself to the many necessary follow-up doctor appointments. If I had been holding down a full-time job, we would have been in big trouble as we have no family to give us help. And no employer would have given me all the time I needed to take care of my spouse. At times like these, I thank God for giving me the ability to earn a living at home doing meaningful work I not only love but can do on a schedule of my own making.

Still, sometimes in the summer when I'm struggling to meet a writing deadline, I look out the window at the neighbor next door as she sits on her porch chatting with a friend or playing in her back-yard pool and I wonder what it would be like to not have anything to do. As one who has the self-employed mindset, however, even when I theoretically could have taken time off for play, my zeal for work and always wanting to do "just one more thing before I quit" has kept me out of the sun all my life. Even if I didn't have to work for a living, I'd be going night and day on one thing or another because it's not my nature to be lazy for any length of time. Only in the past few years have I finally reached the point where I will allow myself to take evenings and weekends off from business. But even then, I'm often scratching ideas or reminder notes or doing business reading. I understand people who say their work is their life because writing is *my* life, and everything I do, hear or see is grist for the mill.

So, to those of you who are just getting involved in a business at home, *be forewarned*. If you love what you're doing and the money you're earning is important to your livelihood, working for yourself is likely to become addictive. And, no matter what you do, a business of your own is always going to be a love/hate affair. If you ever begin to hate it more than you love it, it's time to move on to something else.

A PROFIT-ORIENTED CHECKLIST

Lessons learned equal profits earned
—from a radio advertisement

As you will learn over time, there is a big difference between a business that makes "good money" and one that generates a true profit for all the time and effort expended. Since literally anything and everything can impact the profits of a small business, you must step back from time to time to take a closer look at your business, carefully analyzing its current profitability. Also remember to:

- Accept the fact that the only predictable thing about an art or crafts business is its unpredictability.
- Arm yourself with knowledge about your art or craft, your industry, and all industries related to it.
- Embrace new technology that can help you realize your dreams.
- Introduce new products to your line on a regular basis, placing sales emphasis on your most profitable items.
- Evaluate your prices regularly to make sure the profit is there, and make price adjustments if it isn't.
- Keep looking for new markets for your products or services.
- Consider why you are working as hard as you are, and make sure what you're doing is really what you *want* to be doing and not a trap you've accidentally fallen into.
- Decide how many hours a week you want to devote to business, and set up a comfortable work schedule for yourself.
- Give yourself a break from time to time. Don't think you can work around the clock forever without paying a price.
- Learn how to work smarter and be a better business manager and marketer. Working longer hours is not the only way to increase bottom-line profits.

Chapter Three

Is It Time to Make a Change?

|||||||||||||||||||||||||||||||||||||||||||||||||||

Change is good—a little terror in our lives keeps us on our toes, while complacency breeds boredom and boring crafts.
—MEG SULLIVAN, AUNT MEG CREATIONS

Change is difficult—it affects me somewhere around my stomach, in my belly bowl.
—GAIL PLATTS, INCALICO

As we settle into a favorite chair with a good book for a long evening's read, we may reposition ourselves several times before we're comfortable. Maybe the light isn't just right, or the pillow needs fluffing, or we can't quite reach our cup of tea. Subtle shifts are needed for maximum comfort.

Business is like that, too. Each year, as things around us change, or we change, we may find it necessary to make subtle shifts in the way we're doing business. Our prices may increase in response to market conditions or a change in the economy. Our marketing methods may change because of new technology or because the old ways aren't working anymore. Business or product names may change in response to industry changes or how customers and clients themselves are changing.

Most of us go to great lengths to resist change because it automatically takes us out of our comfort zone and makes extra work for us. A change of name, phone number, or pricing means we have to revise all our printed materials. A change in focus means we have to write new advertising copy for our brochure, catalog, or ads and explore new ways of reaching the larger market we've targeted. Suddenly we need a whole new series of printed materials or perhaps a presence on the Internet.

As we grow older (and, hopefully, wiser), we are sometimes forced to make changes because we've received an important wake-up call, such as a serious illness or life-threatening disease that suddenly shows us what our real priorities in life are. A few years ago, a little dance with breast cancer cost me a lot of time, money, and energy due to surgery, follow-up doctor visits, and six weeks of daily radiation treatments. I was lucky the cancer was caught and halted in its earliest stage, but the experience woke me up to the fact that I was getting older and wasn't going to live forever. This turned out to be a positive life experience in that it forced me to take a closer look at my life and make some important changes in the way I was spending it and running my home-based business.

From time to time, we need to ask ourselves if we are living life the way we really want to; when that life includes a business at home, the questions become all the more pointed. Change, though hard to make, brings its own rewards. Upgrading your business will enhance your professional image and this may prompt your customers or clients to respond differently, perhaps with bigger orders or more business. In the process of making necessary changes to my own business, I discovered another important benefit of change. Satisfaction with the changes I had made lowered my business stress as well as my blood pressure. Best of all, I found myself fired with ambition and energy to tackle new challenges.

Making changes is always painful to one degree or another. When I decided to cease publication of my newsletter a few years ago and gradually close down the book publishing and mail order end of my business, I went through an emotionally difficult and financially painful "withdrawal period." Suddenly, after fifteen years of speaking to a devoted following of readers through my newsletter, I no longer had an active network or a soapbox from which to deliver information, opinions, and advice. My income dropped dramatically, and I couldn't replace it quickly because I was then spending all my time writing new books that would not yield royalty income for more than a year. It was a difficult decision to make, but I'm so glad I did it. I'm back on track financially, and my work is less stressful now that I'm doing the one thing I love most and never had enough time to do before—writing 100 percent of the time. And now that I'm on the Internet, I have my soapbox back as well.

What's interesting to me about all this is that, although I've been a professional writer for thirty years, it took all that time for me to actually get to the place where I really wanted to be. And I couldn't have gotten there at all if I hadn't gone through all the growing pains and changes along the way. Each subtle shift in the way I worked or managed my business automatically repositioned me for something else that wouldn't have come my way if I hadn't moved in the first place.

Based on all the interviews I've done with other business owners through the years, I can practically guarantee that a similar kind of progression will happen to you. So don't get too comfortable where you are right now unless you are already exactly where you want to be for the rest of your life.

STEPPING INTO THE UNKNOWN

Have you ever seen a movie where people are exploring an old haunted mansion, walking up a long flight of stairs leading up to a dark attic? Although clearly nervous about what might be lurking behind the closed door, they continue to climb the stairs cautiously, pausing on each step to take a breath and gather their courage. Why? Because their curiosity is greater than their fear, and they simply *have* to know what's up there.

Building a business of your own is a lot like that. You won't know what's waiting for you at the top until you get there, and each step you take requires a modicum of courage and a shift in both stance and attitude. Are you ready to move to the next level? Have you put off for too long the changes you've thought about making in your business, your product line, your prices, or the services you offer?

Awhile back, Susan Young agonized over her decision to move out of the retail end of decorative painting and into the realm of writing and designing full-time. "It's not that I'm giving up my craft," she says. "I'll still paint for pleasure. But my gut kept telling me I had to change direction. I wonder how many crafters are trying to do it all, yet fail to find what they are best at, or what their customers want to see. There is no way to hit it all and expect to keep equilibrium. Maybe it's a lesson I've learned as I've gotten older. There comes a time when there has to be more focus or concentration, and then the question is what to focus or concentrate on."

A few weeks after making the decision to close her retail shop, Susan was approached by a publisher to write her first book, *Decorative Painting for Fun and Profit,* (Prima), something she wouldn't have had time to do if she hadn't been willing to change directions. So often when we reposition ourselves, we automatically open the door to new opportunities.

Karen Combs had a similar experience. She nervously left her comfort zone in 1995 when she sold her share in a small quilt shop she had co-owned for five years. She had been teaching in the shop and at several shops in a neighboring town, but decided she now wanted to teach nationally and write books and articles. "I could not do this with the shop and a growing family," she says. "It was a hard decision—what if I failed? I would lose everything—no shop income, no teaching income, etc. There was also the possibility that I'd have to explain my failure to friends and family. So I set a goal and worked toward it. I prayed like it all depended on God and worked like it all depended on me."

It proved to be a smart move. The following year, Karen wrote her first book, *Optical Illusions for Quilters,* (American Quilters Society), which soon led to a second, then a third book. After leaving the shop, Karen began to teach nationwide, which led to several television appearances. "I now have many published magazine articles to my credit and my quilts are appearing in art and quilt shows across the country," she says. "My income has tripled and I have more time with my family. Life is good; however, it started with making a hard change and going out on a limb."

Eileen Heifner had a similar experience when she decided to close down her doll manufacturing operation and start buying less expensive dolls from overseas. She says it all started one Christmas season when she and her staff were so swamped with orders she was actually terrified of what the mail would bring. "We didn't know which way to turn," she recalls. "We were working day and night, seven days a week. The week before Thanksgiving was always a time when many men would call with a list their wives had given them of the dolls they wanted for Christmas. But that year when they called, I had to tell them we were taking orders for March delivery. I decided then that we had to go in another direction if we were ever going to grow the business because making our own dolls clearly wasn't the way to do it."

The transition from manufacturing to importing dolls took about eighteen months. "I didn't like having to turn away orders, but things had to change if any of us ever wanted to have a life," Eileen recalls. "My income was drastically reduced during this changeover period, but at last I had some time which I used to learn new software and get my company on the Internet—something that would have been impossible to do otherwise. I now see that my new plan is an investment that will return dividends for the future."

Designer and author Annie Lang says comfort zones more often than not create ruts. "We are comfortable at the time and can't imagine moving on into the unknown territories, but life, markets, and circumstances keep moving with or without us. I've maintained the attitude that I can always go back, but in reality, it's probably more difficult than moving forward."

"You can't expect your business to change if you won't," says Barbara Arena, managing director of the National Craft Association (NCA). "You have to leave your comfort zone, embrace new ideas or alternative methods, and always be on the prowl for new opportunities to expand your business."

Making a major change in the way you work or run your business takes courage. But as my experience and these examples prove, change often leads us in more interesting, satisfying and profitable directions.

By the way, if you think there are a lot of writers, teachers, and designers profiled in this book, you're right. Almost without exception, each of them got their start by making products for sale at fairs and shops. After years of doing shows or wholesaling products, however, many of them decided to change their lives by moving into teaching, speaking, designing, writing, or self-publishing periodicals or books. The how-to's of doing these things are beyond the scope of this book, but I've discussed them at length in my book, *Creative Cash*.

How to Make a Decision

Try this. Take any decision that's troubling you and frame it as a yes or no alternative. Yes, you should do it. No, you shouldn't. Make one alternative heads; the other tails. Then flip the coin. Your instant gut reaction to what the coin comes up with will reveal your intuitive call.

From Sixth Sense—A Whole-Brain Guide to Intuition, Hunches, Gut Feelings and Their Place in Your Everyday Life, Laurie Nadel (Prentice Hall)

HOW MISTAKES PROMPT CHANGE

What do you wish you had known at the beginning that took you too long to learn on your own? If you were to start your business all over again, knowing everything you know now, what would you do differently? By learning about common mistakes others have made, and what they did about them, you can gain perspective on your own situation.

Mistake: Starting Unprepared. "If doing it over again, I would have taken some courses in business and marketing and some further art studies," says printmaker Chris Noah. "Then I would have gone into my business feeling stronger and more prepared."

"I cannot stress too strongly the importance of reading," adds author Kathy Cisneros. "The old adage still holds true: The fool keeps making the same mistake over and over again and never learns. The smart man makes a mistake and learns from it, but the wise man learns from other people's mistakes. Read, read, read! A dear friend once told me that nothing is difficult when you want to learn, and she was right. Attitude is everything."

Mistake: Spreading Yourself Too Thin. Marsha Reed, who for over sixteen years has published *Craftmaster News*, says she has run into her share of roadblocks over the years. "The biggest mistake we've made is spreading ourselves too thin, trying to take on too many projects at one time without ample resources. Six years ago when we had only three employees, we were publishing our monthly magazine, two smaller newsletters, hosting dozens of crafter conferences, and promoting one of the largest shows in Southern California. Oh, yes . . . we were also trying to raise a family and have a personal life, too. I think you get the picture.

"By spreading ourselves too thin, we weren't able to provide as high quality service as we did in the past. Bottom line? Our customer service level wasn't where it should have been. And although we realized we were busy, we didn't immediately realize how much this affected our customer service. Our solution was to redefine what our business scope was. We took a break, rewrote our business plan, and axed whatever additional projects we had that we simply couldn't get to. It was extremely difficult to drop something from our agenda, especially after having put so much hard-earned time, effort, and heart into it. But we realized that things just couldn't continue the way they were. We learned how to focus, and we got back down to the bottom line of providing the best services possible for our customers. Now we feel we've learned from our mistakes. Before committing our precious time and effort to additional projects, we make sure we have the available resources *and* we analyze the project intensely to make sure that what we plan to do is really worth doing and that it will bring in bottom-line profits."

Jewelry designer Jan McClellan says her worst mistakes come when she is tired and pushing too hard. "Most of them concern my mind not working very well. Last summer when some personal family problems upset me, I arrived at one show without taking my tables (how can you forget a thing as basic as that?), and the very next weekend I got mixed up on the dates and actually arrived at a show a day late. I've learned that I'd better not stress myself too much, better keep more lists, and double-check things, especially if I'm feeling tired and spaced out."

Mistake: Failing to Focus. "If I were doing it over again, I would choose one avenue of selling and stick with it," says bead business owner Jacqueline Janes. "I have done wholesale, sold to stores, done shows and craft malls, but I have never really pursued any of these avenues with all of my attention. Had I known that craft malls were going to die so suddenly, I may have concentrated my efforts on a more profitable area."

"I see now that my marketing effort has not been aggressive enough," says artist Carol Carlson, "and I hung in there paying high advertising costs when I should have been pursuing different avenues."

Mistake: Being Too Cautious. "I was too timid, too cautious, and almost prided myself in taking things one step at a time," says fiber artist Elizabeth Bishop. "If launching my pattern line all over again, I would be more aggressive. I should have believed in my ability to launch a very different classic type of doll and grabbed much of the market while it was sensational and new. The first time I exhibited at the Houston Quilt Market, I was bowled over at the response, with lines forming to get to my booth. I was not prepared for the people who wanted to be distributors, nor the shops who wanted models and trunk shows right away. I could have been ready to go all out instead of taking the slow approach. And I lost some of that momentum of being new and different."

Mistakes are always uncomfortable, sometimes embarrassing, and usually costly in one way or another. "Believing the hype I got from a show promoter, I signed up for a week long, very expensive show my third time out," Joyce Birchler remembers. "I not only lost money, but I lost two months of my life getting ready for that stupid show."

Mistakes are also beneficial in that we learn from them just as we learn from failure. "Most of the hardships have taught me lessons that have helped me to acquire knowledge I would not have had otherwise," confirms doll designer Eileen Heifner.

Calligrapher Michael Noyes told me about a friend of his, a marketing VP, who asked him what mistakes he had made lately. "I suggested one or two, but he said that wasn't enough. To be successful, he said, one needs to be trying new things and taking risks. If you're not making mistakes, you're not experimenting enough with new ideas. That made sense to me. Afterwards, I thought of several more mistakes, so maybe I'm on track after all."

CHANGES FORCED BY NEW TECHNOLOGY

The problem with new technology is that it is continually forcing small business owners to do something they never planned to do in the first—place and have no desire to do in the second. Yet they are fearful that if they don't make changes, the competition will get a jump on them.

A few years ago, I was literally forced to purchase a fax machine. I didn't *want* a fax . . . didn't *need* a fax . . . didn't know where I'd *put* a fax in my already too-crowded office. But everyone kept asking, *"What's your fax number?"* until I couldn't stand it any longer, I finally got a fax just to shut them up.

Of course it only took a few days to convince me that the fax was a wonderful business tool that was going to save me time, money, and stress. Now, as a writer who regularly communicates with several editors and publishers, a fax machine is absolutely essential to my work.

The same thing happened where the Internet and e-mail was concerned. Prior to actually using this technology, I felt I didn't need it. The minute I had hands-on experience with it, however, I was hooked for good. In the end, then, most business people are simply forced to accept new technology and make changes in their business—or else. That "or else" might be that (1) others (your competition or clients/customers) will perceive you as being unprofessional or just not "with it"; (2) you will be left at the gate as your competition speeds ahead; or (3) you simply won't be able to do certain things because your computer hardware or software is out of date.

Take Dan Carlson for example. He had been baby-sitting a 286 computer for a long time because it was just perfect for doing invoicing and correspondence. He and his wife/partner Maureen had their Pentium computer for the Internet and graphics design, but the 286 was a great second computer.

"It was still working just fine and I didn't need a faster computer, but in the fall of 1999, UPS said everyone either had to upload their shipping data to their data center or they would not service us for daily pickup. Because Starship, our UPS shipping interface program, would not run on my 286 anymore, I was forced to buy a faster machine. We did not have a way out unless we hand-delivered the boxes to them. Changes like this take time, money, and patience," Dan concludes. "I don't like it when options disappear, but one has to live with it."

Personally, I'm baby-sitting my Gateway 486 computer because I'm a DOS person who hates Windows. I have no need for a Windows environment and want to stay with my DOS-based WordPerfect and dBaseIII software until I'm absolutely forced to switch, which won't be long, I'm sure, since all the new computers come with Windows software and most won't allow DOS software to be operated on them. I recently bought a second 486 machine in hopes that it would enable me to keep working in DOS for a few years longer. I'm only delaying the inevitable, however, and I dread the day when I will literally be forced to buy a Pentium and go through the learning process all over again.

By the way, Dan offers this little modem tip for those of you who are getting ready to buy a new one: "Buy a modem card that has a hardware switch that enables you to select the serial port to be used. I had a problem with one modem that worked only inside Windows. Because I also needed a modem that would work with DOS and my UPS Starship software, I had to install a separate modem on a serial port for this purpose."

NETWORKING SESSION #3: CHANGE IS HARD, BUT WORTH THE EFFORT

The following picture of how different craft businesses are changing offers insight and encouragement to others who may be stuck in a rut, wondering if it's time for a change and how to go about putting a new plan into action.

How do you know when it's time to make a change?

Chris Noah (Paperways): "Like everything else, a crafts business has a life cycle. It seems to me that when I am working as many hours as humanly possible and commanding as good a price as I can in the immediate area, unless I am satisfied with treading water forever, it's time to move on to the next level. One wants to make this a smart move. The effort is commensurate with the rewards, so care-

Keeping Customers Happy

To make changes of any kind, you must have a flexible nature. It's important to stay in tune with the times, to notice consumer buying trends, and, to relate to them accordingly. For example, the fact that we are living in difficult, challenging times is prompting many people to build bunkers (also referred to as "cocooning") at home, which is the only place where they feel perfectly comfortable and safe. So people are naturally padding their bunkers with things that make them feel good, more comfortable, more in control.

"Being flexible is at the core of all successful businesses," says Bill Mason, a former gallery owner who creates eclectic gemstone jewelry. "Every success I have had has been because I was willing to find the way to present the product or service I offered in a way that generated feelings of success, contentment, value, pride, and enjoyment. Products I've made have sold for as little as a dollar and as much as $25,000, and it's always the same in terms of finding the customer's 'happy spot' and feeding it. If a client is not in the happy-spot position, it is my job to change what I can—product, presentation, price, location, or client."

"If you see a trend in the craft industry changing, you must go with the flow," adds doll pattern designer Eleena Danielson. "Learn to adapt. Don't be a dinosaur. Maintain your unique style, but be able to adapt to what's hot in the market. Always strive to be one step above the rest. Never become complacent. If sales seem to be slowing down for you, that's your cue to take more aggressive approaches and affirmative actions in succeeding in your goals."

ful choices need to be exercised. Different avenues come to mind—major shows out of the area, reps, a line of art prints, tooling up for more production (which could mean hiring people), prestigious stores and galleries, magazine articles. Changes like these can also mean extensive, expensive travel with little to show for it and lots of slides sent with no replies."

Annie Lang (Annie Things Possible): "Any change is difficult, and most of us will reach a crossroads at one point or another in our careers. Pros and cons must be carefully thought through before acting, but I think all of us know intuitively when and what necessary changes need to be made. Moving from mass producing-handcrafts into designing for publishers and manufacturers was absolutely terrifying to me, but I knew in my heart it was the right decision for me at the time."

Pamela Spinazzola (Pamela's Studio One): "Artists and craftspeople have a multitude of opportunities. One just has to choose what is best for timing and goal achievement, making decisions by market research, or just common sense. Good decisions from gut-feelings are most likely to come from an educated mind."

Kathy Wirth (Kathy Wirth Design Services): "I've found that sometimes serendipitous events will occur to change the direction of my career. For instance, it had never been a goal of mine to write a full-length book. I guess I didn't see that as a possibility for me. But last summer, I happened to meet an acquisitions editor, and he saw something in my portfolio that interested him. Although this particular book idea didn't work out, I now see the idea of writing a book an interesting challenge."

Chris Maher (Selling Your Art Online): "Two things prompt change in my creative/business life: outside conditions, and some sort of inner discontent. The outside factors—mostly changing market conditions—cause me to drop unsuccessful ways of doing things. The second thing, inner discontent, can cause me to drop successful ways of doing business. I have come to understand that there is more to me than the logical part of my brain that can plan, target, and archive goals. To ignore that inner disquietude is to risk a serious case of burnout."

What kind of changes have you recently made to your business?

Michael Noyes (Calligraphy by Michael Noyes): "When I first came out with my framed prints, I was weak in knowing what would and would not sell. As the buying public critiqued my work (with their purchasing choices), my tastes in color and subject material came more into line. Sales improved dramatically when I moved from selling through evangelical bookstores and church craft shows to seminary bookstores and at high-end retail arts and crafts shows from Michigan to New Jersey. These venues have brought more sophisticated buyers."

Kate Harper (Kate Harper Designs): "Every day, I change something in a small way to refine it and make it mine, to adapt to my easygoing lifestyle. For example: I never purchase products from anyone who doesn't deliver because I don't want to be running around anymore. I used to actually dig through art store recycle bins to find boxes to pack my orders in. That's bad, but I didn't have the funds to buy boxes then. Most things I did then, and do now, were actually a wonderful experience in going through the changes and growing. In the beginning, I would have hated someone next to me always telling me what I should do. The discovery process has been the most joyful part of the experience."

Annie Lang: "Time and change are inevitable and opportunities don't drop out of thin air . . . you have to go find them or make them happen. One change I've made is a commitment to attend at least one trade show and educational seminar a year. Not only does this allow me to travel, but it keeps the creative juices going and opens the door a little wider to opportunities."

Robert Houghtaling (Sculpture and Design): "Besides my commercial and fine art sculptures, I've been doing humorous frogs for over

thirty years, and I'm finally moving on a line of collectible ornaments and figurines based on these designs. I've dubbed them The
Figgy Mountain Frogery ("Art That's Finer Than Frog Hair").

Charlene Anderson-Shea (Anderson-Shea, Inc.): "I used to sell in galleries but found I could make as much money making one item and
writing how-to articles about how I made it than I could earn from
making several for sale. And I still have the project when I'm done."

Jacquelyn Fox (Waxing Moon Designs): "After months of urging from
other designers I network with, I finally committed the time and
money to attend a major needlework trade show. Time will tell whether
that decision merits a pat on the back or a knock on the head."

Carol Carlson (Kimmeric Studio): "I have changed marketing methods, gone to school, and taken charge of my life to make this a real
career. It's amazing how that works after you get a divorce and you
are responsible to yourself for the first time in your life. The idea of
getting a 'real' job scares me to death. I don't think I would know
how to do that because it's been more than twenty years since I've
worked for someone else. Even if I don't see the rewards right now,
I figure that what I've learned will kick in when I least expect it (a
lot of faith going on here)."

Derek Andrews (Sunrise Woodcrafts): "I am concentrating on more
profitable lines and direct sales. I plan to pursue Internet sales more
vigorously and try to break into the corporate gift market. I'm hoping the Net can help make sales from January to May when my
shop income from the tourist trade is negligible. I also plan to do
some teaching and set up a display at the public library to promote
woodturning and my courses."

**Change always demands its price, so I'm wondering what it
has cost some of you to make changes in your business.**

Karen Lyons (K.J. Lyons Design Studio): "I'm losing money as I
develop my new gallery line, but I really needed to get back to my

roots. I started my business because I loved sculpture. Over the years, working for the toy companies, my business became more and more commercial. I still did figurative clay sculpture for relaxation, but I seldom used it in my business. I was getting really burned out. So when I had an opportunity to design this gallery line I'm working on, I was ecstatic. I could do a realistic clay sculpture and use it as a model for my creature. It was quite a challenge, but I feel as though I'm really learning and creating again. Hopefully, it'll make me money, too."

Gail Platts (InCalico): "Transition and change are painful not only because of the leap into the unknown, but because your self-image is tangled up in your work. Shortly after I started my business, my work gradually changed from country to bright and whimsical, and although it was a good move and some folks embraced the change, it was a bit painful when I lost customers because my work no longer fit their taste. Rejection of any kind is never fun, but change is a necessary part of life, to keep interest in your work and to find new challenges. The scary part is the self-doubt about whether a change is a move in the right direction. Sometimes you just gotta pack a parachute, close your eyes, and take a leap of faith."

Robert Houghtaling: "Right! Sometimes you just have to jump the fence and go in a different direction. Recently I've been focusing on developing my own product and getting it to market rather than doing contract work just to pay the bills. No matter how hard you work on contract stuff, you are doing piece work, and five years from now you will still be doing piece work. I keep reminding myself of that old saying, 'If you keep doing what you've always done, you'll keep getting what you've always got.'"

Susan Gearing (Susie's Crafts): "When I moved from Maryland to Tennessee, I had to change the way I did business, shipping more things by mail than usual, trying to find new sales outlets in my area, and so on. Work involved on building a new house forced my business to the back burner for awhile. This wasn't bad, except for lost income, because it gave me some time to ruminate on where my business will go next. Sometimes our downtimes can lead to a good change and greater productivity—perhaps in another area of this business. I'm now interested in developing my design and writing skills."

Wendy Van Camp (IndigoSkye Bead Fashions): "Before my entry onto the Internet three years ago, all my business was geared to the local area. I was a video producer/consultant in an area where there was a saturation of such skilled people. When I made the shift to selling beaded jewelry via local shows and my Internet Web site, I did take a loss for the first year and had to support myself through a second job. However, the second year I was in business, my jewelry business began to support me and I began to realize a truly global market for my wares. Currently I am also applying what I learned through my bead jewelry business to my video skills and finding new avenues are opening up in this way as well. Work is pouring in from many quarters. So, while the transition to become more Internet-based was a painful one full of mistakes, in the end, it has proven to be a fruitful venture for me."

The trouble with being self-employed is that we not only have to crack our own whips but are usually the only one around to pat ourselves on the back. What have you done recently that deserved a pat on the back?

Kim Marie (Kim Marie Fine Pottery): "Oh boy! Patting myself on the back . . . what a concept! I usually look for the 'Atta Girl' comments from somebody else, but I'm still waiting so, yes, I'd better learn to pat myself on the back."

Jacqueline Janes (Arizona Bead Company): "I applaud myself for having the courage to support myself with my business. Some days I just want to go and get a job to get a steady check and have some time to myself."

Leila Peltosaari (Tikka Books): "I keep reminders of my past successes around me in my office to inspire me and say quiet bravos to myself. When I wrote my latest book, I bought myself a bouquet of roses and wrote a card, 'Congratulations to myself for having the courage to write a new book.' It felt good. I talk to myself aloud in the car while I am driving ('Way to go, Leila, you can do it'), and recite a certain little prayer several times until I feel blessed, guided, protected, and helped. I also collect inspiring quotes like this one: *Still round the corner there may wait, a new road, or a secret gate.* (J. R. R. Tolkien)."

I didn't get many responses to my pat-yourself-on-the-back question, which only proves that most craftspeople aren't doing enough of it. It *is* okay to pat yourself on the back when you've just designed a new line of products that excites you . . . when you've learned how to set up and maintain your web site . . . when you've mastered another software program or fixed a computer problem . . . when you've just gotten a new landmark client or account that could change the course of your business . . . when you've achieved a secret dream . . . reached a new goal . . . won an award . . . gotten another step past your fear barrier . . . made a bigger profit than the year before—the list is endless. Create your own and follow Leila's lead by giving yourself a well-deserved bouquet from time to time.

A "MAKING CHANGES" CHECKLIST

Are you overdue for a change? Is it time to reconsider your business and the direction it's taking? Remember that old saying, "If you keep doing what you've always done, you'll keep getting what you've always got." And this one, too: "Fear makes the wolf bigger than he is."

Also remember to:

▸▸ Stay flexible. Go with the flow.
▸▸ Maintain your unique style, but be ready to adapt to what's hot at the time.
▸▸ Strive always to be one step above the rest. Don't allow yourself to be complacent about your business.
▸▸ Accept the fact that nothing stays the same and that the only way to grow or get ahead in life or business is to be willing to make changes.

▶ Welcome change because each shift you make in the way you work or manage your business may reposition you for something else that wouldn't have come your way if you hadn't moved in the first place.

▶ Experiment to find the path in life that is most satisfying to you.

▶ Follow your gut instincts and the dictates of your heart. (To thine own heart, be true.)

It's not easy to make changes in your personal or business life, but sometimes you just have to bite the bullet and do it. As you think about this, consider these words of advice from S. H. Payer in his poem, "Live Each Day to the Fullest:" "When you are faced with a decision, make that decision as wisely as possible, then forget it. The moment of absolute certainty never arrives."

Chapter Four

Building a Business With Computer Technology

||||||||||||||||||||||||||||||||||||||||||||

The computer has evolved from a building-sized monster to a tool so simple it can be used as a toy by a four-year old. It is seeping into every aspect of our lives. In five years, a computer-illiterate person will have the same disadvantage as the non-reader of the last decade.
—LAVERNE HERREN, *Arts & Crafts Show Business*

We are living in the most interesting, exciting, and frightening time in history, where computer technology is the fuel that now runs the world and where each day brings news of yet another technological advance that can both empower and terrify us at the same time. The technological advances we have seen in the past year alone have left most of us standing in awe, totally overwhelmed by all we need to learn just to stay even in our businesses, let alone get ahead. Without question, technology is quickly and dramatically changing the way we all live and work, the way we communicate, the way we create our products and services, manage our businesses, and sell our wares. And the changes we have been told are coming soon are still unimaginable to most of us.

The good news about technology is that it has enabled even the smallest home-based business to compete with Fortune 500 companies. "We've certainly come a long way since you first convinced me that purchasing a home computer would be one of the wisest business investments I could make," says Annie Lang, one of my long time readers. Annie began as a selling artist and gradually evolved into a successful designer and author who has published several books and licensed many of her designs to manufacturers.

"In addition to my office computer, I have a laptop for travel or use outdoors when weather allows," she says. "The laptop also allows me to work on two simultaneous projects without interruption. My son, now twenty, began building computers when he was fourteen. He became an IBM-certified technician when he was fifteen and now works on business computers for a corporation. He has kept me upgraded with all the latest in scanners, printers, programs, and computer gadgetry ever since. I told him he can never leave home!"

I chuckled at this because my sister Mollie Wakeman, who runs a full-time piano-teaching business at home, has two "techie" sons who are always updating her system with the newest software and peripherals. She designs a lot of jazzy handouts for her students, beautiful programs for her recitals, and all kinds of other well-designed printed materials. She admits she doesn't understand much about how anything works, but that doesn't bother her because help is always near at hand. I'm sure many craft businesses that are now computerized owe a big debt to at least one child in the family who's a computer whiz.

Periodical publisher Marsha Reed credits a lot of her success to her son, Tim, who runs her business with her. The way Marsha and Tim run *Craftmaster News* offers a good example of how the proper use of computers in a home-based business can dramatically increase both productivity and business profits.

"Tim was a systems engineer for over five years before he decided to join me in my business," Marsha says, "and the computer work he has done has dramatically changed our business. Since everything is integrated into one solid system, our business reports are available daily with the click of a button. For example, three years ago, it used to take us at least two days, with two employees, to handle all our customer invoicing. Now it takes just twenty minutes with one employee. Talk about saving time and money! And with the work completed so quickly, it allows us to get back to what we really should be doing—serving our customers and increasing our sales."

Marsha has four computers now, plus a laptop. "One is in my office in the house; three others are in a separate building on our property where we run the business. Instead of multiple stand-alone systems, we now have everything networked together. Finding files, tracking customers, etc.—everything is easier. Our response time is ten times faster than it used to be. When you sit down at one computer, you know that everything on it will be the same as the others. Now, instead of digging through files when customers call, we can find their account information with a couple of keystrokes."

This is important since Marsha can answer her business phone either in the house or in her business workplace. "When someone calls after hours, which they often do, I have everything at my fingertips."

Like Marsha, Susan Young has also increased her efficiency by networking her main office system at the far end of the house (her office) to a secondary system serving as a kitchen workstation. "That way," she says, "I can work at either computer and send files to either printer, depending on quality and effects desired. When the situation demands, I can work on my kitchen computer and keep an eye on dinner—especially nice when I suddenly find I'm having company on a day when I'm also trying to meet a publishing deadline."

Many professional artists and craftspeople are quick to see the benefits of computerizing their business, but it takes some people longer than others to "see the light." Many feel that as long as things are working well the old way, there is no need to change. Although Geoffrey Harris was a software systems engineer for seven years, developing computer-based business applications for large companies, he has managed quite well without a computer in his Harris Collectibles art business, his livelihood since 1992. "I just go to Kinko's to create my show and thank-you postcards, artist bios, resumes, business cards, and price tags," he says. (See illustration.)

Geoffrey's success proves you can succeed in an art business without a computer, but it has not slipped his attention that a computer could be very helpful to him in handling his accounting, customer database, and correspondence. Recently, he also saw the need to get his art on the Internet. "I guess I'll have to purchase a computer now so I can set up and maintain my own Web site," he said. "It will have all of my current inventory with a price list, show schedule, artist bio, etc."

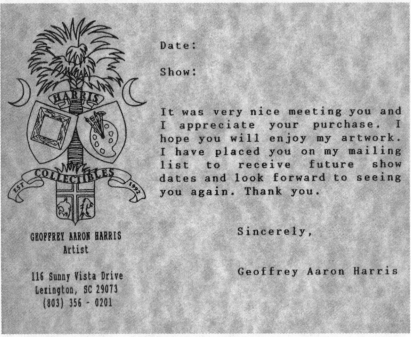

Date:

Show:

It was very nice meeting you and I appreciate your purchase. I hope you will enjoy my artwork. I have placed you on my mailing list to receive future show dates and look forward to seeing you again. Thank you.

Sincerely,

Geoffrey Aaron Harris

GEOFFREY AARON HARRIS
Artist

116 Sunny Vista Drive
Lexington, SC 29073
(803) 356 - 0201

Sample of a thank-you card used by Geoffrey Harris.

You may be doing quite well in business now, doing everything the old-fashioned way, but sooner or later there will be a price to pay if you don't join the rest of the world by computerizing your business and having several different options for communication. You will either (1) have to work harder than others to accomplish similar tasks; (2) find it difficult to compete with others in your field; or (3) miss out on certain opportunities. For example, once I decided to do interviews for this book primarily by e-mail, I found I could not efficiently work with people who didn't have e-mail (or at least a fax) because I was simply moving too fast on the book to wait for them to send responses by mail. Thus, a few people I would have liked to have more input from were simply eliminated from my interview list. Geoffrey Harris was one of them.

True, the process of learning how to use a computer in business and then keeping your system upgraded will be stressful. But as this book proves, a business with "computer power" can go a lot farther, a lot faster, than one without.

Computer Buying Tips

"Buy the best your money can buy," advises newsletter publisher Rita Stone-Conwell. "While computer systems become quickly outdated, you can improvise with each system. Whether you buy a Macintosh or IBM computer, be sure it meets current needs, has plenty of growing abilities, includes a modem, and is Internet-ready."

"Always ask about service, warranty, and online help," emphasizes Susan Young. "I recommend the made-to-order systems such as Gateway because they offer toll-free service and their technicians will walk you though any problem you may have. The main benefit in buying a made-to-order system is that you can order exactly what you want and you don't have to pay for things you'll never use. You save time because you don't have to go to discount houses or browse catalogs to find the software you want. Gateway's prices are competitive, and the software I wanted came with the system."

With over twenty years experience with computers, Susan knows the value of using top-quality surge protectors with all electronic equipment. She recommends SurgeSTATION, which has eight outlets, two of which are always on. Surge protection is guaranteed for life, with coverage up to $10,000 for the Professional Series and $25,000 for the Network Series.

NETWORKING SESSION #4: TECHNO-STRESS

Creative people everywhere are using computers in a multitude of ways, saving time, energy, and money in the process, but few of them would say the learning process was easy. In fact, fear of technology is a big problem for many people who are just now computerizing their businesses or trying to find the courage to consider this step. If you suffer from "techno-fear," perhaps you will take comfort in knowing you are not alone and that the effort it will take to "get with it" will be priceless to you in the long run. As I once heard someone say on the radio, "You've got to turn off the fear impulse so it doesn't reach the chicken portion of your brain."

Once again, I invite you to sit in on a discussion among several business owners in my network.

Some of you who have resisted the computer all these years—especially those of you who are older—may wonder if all the learning this will require is worth the effort.

Ginger Kean Berk (designer): "I've had a successful crafts and design business for many years, but maybe it would just be easier to retire at this point. I feel so much behind the times with no computer, fax machine, or any of the great new technology. But I'm still doing designs for a publishing company that produces several magazines and am kept busy enough so there isn't too much deadline pressure."

Of course it's not time for you to retire Ginger! As an established designer, you can probably continue to work indefinitely without a computer; on the other hand, if you could just motivate yourself to invest a thousand dollars into a computer, your whole business (and life) would suddenly be revitalized. Although it's easy to say, "I got along without a computer all this time, I can get along without one now," I see that most people who have gotten past their fear of computers absolutely love the benefits of computer technology.

Sue Johnson (Gramma's Graphics, Inc.): "I got into the computer scene years ago just to introduce our children to it. I now use and rely on it daily and am convinced it has helped my businesses grow. Upgrading, learning new programs, etc., is stressful, but worth the effort."

Tori Hoggard (Harmony Artworks): "I once thought I'd never be into computers. But when I was able to make more professional promotional materials, organize my bookkeeping and other things, and find resources on the Internet, I changed my mind. I'm no longer a purist living in the dark ages."

Wendy Van Camp (IndigoSkye Bead Fashions): "The computer is a godsend to my business and personal life. It has connected me to suppliers, fellow artists, and marketers on the Internet who have helped to shape my business and teach me the basics of what I needed to do to make my small home-based business a success. I have made fewer mistakes by following their advice than if I had attempted this on my own. My accounting software also serves as an accountant for me and keeps my records straight. My sales tax figures for the year are calculated with the single press of a button. I can't even imagine life without my computer now."

Kim Marie (Kim Marie Fine Pottery): "I think the difference between caving in and meeting things head on is all in knowing yourself. Knowing for yourself what aids in motivation and what makes things seem overwhelming can really make the difference. Attitude is the key."

Even with the right attitude, however, craftspeople are experiencing higher levels of stress these days as they try to figure out how to reposition their businesses and products in our quickly changing times and marketplace. It's as if we're all living in the margins of life and there isn't any time left for normal living because there is too much to learn just to stay where we're at in business, let alone make gains. Certainly I feel stressed by all the high-tech changes forcing their way into my life, and some days I'd just like to pull the covers over my head and let the world go on without me. How do you folks feel about this?

Pat Endicott (House of Threads & Wood, Inc.): "I thought I was alone in my computer-tech stress mode. I appreciate hearing it is more common than I thought. Personally, I need a 'dummy' book on this topic. I think that many of us (the fifty to sixty-something peo-

ple) feel the world is running over them. Somedays we would sooner let the train roll on and rest! It is passing down to our children
also, as everyone seems just too pressured and going too fast."

Susan Young (Peach Kitty Studio): "Sometimes I don't know
whether life is passing me by, or trying to run me over. If I see a light
at the end of the tunnel, it's probably an oncoming train."

Marsha Reed (*Craftmaster News*): "I'm the first to admit that at times
I have been absolutely terrified by all the technological advances
over the years. Yet I'm also quick to admit that I've finally realized
the importance of keeping up with the technology. If we don't do
this, we will simply be passed by and somebody else will take the
business that could otherwise be ours."

Anita Means (Cottage Crafts): "There is a certain amount of stress
related to keeping up with the technological advances that constantly change the way we do business, but I feel it is a necessary
evil. For example, when I hired a mailing house to do my mailings
for me, my challenge was to enter all the names using a program
capable of detecting duplicates and compatible with the mailing
house's program. I had to buy a ZIP drive and new software to
accomplish this—which was stressful—but well worth the effort."

Tori Hoggard: "I am so old-fashioned when it comes to technology.
Initially, my thoughts were that it was the exact opposite of what I
tried to convey in my work, which is entirely handmade. Well, I've
since discovered that computers make nice companions when it
comes to labeling, marketing, etc. We need to stay strong. We craftspeople are a big part of what will keep the world balanced as technology continues its course."

**A few of you report no computer stress at all, but you are clear-
ly in the minority.**

Bob Gerdts (Bob & Carol's Egg-Art, Ltd.): "Even though I'm from
the manual generation (age sixty-four), I'm not stressed by technol-

ogy. Until 1985, I made my living from computers, and that is where stress was at the time. Now, I embrace the Internet and use it to gain a wider scope for our business."

Chris Noah (Paperways): "I am not personally stressed by the concept or the reality of computer technology. I see it as an aid and a resource. I can choose how far I will go with it. Right now, our computer is used for record-keeping, designing, and marketing resources. I think that's great when I consider how I used to do it."

Although some of you are not stressed by computer technology itself, there is some indirect stress as a result, isn't there?

Meg Sullivan (Aunt Meg Creations): "I find technology an exciting challenge. It has enabled me to create cross-stitch charts on the computer instead of by hand, where turning a component or moving it over three spaces is just a cut-and-paste operation, not starting again. My stress is in the growth of the business and keeping up with demand."

Kathy Wirth (Kathy Wirth Design Services): "The main stress I feel is simply keeping up with the increase in correspondence and information. I've been using computers since the mid-80s, so I feel pretty comfortable with the technology and can keep up enough to suit my needs. But e-mail and the Net have drastically increased the volume of communication one has to deal with. I feel as though I have to keep up with all the information that's out there—all the industry Web sites, e-mail lists, chat rooms, etc. Needlework design is a labor-intensive field that allows little time for all this 'techie stuff.'"

Kim Marie: "I'm comfortable with having to make changes and I have confidence in my work; however, that doesn't mean I don't feel the stress. I have a much harder time relaxing now. I always feel I should be reading, learning, changing."

Betty Chypre (*Choices for Craftsmen and Artists*): "The stress level is incredible at times, but some of this high-tech stuff is so fascinat-

How to Deal with Technological Advances

Tips from Marsha Reed, Craftmaster News

▸▸ Even if you don't have a computer whiz at your fingertips, be sure to stay aware of technological advances that can make your business and life easier.

▸▸ Don't take the advice of just one person, and don't dive into an investment (like a new computer system) without getting multiple suggestions from different people. And be sure to include planning for the future. The last thing you want to do is write-off a new system as a loss before it's even depreciated in the books.

▸▸ Try to look at things in a positive way. Although we tend to stick to the old ways of doing things the older we get, we need to give new technology a chance. By doing so, you may be surprised at how much time and energy you save and how much more profitable your business can become by simply stopping and listening for a bit.

Marsha has updated her computer systems several times in the past ten years and says this has taken a great deal of time and caused untold hours of stress. "At times, learning a whole new system seemed such a burden that we simply didn't use it and went back to filing everything on paper for awhile. I now believe, however, that when we look at the new and modern technological advances available today, we have to learn to look at them with an open mind and realize that the benefits will definitely outweigh the costs."

Recently Marsha's accountant told her she was getting uncomfortable about writing off all the new computer purchases she was making every year, saying the IRS didn't like that kind of deduction. "I told her that was too bad because I needed to stay up on technology or be left behind," Marsha countered.

Perhaps if the IRS had kept their computer systems upgraded through the years, they wouldn't be in the mess they are now reportedly in. It will be interesting to see how well the IRS survives the Y2K rollover. Since many believe our tax system is likely to change soon, this book contains no tax information whatsoever.

ing, I can't seem to learn fast enough. I'm always hungry for more. I love monkeying on the web. I am taking courses now because I want to fill in the holes in my knowledge bank."

Charlene Anderson-Shea (Anderson-Shea, Inc.): "Computer technology can be overwhelming if you let it. You don't have to know everything about everything, just make sure your electronic equipment does what you need it to. You may need a Web site, but nothing says you have to design it yourself."

HOW CREATIVE PEOPLE
DESIGN ON COMPUTER

For many creative people, the computer has unleashed a flood of creativity as they have learned to use different software programs and related hardware to create art and design products for sale. Here are a few examples.

Creating Artwork. Annie Lang uses Adobe PhotoShop and Adobe Illustrator software to design projects for her books and designs she licenses to manufacturers. "I can create and manipulate almost any type of linework, scanned artwork editing, layout, and color scheme to suit everything from pattern layouts to the creation of fabric print wallpapers and repeats. I use Microsoft Word for text and documents. Though I have manuals for all these programs for reference, I found that a week or two of hands-on self-taught training works best for me when learning how to use a new program."

Calligrapher Michael Noyes uses his Macintosh PowerBook to manage his entire business and his Web site. "Computers have been my saving grace," he says. "I design on computer using Illustrator and PhotoShop software (both Adobe programs). I scan in penwork or brushwork and then manipulate them on screen. I also do direct digital drawing with a digital pen and tablet. I can print in full color, and in very short runs, simply by pressing a button. I can retouch, colorize, and otherwise modify my calligraphy fast and effectively. Custom work is quick and profitable."

Printmaker Chris Noah also uses her Macintosh computer to first draw her art, then scans the image using PhotoShop and compos-

An example of one of Chris Noah's drawings (a Double Distilfink, a much-loved Early American image), which will later be traced to a copper plate for etching.

ites it with Freehand software. "The composite is then printed onto tracing paper so I can trace the image onto a copper plate for etchings. Our goal is to have handmade art, but the use of high-tech is like the dark matter of the universe: You can't see it, but it pervades everything. We are still climbing up the learning curve on the use of graphics software. Every time we use it we learn something, including the fact that some things can be done by hand faster than by computer. The goal is optimum use of the computer, not use of the computer for its own sake."

Sculptor Robert Houghtaling, yet another Mac user (notice how artists seem to prefer Macintosh computers?), uses Macromedia's Freehand and ClarisWorks to do design and renderings. "I once designed a Star Trek plate for The Hamilton Collection, all on computer, then printed and mailed the color comps to them," he says. (See also sidebar, "Using a Video Camera," for more on how Robert communicates electronically with his clients.)

Needlework Design. There are a variety of charting programs needleworkers can use to design on computer, but it will take time and experimentation to find one that's right for you. "There are several trial versions (demos) of cross-stitch design software on the Web," says Jacquelyn Fox, who publishes her own needlework design leaflets for sale to shops. "To find them, read cross-stitch

Using a Video Camera

Sculptor Robert Houghtaling explains how he uses a video camera in conjunction with his computer and the Internet to communicate with his clients on how a particular sculpture is coming along:

"Like most computers today, mine has a video card and the software to use it. (I don't need Snappy, a commercial software program, but it is the same process.) A digital camera can give you better resolution but what I like about using the vidcam is I can set up my sculpture right on the desktop, view it in real time on my monitor, and when I've got it just the way I want it, I can capture the pictures. I then run it through a converter program for display online. This really helps when I am dealing with remote customers. I can e-mail them pictures of the sculpture in progress, and we can talk about how it is going.

"Once you have a video camera, you have to check the kind of output cable or cables it uses and the kind of input your computer has. Then check your local camera store or Radio Shack for the proper interconnect cable. After you hook things up, it's just a matter of turning on the lights (ordinary room light works fine) and zooming in on your subject. When you see the image you want on the monitor, just hit SAVE, give it a name and, bingo, you're in business. When you have the pictures you want, run them through a graphic conversion program and change them into the JPEG format required by e-mail. If you have the above-mentioned hardware/software on your computer, you can also hook up your VCR to your computer. This allows you to capture images from tapes and also to watch TV on your computer.

continued on following page

continued from previous page

"I like the digital camera a friend of mine bought—a Sony MVC-FD 71. It has a 10X optical zoom lens and can take up to 2,000 shots, or up to 2.5 hours on a charge. The really cool part, besides the zoom, is that it stores the photos on a removable 3.5 inch floppy disk. You can just plug the disk right into your computer. Each disk holds about twenty images, depending on the resolution you choose. You can even set it to take photos that are ready for your e-mail. I love computer technology and really use it in my business and private life, but it does take up a lot of time. I sometimes wonder if the time saved or the knowledge learned is equal to the time spent.

"The big change I see coming in my field is the use of the computer for modeling and printing 3-D images. This concerns me because it could do away with a lot of hand-sculpture work. I thought this technology was far from being perfected, but I've recently learned that all the business from the major houses, such as Disney, is no longer going to individual sculptors like me but being sent instead to companies that have the 3-D computer output devices. Just one more example of how technology is affecting the art/crafts business world."

magazines and pick up on ads for them." Jacquelyn is looking for a new program to do her charting, but currently she uses PrintMaster Platinum (Mindscape) to create her design leaflets. "This is an all-purpose program you can use to lay out pages, make greeting cards, calendars, newsletters, business cards, and more."

Charlene Anderson-Shea does both cross-stitch and knitting designs with Stitch Painter software (Cochenille Designs). "This is a grid-based program," she explains. "For cross-stitch, I just scan in or draw a design under the grid and fill in the blanks accordingly. It's also great for doing complicated stitch patterning. This software produces a chart that is great to knit from. I'm also using a program called Garment Styler to do the actual garment design (that is, the shape of the garment as opposed to the actual stitches in the garment)."

Although Charlene is a dyed-in-the-wool Macintosh user, she purchased a Gateway laptop for designing and downloading designs to her Bernina Deco embroidery machine. "A Mac version of the hardware/software did not exist," she says, "and to jerry-rig something would have cost more and been slower than buying the PC laptop."

WRITING AND PUBLISHING BUSINESSES

A computer is absolutely essential for today's writers and publishers. Looking back, it's hard for me to believe that I wrote the first editions of my early books on a typewriter, retyping page after page after page, trying to get all the words, sentences, and paragraphs just right. Today, with my WordPerfect software, I can manipulate words and move large blocks of copy from here to there with the flick of a finger. Having this kind of control has not only made me a better writer, but has enabled me to quadruple my writing output. Here are a few examples of how other professional writers and periodical publishers do their work on computer:

» Kathy Wirth uses Microsoft Word to write how-to project instructions. "I submit text for project instructions on disk when an editor requests it. I know some designers who do not use computers to type their instructions, but I think they are missing the boat. I can store instructions in the individual magazine's format and then reuse the format for the next set of instructions."

» Author and needlework designer Sylvia Landman uses WordPerfect software to write her books, columns, and how-to instructions for knitting and crochet. "I have 'taught' it all the common abbreviations. I do my first-draft writing instructions from handwritten notes as I work. Then, I pull up first and second windows and split screen for editing, clarifications, etc., which of course becomes my final draft. Rather than describe a project, I actually place it on my copier, enlarging or reducing as needed so editors can see exactly what the work will look like close-up."

▸▸ Patricia Kutza, a neckwear and home decorative accessories designer/writer, likes Inklings software for manuscript submission management. "I can track magazine/Website submissions in vertical or parallel markets, set up memory joggers and manipulate the data for a variety of reports."

▸▸ Morna McEver Golletz, who publishes *The Professional Quilter* on a Macintosh, says she is pleased with how her skills have developed as she has learned to use QuarkXPress (a high-end page layout program), Adobe Illustrator, and PhotoShop to prepare her magazine. "I receive many articles via the computer and do all the editing with copy editors over the computer, and I develop ideas via contact with other quilters on newsgroups and lists. I also send my files electronically to my printer in Pennsylvania. When I moved to a different state, I thought about changing printers but found the costs were higher. Also, I knew my printer and he knew me. We had a good understanding of the quality of printing I wanted, and I didn't want to give up that personal relationship. Because my printer and I both use Macintosh computers and QuarkXPress software, it's a simple matter to send my magazine as an attachment to e-mail. I also e-mail a copy to my proofreader who opens it up, prints it out, and checks it for errors."

▸▸ Dan Engle, who publishes *Arts 'n Crafts ShowGuide,* still works the old-fashioned way, delivering camera-ready "boards" to his printer. That's because his printer's computer software is not compatible with his. "I use a lot of different graphic programs that don't translate well when transmitted electronically. I switched from a Macintosh to a PC Windows-environment five years ago because everyone seems to be using Windows these days. There are more software options for Windows users, and I was getting tired of continually having to translate files from my Mac to the PC where I do all my word processing and database work."

▸▸ When Rita Stone-Conwell decided to launch *Crafts Remembered,* an events-oriented newsletter for professional craftspeople in

New York state, she decided to buy a Mac because that's what her kids were using in school. "I found it easy to learn, and the software that comes with it (ClarisWorks) has everything I need to run my business and produce the newsletter. It has word processing, database, and spreadsheet capabilities as well as a draw-and-paint program. I am currently on my fifth Mac, and this latest one came with a ZIP drive, which makes the job of backing up data very easy."

What a Scanner Can Do for You

The first thing Liz Murad did when she wanted to buy a scanner was visit the crafter.com chat room on the Internet and ask a few people what scanner they had and why they chose it. Then she visited a couple of stores to take a look at her options.

"After going to two local computer stores to look at their big, screaming, come-get-me advertisements and being unable to find anyone in the store who knew anything about scanners, I went home and got back on the Web," she recalls. "I hit the Hewlett Packard Web site, checked the prices, and ordered a scanner that cost less than the store prices."

Liz used to sell original calligraphy and artwork only, then found it tedious to do the same work over and over. "I explored printing options," she says, "but they were very expensive. Now, with the new technology in copiers and scanners, I can produce my work

Technical Acronyms

New acronyms related to technology are popping up every day. One mentioned in this and other chapters is JPEG, which stands for Joint Photographic Experts Group. It's the standard used for sending pictures electronically by e-mail. My favorite technical acronym, contributed by Chris Maher, is TWAIN, the name given to the interface for scanners and digital cameras. It actually stands for "Technology Without an Interesting Name."

I can only handle one complaint per day.

Today is not your day.

Tomorrow's not looking too good, either.

Calligraphy by Liz Murad, who scans images into her computer, prints them on parchment paper, then hand colors and frames them for sale.

with the same integrity I have had in the past. By producing my designs on white paper, I can transfer them onto colored parchment paper; then I add color to each design individually to coordinate with the matting and sign each work."

Scanning is great!" says Sylvia Landman. "I scan both images and text and can send copyright-free clip-art to my computer. To put actual swatches of a hand-dyed variegated vest knitted from silk ribbon, I laid the garment on the scanner, sent it to my computer, cropped it, and, viola! It now appears on my Web site."

"My HP4100C scanner is fantastic," says crafts business owner Sue Johnson. "For publicity opportunities, it and my HP Deskjet 722C color printer have revolutionized the way I can share color photo examples of what our Sun Print Kits can do. By scanning photos and my book cover and putting them onto disk, I'm able to give magazines and newspapers the best and clearest medium to reproduce pictures of my work, plus it's less expensive than sending photos. I also have a Kodak digital camera and it, along with these other two machines, has unleashed a wealth of creativity. The abil-

Even 3-D objects, one laid on top of the other, scan beautifully. These wood pieces, handpainted by Susan Young, are laser-cut items copyrighted by West Coast Wood Craft Supplies. They may not be reproduced without permission.

ity to manipulate photos and scanned objects makes creating brochures and publicity packets fun and exciting. I use Picture Easy with the camera photos, then manipulate them further in Adobe PhotoDeluxe."

"Scanners are wonderful creations," says Jacquelyn Fox. "If I'd known then what I know now, I would have invested in my new computer, scanner, and printer right off the bat. I could have saved nearly $1,000 on professional four-color printing of my promotional flyers if I'd been able to lay out and print them myself and just run off as many as I needed. Instead, I had to pay a printing company big bucks for 2,500 color flyers (the smallest quantity I could order). I still use those flyers, but it'll be a long time before I ever use them up. Now, whenever I put out a new set of designs, I lay out a brochure that features color photos of each design, include all the ordering information, and just run off as many as I need to reach the shops on my mailing list."

Susan Young uses a Hewlett Packard OfficeJet Pro 1170Cse primarily for high quality printing and or scanning photographs.

"Although the manufacturer probably wouldn't endorse my personal practice of scanning actual ⅛" painted wood cutouts, I do it frequently and have had no problems with scratching the screen. These scanned images are saved as any other file is saved. In dealing with out-of-state clients, customers across town, or a magazine editor, I can send a file attachment with e-mail concerning a project or design submission. The time this method saves me is invaluable. Text material can be scanned into word processing software, then saved."

Annie Lang believes a full color scanner, Pentium processor, and CD-ROM are basic necessities for anyone working in graphics. "I've also found a ZIP drive a necessity to save and work with graphics. I scan digital pictures and use a digital color photo printer to create and crop project photos for submissions in lieu of running back and forth to get photos developed. This is also helpful when I'm dealing with editors who like to see a project by e-mail. I can attach a JPEG file and get an immediate yes or no as to whether I should continue with the project."

A Little Scanning Tip

"Scanning photos at a resolution greater than 100 dpi will not improve picture quality," says Susan Young. [Although some newer applications, such as inkjet photo printing can require higher-resolution images.] "For higher resolution, see the options within your printer/scanner software. If you are scanning a photo or small item for a Web site or display screen, most screens only display at 72 dpi, so there is no reason to scan at a higher resolution or bit depth than you need. It doesn't improve your quality and only takes up more space on your disk. With HP Scan Picture (HP OfficePro software), I have the capability to scan pictures/photos directly into any document I'm working in, whether it's WordPerfect, Microsoft Publisher, or Microsoft Word. The option 'Scan Picture' became automatically listed on the file menus of all my resident software programs upon installation of my HP OfficePro software."

A note to designers without e-mail: Are you beginning to see that if you continue to try to deal with editors only by mail, you are going to lose ground to your competitors? By communicating electronically with editors, they can get their foot in the door faster than you can lick a stamp!

A "BUILDING YOUR BUSINESS" CHECKLIST

Technology is quickly and dramatically changing the way we all live and work, the way we communicate, the way we create our products and services, manage our businesses, and sell our wares. For that reason, no one in business can afford to operate without a computer. Even the smallest home-based crafts business will benefit from computer technology. Remember to:

- Buy the best computer system you can afford—one that meets current needs, has room for you to grow, and is Internet-ready.
- Expect a stressful learning period, but look ahead to the rewards awaiting you when you've got a handle on everything.
- View computers and related technology as helpful friends who can save you hours of work and tons of stress once you've gotten past the initial learning process.
- Keep learning and working to "fill the holes" in your knowledge bank.
- Periodically analyze what you're doing in light of new technology that could make your work easier.
- Don't let fear of technology prevent you from exploring new technological turf. Remember, the trick is to "turn off the fear impulse so it doesn't reach the chicken portion of your brain."

HELPFUL PERIODICALS MENTIONED IN THIS CHAPTER

Arts & Crafts Show Business, P. O. Box 26624, Jacksonville, FL 32226. LaVerne Herren publishes this monthly magazine, which lists shows, festivals, exhibits, etc., in Florida, Georgia, North and South Carolina. www.jacksonville.net/~artcraft.

Arts 'n Crafts ShowGuide, ACN Publications, P. O. Box 25, Jefferson City, MO 65102. Dan Engle publishes this magazine, which is devoted entirely to the business side of craft fair exhibiting and includes a comprehensive national list of shows and supplier resources; www.acnshowguide.com.

Choices for Craftsmen and Artists, P. O. Box 484, Rhinebeck, NY 12572. Betty Chypre publishes this quarterly "Yellow Page Directory of Craft Show Information" about shows in Connecticut, Massachusetts, New Jersey, New York, Pennslyvania, and Vermont; www.choices.cc

Craftmaster News, P. O. Box 39429, Downey, CA 90239. Marsha Reed publishes this monthly show-listing periodical for professional craftspeople on the West Coast; www.craftmasternews.com.

Crafts Remembered, 1046 Madison Avenue, Troy, NY 12180. A show-listing periodical with articles and other business information, published by Rita Stone-Conwell for artisans in the New York state area; www.taconic.com/crn.

The Professional Quilter, 22412 Rolling Hill Lane, Laytonsville, MD 20882. Published by Morna McEver Golletz, this quarterly business journal provides business and marketing information for quilters, designers, and teachers interested in making a career in quilting; www.professionalquilter.com.

Chapter Five

Business Planning and Goal Setting

||||||||||||||||||||||||||||||||||||||||||||||||

The point in having a business plan is that it gives you a starting point for review, growth and adjustment. If you don't know where you want to end up, how will you know how to get there, if and when you get there at all?
—MORNA MCEVER GOLLETZ, *The Professional Quilter*

What happens if you don't make written plans? As one craftswoman put it, "I didn't have a real plan. What happened, happened."

I don't think that's how you want to run your business. Certainly this is not a profitable way to run a business. Although a plan can be something as simple as a list of things to do, you need more than this if you want to analyze certain aspects of your business and learn how to:

▸▸ measure the annual growth of your business,
▸▸ see how it's changing from year to year,
▸▸ calculate true overhead costs,
▸▸ identify your most profitable products or product lines,
▸▸ spot sales trends that signal a need for new products,
▸▸ stay focused on your various goals.

In the last chapter you learned the importance of staying up on computer technology. This chapter's focus is on the importance of planning and how to use both computerized and handwritten notes, files, and records to create business or marketing plans that will translate into extra profit at year's end.

WHY YOU NEED A WRITTEN PLAN

"Every business needs a plan to grow, and the key to good planning lies in keeping good records," says association director Barbara Arena. "Running the business is as important as designing the products you plan to sell. Over time, the plan will clearly show you both your strengths and weaknesses. You must constantly evaluate and re-target your efforts to meet the current customer demand. This is all the more important now with the impact of the Internet as a viable marketing tool. I feel our growth is directly related to planning and keeping an ever-watchful eye on changes we discover from our business records."

"I've found a written business plan to be an absolute necessity," says designer and author Annie Lang. "It is tangible evidence that your business is indeed yours to control. I can't drive to most destinations without a good map; likewise, I cannot meet my business objectives without a good plan of action. I don't expect everything to go according to Hoyle, so I make sure my plan is both flexible and practical."

"Having a written business plan saves me time and money," says bead jewelry artist Wendy Van Camp. "Being creative, I tend to go off in many directions easily. Having a plan written down and posted on the wall next to my computer reminds me of the goals I have set for this year and keeps me from flying away with my active imagination."

"Putting things in writing really opens your eyes, helps you get focused, and makes you stay on track," says crafts wholesaler Pat Endicott. "For over ten years, every November and December, we would discuss what went right or wrong during the year, what we liked, wanted to try new, etc. I finally wrote my first business plan after taking a night class on that subject. An SBA [Small Business Administration] booklet I'd gotten from a SCORE [Service Corps of Retired Executives] adviser was also helpful to me. It took weeks of research, but it was all worth it. I went back five years and recapped all sales and expenditures. Pulled past price sheets, hang tags, and catalogs, and analyzed them. The complete study made it easy to see how the business had grown, how certain product categories were up one year and not the other. I was able to more accurately calculate our true overhead costs and determine a figure that could be applied to all our products. Each year now I review the whole plan and add an annual update."

"Planning shouldn't be too detailed," cautions greeting card publisher Kate Harper. "Always look at the bigger picture. Ask yourself 'What is priority?' every day. My first priority is always the shipment of orders. Everything else can wait. If you don't have a general yearly outline hanging on the wall where you can see it, you will end up putting out fires every day and wonder why things aren't getting done. This kind of planning brings in more business because stores start to realize you are more organized than other sellers, and they will know they can depend on you to do what you say you'll do."

When is a good time to write your annual plan? "I normally set aside the week after Christmas to analyze my yearly sales," says Annie Lang. "At the same time I also work out a budget, set my objectives, review my wish list, set up tentative travel plans for annual conventions I want to attend, and fill in any necessary calendar deadlines so I can better manage my productive time."

Once written, a plan must be implemented. Here's how Annie does that job. "After writing a plan, I go back and prioritize my list. I fill in my calendar time slots to coincide with those objectives and set specific objective deadlines. For instance, if my objective is to be published in *ABC Magazine* my plan of action would be to: (1) research back issues; (2) query the editor and request publication deadline schedule; (3) create several projects that will fill their needs (if not, list other publications that may be interested in purchasing the designs); (4) submit the project and then follow-up if necessary.

"If my objective isn't met within three months, I'll submit the project to other publishers on the list," Annie continues. "Working in this methodical manner, I save both my time and the editor's by not submitting projects that don't fit her format or editorial needs. Stress is kept to a minimum because I'm working at my own pace and not 'under the gun.'"

How to Use a Business Plan

"I do a formal written plan shortly after the first of the year, when I have all of the end-of-the-year reports done. This way I can evaluate the progress from the previous year and make plans based on that information. I review the plan every three or four months to see if I am on target or need to revise something. For me, the sales information from the previous year or previous quarters—not only the total dollar amount per item, but how these sales were obtained—are key in planning for the continued growth of the business.

"In every business plan, I include a statement of purpose and business description. In looking over plans from previous years, I can see how the purpose and—often—the description have changed as the business grew and changed in response to an ever-changing market and customer demands.

"This part of the plan is an analysis of who our target customer is; why they need, want, or will buy our product or service. Here I detail each part of our selling program—again, guided by sales report information I've pulled previously. This provides a road map to where we will put more time and effort and where we should spend the least time. Time is money, so we need to spend it wisely. Without evaluating on a regular basis, it is easy to follow the same old route, which can be costly if you are not on the right road.

"Using notes I've kept from talking with customers and networking with others within the arts and crafts industry, plus the sales reports at hand, I do an overview of what I have so far to decide if any new products could be added to generate additional income.

"Finally, we look back at previous plans to see where we came from and where we are headed as we develop a new plan. It serves as a goal or target to work toward, one step at a time."

by Barbara Arena, Managing Director, National Craft Association

NETWORKING SESSION #5: DIFFERENT WAYS TO PLAN

List-making is a simple kind of plan we all do, from writing down what we're going to buy at the grocery store to making a checklist of jobs we want to accomplish in our office on a particular day. Tell me about the lists you make.

Eileen Heifner (Create-an-Heirloom Doll Kit Co.): "My business is no longer in my home, but every day, just as I did when I worked at home, I make a work plan, or on very busy days, just a list. This helps me to keep focused on the most important things that need to get done that day. On some 'brush fire' days, the only thing I get to do is look at the list, so even the best-laid plans do not always come to fruition when you want them to."

Jan McClellan (Heirloom Jewelry): "I'm a great list maker. I make long lists of things that need to be done in certain time frames. For instance, in January and February I send off jewelry to a professional photographer for new slides, then sort out and enter fairs or list fairs to do and applications I need to write for. I also have a list for things I need to do to update my Web site, and I also inventory and assess what jewelry I need to make."

Deb Otto (Henri's): "I forget the simplest things at times, so lists are invaluable to me. But it takes too much time to write them out from scratch, so I have a number of standard reminder checklists I've created on computer using my spreadsheet program. One column becomes my list and a narrow column of boxes next to each item is for checking off. These lists can be customized for several things I do on a regular basis. For example, I have checklists of things to take to a craft show; on overnight trips; what to do when company is coming (including a list of all the ingredients to make a certain meal for guests so I don't have to plan the meal all over again); end-of-month business things to do (commissions to pay, reports to print, sales tax due, etc.); monthly errands list; and a master list of grocery items I normally stock, so I can just check the items I want on shopping day. I print several copies of some lists and keep others in a LISTS folder and print them as needed."

Gail Platts (InCalico): "I've learned the importance of writing down time needed to get things done. I've found that things like running to the store, which only takes one line on a to-do list, can easily erode an hour and a half of my day. If I didn't take into account the time needed when planning my schedule, I would wind up over-scheduling myself, not meeting my goals, and getting frustrated and depressed. Thus I give myself a visual picture by writing the tasks, the time needed to complete them, and a due date."

Tori Hoggard (Harmony Artworks): "I end each day by writing a to-do list for the next day. This saves me time from gathering and reorganizing my thoughts each morning, keeps me on schedule, and ensures that I do not forget anything important."

Kim Marie (Kim Marie Fine Pottery): "Having a to-do list is grand, but if the length of it makes you want to run and hide, then something has to change. For me, after I make the to-do list, I go for a priority list. If I feel overwhelmed I stop and think, 'It will all get done if I start by taking one thing at a time.' I've also keyed in on certain beliefs I have that keep me working, like 'The more I do, the more I *can* do.' I also like small reward systems. For example, if I meet my production goals, I'll take a free Friday and just work on ideas I've wanted to develop or pieces that make my soul sing."

Elizabeth Bishop (Seams Sew Creative Patterns): "Making lists is a compulsion of mine. If I can get it down on paper, it unclogs my mind. I use a spider-web type of list I once found in a book, whereby each spoke represents an area of work, then subspokes evolve from that."

I, too, have often used this method of "emptying my brain," especially on nights when I'm having trouble sleeping. For those unfamiliar with this kind of list, you just start with a circle in the middle that represents your main concern, such as a

deadline date or problem you must solve. Then, as you think of things related to what needs to be done, draw lines from the circle, writing a note on each of them. In turn, those notes will suggest other things that need to be done, so draw shorter lines off your main lines, and keep on adding main and subhead lines until you have literally outlined every thought in your head. I have found this exercise to be a great stress reliever as well as a good outline of everything that needs to be done. (P.S. Start with a BIG piece of paper!)

In addition to making lists, how many of you also keep card files, idea notebooks, or journals?

Bobbi Chukran (Wildest Dreams Designs): "I jot down ideas on colored 4 x 6 index cards and stick them in a wooden file box that I have divided by subjects. This keeps all those little scraps of paper, sticky notes, etc., somewhat organized. I tried doing this on computer, but that didn't work as well for me. I can carry the cards around with me everywhere I go, and I have them stashed all over the house in drawers, nightstands, in the car, my purse, etc., always ready to capture a new idea."

Tabitha Haggie (Bunny Hutch Handcrafts): "I keep a spiral-bound notebook I carry everywhere. I write down every idea from booth display ideas, projects, marketing ideas, crafting tips, packaging tips, whatever. I then periodically transpose that information to my computer (using Microsoft Excel software) and print it for my three-ring binder."

Jacquelyn Fox (Waxing Moon Designs): "I find it handy to have all my ideas in one place. In a stenographer's notebook, I jot down marketing ideas and brochure layouts, make notes about costs of upcoming design projects (printing, model creation, kit costs, etc.) as well as the projected income of the project. I've had some real eye-opening experiences about the projected income part. When I first started, I thought I could wholesale many designs directly to the needlework shops, but found instead that most prefer buying my charts through

distributors. (They take a twenty-five to thirty percent cut of my profits, so the projected income is a bit lower than I originally anticipated. I look back on those notes now and think how naive I was.)"

Eileen Heifner: "I make several small business plans a year in a
notebook that usually involves headings of topics I wish to pursue.
When I feel it is time to explore that particular topic, I will take
action by gathering information. Sometimes things just get too
hectic, and it may take a lot longer or even become obsolete if
something better comes along. Any time I hear of a new idea or
opportunity, I put my idea there to look over when I'm ready to take
another step forward."

Wendy Van Camp (IndigoSkye Bead Fashions): "Since I virtually live
at my computer all the while I'm in my office, I do all my writing
and planning as I'm working. Often, my best ideas come when I'm
in the middle of a particular writing job. When the muse strikes, I
simply pull up one of my many idea files on computer, jot a note to
that file before I forget it, and go back to the job at hand. (One thing
I love about word-processing software is that I can have several
screens going at the same time, so pulling up a new file to add
something to it takes only a moment and doesn't disrupt the flow
of my work.) I also keep a clipboard with a scratch pad beside my
computer that I write new ideas upon. Many of these new ideas are
incorporated into next year's plan after I've had a month or two to
mull it over and do a small test of whatever the idea is."

Kate Harper: "I organize everything into looseleaf notebooks
because things change a lot. I have different notebooks for each of
the following topics: Sales Stats, Store Account List, Store Chains,
Potential Accounts, Rep Territories, Potential Reps, and General
Business Procedures. Even though all this is on the computer, it's
much more usable in notebooks. I can make notes while I'm on the
phone or jot them down when I'm away from the computer."

**I agree. Although I have all my notes and idea files in comput-
er documents, I need hard copy in hand to use them because**

my brain reacts differently to words on a computer screen versus words on paper. As I work with my notes, I modify them on paper, then go back to the computer to update the files. Often, in rereading my notes, I see things that weren't obvious to me at the time I originally wrote them. That's why I always encourage business owners to keep a journal of their daily business activities, ideas, plans, and accomplishments. Rereading them from time to time is not only personally satisfying but often revealing. I think some of you have already discovered this for yourself.

Susan Young (Peach Kitty Studio): "Yes, I certainly have. I've kept handwritten notebooks, sketchbooks with designs, and logs of activities and correspondence for the past eight years. Recently, I retrieved a spiral notebook from 1992 and, though I had other things vying for my time, I became lost in reliving what I was doing/designing/marketing seven years ago. When I put the book back on the shelf, I was smiling because that notebook was proof I was becoming successful even then—when I didn't think I was getting anywhere. It showed me how I've grown in spite of some day-to-day disappointments, and how I'm still growing. And isn't that what it's all about?"

HOW TO USE CALENDARS

Calendars are helpful time management and organizing tools we all need for maximum efficiency. Greeting card publisher Kate Harper keeps a general yearly calendar of things that have to be done by a certain date. "It's here that I schedule what has to be done with each card in my line. For example, in June, I plan Valentine cards; in July, I print them; in August, I mail them to reps."

Tabitha Haggie monitors craft show sales with a project planner that she starts for the next year during her fall selling season. "Then, in January, I refine it and continue to do so throughout the year. This has been an invaluable tool for me. At any given moment I can see exactly what I have on the table, what it will cost to produce, and what my profit can be. After my shows start, I add a column for each show. Then I enter the number sold for each item. This enables me to keep track of what sells at what shows and at what time of the season certain items start to move, such as Santas and Snowmen."

Pat Endicott has used a daily calendar for five years. "It includes personal and business notes. Some days it holds a wealth of discoveries; other times it is boring. It is especially good for noting what worked or didn't regarding shows/traveling/product development (correction of errors in the corporate world) as well as noting moods. Sometimes in reading back notes, my eyes are opened to repetitious things that should be changed."

Here's a tip that has always worked for me. When you have a deadline looming, you can get ahead by working backwards. For every task with a deadline attached to it, make a plan that starts at the point where you must be finished and work backwards to the beginning. Estimate the amount of time each step will take and plot it to a calendar. As you work on your project, you can see whether you're still on schedule or running behind and you can see and make adjustments accordingly.

As both a full-time writer and home-business owner, I use a variety of calendars to help me manage my time, my writing, and my money. To organize my writing work, I make lists of all the various topics and people I might write about for each of my columns and books, keeping this information in various document files on computer. I also create a written plan that summarizes the topic of each column I must write, along with its due date, and print out a copy for quick reference. Then, on my Writing Calendar, I put colorful stickers on the day I need to start the research or writing for each column so my brain registers the fact that this is *the day* I've got to start writing something that's on my schedule.

In addition to my Bill-Paying Calendar (see Chapter Six), I keep an Income Calendar onto which I plot when writing income is due from my various publishers and how much is expected each month. This helps me do cash-flow planning.

When I'm working on a book, I keep a Book Calendar, noting each day how many hours I've spent on the book doing various jobs related to it. Because I had recorded every hour spent on research, telephone interviews, writing, rewriting, editing, and

Writing a Mission Statement

A mission statement is a document you write for yourself that outlines your overall plans and goals for your business. It helps you to fully understand the business you are in and where it's headed. Some mission statements are just a sentence or two, while others are longer. Here are some examples:

▸▸ *To create innovative, high-quality products at a reasonable price; to give the customers more for their money. —Eleena Danielson, Cranberry Junction*

▸▸ *To become more proficient and prolific as a designer and writer, to enrich my life and the lives of others by expanding and strengthening my professional and personal relationships, increasing my knowledge and sharing my creativity. —Carol Krob, Carol's Creations*

▸▸ *To create unique custom works of art for a highly discriminating audience; Develop and support the availability of special quality limited art items for those who wish to take advantage of my creativity for gifts to special individuals and for special occasions; Support the reproduction of certain works of art for larger audiences who may desire the artistry for remembrances, keepsakes, and commemorations; Dedicate time and energy to the exploration and enhancement of creative artistic styles and expressions; and Work diligently to satisfy the needs for timing and delivery of artwork. —Pamela Spinazzola, Pamela's Studio One*

If you can put into writing what you stand for (your values) and link it to what you are seeking to accomplish (your vision), you will create a mission statement that outlines exactly where you want to go and what you must do to get there. Once written, post it where you can see it, for it will give you extra motivation to achieve your goals.

proofreading my last two books, I knew when I started this book that I could turn out an average of 168 words of finished copy per hour. That may not sound like a lot, but it translates to around 1,200 words of finished copy a day, which means that if I can work on a book five days in a row, I can probably complete a chapter of 6,000 words or more. This is invaluable information to me because now, when a publisher asks me how long it will take for me to write a book of 100,000 words (the size of this one), I can calculate the answer. (Of course, the real trick here is building in extra time for other work and "life's little interruptions." This particular book took five months to complete.)

THE BENEFITS OF WRITTEN GOALS

If "business planning" sounds too hard, just write down your goals every year and let those written goals serve as a plan. Keep your goals large enough to motivate you to go forward, yet small enough to be easily achieved. If she were doing it over again, newsletter publisher Rita Stone-Conwell says she would have started with smaller goals in mind. "I wanted to be the best imme-diately," she recalls. "This is not a rational idea; taking smaller steps would have put me on an easier track and still gotten me to where I am now."

Putting your goals in writing helps you stay focused, says cloth doll designer Gail Platts, who follows the SMART rule that reminds us that goals are:

▸▸ **S**pecific
▸▸ **M**easurable
▸▸ **A**ttainable
▸▸ **R**elevant and
▸▸ **T**rackable

"I wear so many hats that I get distracted at times," says Gail. "So I write my goal, decide how I will reach it, within what time frame, and what steps I need to follow. It also helps to have a couple of friends in your business that you can meet with periodically, in person or online. It's nice to have someone who will check in to make sure you are staying on track, and help you evaluate if things are going they way they should."

Quilt designer Karen Combs makes lists in her planner of monthly goals. "From this list, I pull daily goals," she says. "It helps keep me focused, and I don't forget as much as I used to. I also keep a small notebook in my purse. As I think of something I need to do or want to remember, I write it in the notebook. When I get home, I transfer it to the planner. As I get older, I can't seem to remember as much as I need to. It could be that I'm getting older, or maybe just busier, but I find I need to get all my 'need to do' things out of my brain and onto paper."

"I try to implement a goal and do something that effects the sale or future sale of my product at least once a day," says soap maker Linda Beattie Inlow. "Unless one is focused on the end result, such as selling 100 items in a month or making so many dollars per day, and does something each day to achieve it, the goal may have to be readjusted when it comes time to evaluate the plan and/or goal of the business."

If you know what you want in life, put it in writing in the form of a goal as Tori Hoggard has done: "My plans for attaining full-time status are to teach more regularly and write a book that focuses on integrating art into everyday life. I am also working on getting better known as a muralist and furniture painter and getting commission work. By having my hands in several things, whichever makes the money may be the one I choose to focus on."

Once you've written a list of goals, they must be reviewed from time to time. Early each year, designer Kathy Wirth reviews her goals from the previous year and writes new ones. "I focus on income expectations, name-recognition goals, and accomplishments I hope to add to my resume," she says. "Then I jot down ideas on how to achieve these goals. I try to evaluate which business activities in the previous year yielded the best results and plan to pursue more of them."

I like the way Annie Lang records and reviews her goals. She keeps a "Wish Box" on her desk that includes notes about all her goals— large, small, business, or personal. At the beginning of each year, she adds a bunch of new goals for that year. Then, every couple of months or so, she goes through the box and reads through her wish list, pulling those she has achieved while adding new ones. "Everything I want to do, wish I had, or hope to achieve goes into this box," she says.

A "Q&A Goals Statement"

Eleena Danielson of Cranberry Junction has documented her goals in an interesting question-and-answer format that may inspire you to write a similar document for your own business:

Q: What is Cranberry Junction's mission statement?
A: *To create innovative, high-quality products at a reasonable price; to give the customers more for their money.*
Q: What ways will we be able to increase sales?
A: *a) Advertise, advertise, advertise*
b) Incentives/promotions
c) Automatic shipment on future patterns
Q: Marketing strategy: How will people find us? Where will we get the best exposure for the money?
A: *a) Internet*
b) Magazine advertisements
c) Trade shows
d) Mail order catalogs
Q: What do we want to make this year, broken down by months, by days? What will it take to achieve this goal?
A: *a) $250,000 a year would mean. . .*
b) $20,833 a month, with. . .
c) $694 worth of orders per day

Other questions to consider: Where do we see our business going in three years? Five years? Ten years? What are my strengths in helping this business to grow and succeed? What are my weak points, and what steps/action need to be taken to turn that around?

Gail Platts emphasizes that the difference between a *want* and a *goal* is, "with a goal, you have a plan. The best business advice I ever got was to 'work at your business every single day,' but unless you have your eye on the goal, how can you reach it? Putting your goals in writing helps you make a commitment to them and helps you to keep them in focus . . . or, as Yogi Berra reportedly said, 'If you don't know where you are going, you might not get there.'"

BORROWING MONEY TO ADVANCE YOUR BUSINESS

"When my partner and I wanted to launch our business, we tried to borrow money from a bank," says a business owner. "But they would only lend us money based on our husbands' assets as collateral. This may have been a smart move on the part of the bank, but it was demoralizing to us." I've heard this story over and over again. Although today women-owned businesses get more respect from bankers than they did ten years ago, no bank will loan money to launch a home-based business.

More than one business owner has gotten crafty when it comes to borrowing money, however. Years ago when Leila Peltosaari needed money to print her sewing books, the banks considered it too risky and refused. "But it was easy to get credit to buy a car and take a vacation, so we told our bank we needed a new car and wanted to make a trip to see our parents in Europe, and then we used the money to print the book. With the profits from book sales, we then bought a car, a house, a swimming pool, and trailer tent, made a fabulous European trip and invested in our retirement, too. I understood that banks had no confidence in our intentions, so we just played their game and it all worked out fine."

I know exactly what she means. When I was eighteen and holding a secretarial position, I found it easy to borrow money for my first vacation (a dude ranch in Colorado). But when I wanted $5,000 to start my home-based publishing business in 1981 and had a high-paying salaried job with money in the bank, I was turned down because I had no collateral. I was advised to borrow from my savings, which is what I ultimately had to do.

Lack of money can definitely delay business success. "I have never borrowed money for my business, and I really feel that my reluctance to do so has been a handicap," says Elizabeth Bishop. "Frugal and conservative traits can rob one of momentum."

"The lack of extra funding has hampered the growth of my business greatly," adds Wendy Van Camp. "However, I find that banks are weighted against women getting business loans. Even with the extra help that SCORE provides for female entrepreneurs, I find the odds too hard to fight."

"I, too, found borrowing money to be difficult," says Rita Stone-Conwell. "In our area, getting banks to take you seriously is a real problem. Even after you prove you've been in business for over the required length of time, the fact that large amounts of profit are not seen causes many to turn you down and sometimes even to laugh at you. Because of the constant runaround I've gotten, I have used one of our charge cards to finance business expenses."

Often the worst that happens if you can't borrow money is that you just grow more slowly than you originally envisioned. And that's not necessarily bad. In fact, having an excess of money has gotten a lot of small business owners into trouble because they spent it too freely and fell into some financial potholes as a result.

"It would be great to have a large infusion of money to develop a new line and just do it all at once instead of piecemeal when there is extra money for it," says Carol Carlson. "I've talked to the bank about a small business loan, but they said I would have to do a home equity loan and use that. But what if you don't own a home? (I do, but I didn't want to go this route.) I have decided instead to take money out of my mutual funds because I see this as an investment for my future."

"We have never borrowed money to get us through cash flow problems, and this regimen has made a distinct difference in our pattern of growth," say Camille and Bill Ronay. "However, the discipline of pay-as-you-go has created a high level of appreciation for what we achieve."

When *should* you think about borrowing money? Taking out a short-term loan to buy a computer system or piece of machinery or equipment that is going to increase your productivity or profits makes good sense. "After being in business for six years, I got a bank loan to buy a needed piece of machinery that could boost my productivity," says Joyce Birchler. "I was nervous about doing this, but got encouragement from my husband. I talked the bank into lending me the money by showing them my retail and wholesale show schedules and accounts I already have. The biggest thing going for me was the fact that my business had doubled in two years and could more than triple in six months with this machine."

"When I started the business, I went to my local bank for a loan and was pleasantly surprised to find I was eligible for a special, low-interest (6 percent) rate for local small businesses," says Jacquelyn Fox. "I would recommend that anyone starting a small business talk to their local bank about possible inclusion into such a program. Many towns are now trying to encourage local entrepreneurs in various ways because it boosts the local economy."

Borrowing to establish credit is a good idea for those who know how to manage their money. "When I first started my store in 1975, I took out a loan to buy inventory," says Chris Gustin. "This did help increase my business. I paid the loan back on time and the next time I needed money, I was able to get a signature loan."

After you've been in business a few years, have a track record of success, good financial reports, no debts, and no apparent need for money, you can probably get a line of credit with no trouble at all. Banks love to lend money to people who don't need it. The trick is getting that credit line at a time when you *apparently* do not need it (like just before you actually need $5,000 for a major expansion of your business).

When a bank loan is out of the question, many people borrow on their credit cards. Properly handled, credit card loans can launch a business or be a lifesaver for businesses whose income is seasonal or comes in spurts. Derek Andrews uses a credit card to get his business through the first six months of the year, keeping one card specifically for business expenditures so the interest can be documented for accounting purposes. Gail Platts jump-started her business with a $500 loan from a credit card that got her a booth and printing for her first wholesale show.

In deciding whether you ought to borrow money or not, you need

A Good Plan of Action

In Step With Today's Creative Spirit

In Carol Krob's plan for her business, Carol's Creations, under "Plan of Action," she includes a note about striving to overcome her biggest hurdle, which may be a hurdle for you, too: *procrastination*. Six other items on Carol's list offer good advice for every reader of this book (myself included):

1) Develop a proper mental attitude; make up my mind to tackle chores and develop projects whether I'm 'in the mood' or not.
2) Don't use fatigue as an excuse to avoid scheduled activities, but do allow for adequate rest, and take a break from work when exhaustion clearly begins to hamper performance.
3) Break down all jobs into small, manageable parts.
4) Temper ambition with a dose of practicality.
5) Regard mistakes and problems as learning experiences, not insurmountable obstacles to eventual success.
6) Approach every endeavor in a realistic, optimistic, enthusiastic frame of mind.

Above all, Carol emphasizes, "We should critically review our daily activities in terms of their contribution to our long- and short-term goals and constantly strive to make improvements. And never lose faith in our ability to achieve success."

to consider your present financial situation and your ability to pay back the loan. "Also," says Wendy Van Camp, "you need to balance the growth idea with why you started your business in the first place. I wanted a job that would pay bills I needed to cover and that would be as stress-free as possible. If my business grew too big, it would not be beneficial to my health. I have reached that goal at present and have been able to grow my business with the profits now coming in. In my case, this seems to be the best of both worlds and unless I decide to open a boutique or a mall cart, I won't bother trying to seek out a business loan."

A BUSINESS PLANNING/GOAL SETTING CHECKLIST

Business planning never stops. It is something you must do at the beginning, in the middle, and even at the end of your business. By putting your plans in writing, you will more easily achieve both your personal and financial goals. Keep these tips in mind:

▸ Before you write a business plan, first write a *mission statement* that links what you stand for (your values) to what you are seeking to accomplish (your vision). Include this mission statement in your annual business plan.

▸ Also include in your business plan a complete description of your business and each of the individual products and services you sell.

▸ Keep good records so your business plan will contain the kind of details you need to analyze various aspects of your business.

▸ Review your plan each year, adding annual updates as needed. Use your plan as both a guide and a goal to work toward, one step at a time.

▸ A three-ring notebook is a good way to organize various idea lists, projects, marketing goals, sketches, and so on.

▸ As your business grows, you may find it helpful to have several notebooks, one for each area of your business. Although everything should always be on computer, information is much more usable in notebook form.

➠ If valuable information or ideas cannot be put on computer, make photocopies of this information and put it in a safety deposit box or fireproof drawer to protect it against loss.

➠ Plot deadline dates and income expectations to a monthly calendar to help you complete projects by scheduled deadline dates and avoid late-payment charges on bills.

➠ Make a "To Do" list every day to help you stay on schedule and ensure that you don't forget anything important. Be sure to prioritize the list because some things will probably have to be carried forward to another day.

➠ Throughout the year, make lists of things to research, books to read, people to contact, ideas to explore, etc.

➠ Frequently reread notes, lists, and other things you've written. This can be a great idea-stimulator that often points to things you couldn't see when you first jotted the note.

➠ Put all your goals in written form since they will automatically become a plan. Keep them large enough to motivate you to go forward, yet small enough to be easily achieved.

➠ Try Annie Lang's idea of keeping a "Wish Box" in which to drop notes about everything you want to do, wish you had, or hope to achieve. Periodically go through the box, pulling goals accomplished and adding new ones.

➠ Critically review your daily activities in terms of their contribution to your long- and short-term goals, constantly striving to make improvements.

➠ Never lose faith in your ability to achieve success.

Free Help from the Government

The mission of the U.S. Small Business Administration (SBA) is to help people get into business and stay here. Help is available from local district offices of the SBA in the form of free business counseling and training from more than 8,000 SCORE (Service Corps of Retired Executives) volunteers nationwide. For more information, call the SBA Answer Desk at 1-800-827-5722; or SCORE, 1-800-634-0245.

Chapter Six

Business Management Tips and Strategies

||||||||||||||||||||||||||||||||||||||||||||||||||||

. . . if you want to run a business successfully, you must run it like successful businesses are run. You must do the things that 'businesses' do."
— ROBERT E. FLEURY, *The Small Business Survival Guide*

tatistics from Dun and Bradstreet and the U.S. Small Business Administration confirm that between 55 to 60 percent of all businesses fail within the first five years, and about 95 percent of these failures are attributable to poor management. Thus, even the smallest home-based business must be concerned about its business management techniques and strive always to improve them.

"No matter how many hours you devote to your business or how much it contributes financially, treat it seriously," advises Pat Endicott, House of Threads & Wood, Inc. "When I had a full-time job, I didn't pay enough attention to the details of my home-based business, such as how to read profit-and-loss statements and study training materials (sales-business improvement, show research facts, etc.). When I had to rely on this business solely, I felt fairly stupid to ask many of these questions after being in business for so long. My SCORE advisor said many people are already drowning when they realize something is wrong, and often it is too late to correct the problem. He was very encouraging and understanding as he answered all my questions."

In the two previous chapters, you learned the importance of computerizing your business and making good business plans. Along with some money-saving tips, this chapter illustrates how creative people handle different office and business management tasks and the various software programs they use for specific tasks.

BUSINESS MANAGEMENT/ACCOUNTING/ RECORD-KEEPING SOFTWARE

There are literally hundreds of software programs that can be used to manage a small business, but QuickBooks (by Intuit) seems to be one of the most popular and best bookkeeping systems for small businesses. It was designed to accommodate the small business owner who needs to do accounting, invoicing, inventory management, and mailing lists. Dodie Eisenhauer, who wholesales her line of handcrafted gifts through sales reps and trade shows, says this software is perfect for her needs.

"This is my whole accounting and record-keeping system. When I type in the name of a shop and all the customer data on it, I include information on where I acquired them and who the rep is so I can sort my mailing list by category. If I want to send something to everyone who came to a particular trade show, I can sort on that data field; or, I could contact all the customers generated by a particular sales rep or in a particular area of the country. Mailing lists may also be sorted by ZIP code or alphabetically by name. At the end of each year, I run a directory of accounts so I can see if I have accounts in a particular state or just look up someone without going to the computer."

Chris Noah-Cooper and husband Tom use Microsoft Excel to keep track of inventory and prepare price lists and sales records for their printmaking business. "Excel is so broad in its utility that it is a challenge to apply it to our specific situation," says Tom. "To keep track of finances, we use M.Y.O.B. (Mind Your Own Business). We recently bought a Mac with Adobe PhotoShop and Macromedia Freehand. We scan things in with an Astra scanner. (Note: These programs are memory hogs—we bought 128 MB of RAM, and even that can be used up with this software.)"

Potter Kim Marie also does her accounting with M.Y.O.B. software. "With it," she says, "I can track inventory, keep pending invoices for work on consignment, set up contact logs for my customers and vendors. It has some great analysis features and reports.

At the end of the year, I give my accountant the income statement, answer a few questions, and we're done."

Not everyone likes M.Y.O.B. software, however. In Steve Appel's opinion, it's a royal pain. "I even brought someone in to show me how to use it, and it still made no sense. I plan to go back to using a Quicken spreadsheet to keep my inventory up-to-date," he says.

Emily Pearlman uses her Quicken software to categorize and graph her pottery-making expenses. "This enabled me to see how I was doing each month. The first thing that became obvious was that my firing charges were much too high in proportion to my gross income. This forced me to focus on that problem and realize that I had far too many seconds each firing. That, in turn, allowed me to look at the 'seconds problem' and analyze what was causing a second to happen. As a result, I became more careful in stacking the kiln, changed some problem glazes, changed some firing procedures, and eventually cut my firing charges in half.

"The same was true for packing and shipping expenses. After focusing on my shipping expenses, I realized that it cost less to use larger (oversized) boxes and pay UPS at the 30 lbs weight—even though the box weighed only 20 to 25 lbs—than to ship in two smaller boxes adding up to the lesser weight."

Michelle Temares, the principal of a product development and design company, has learned the importance of tracking the results of her marketing and advertising efforts. While some do this kind of analysis with database software, Michelle simply uses her Excel spreadsheet software. "You can't sort extensively on a spreadsheet, but you can do analysis," she says. "I set up a file for each customer that included contact information, type of company, and how the business was obtained (a source code). By indicating a source-of-business column, I was able to determine which of my marketing and advertising efforts paid off the most handsomely and which were a waste of time. It was really illuminating to see all of the data organized and laid out for the first time. I was quite surprised to see that 'cold calling' generated a significant percent of my business. I thus made it a goal the following year to send out one informational package per week to select targeted companies that I had not previously contacted. Now my spreadsheet record functions as a contact sheet for me as well. I enter

CRAFT SHOWS 1999

	SHOW SALES	LESS CGS	SHOWFEE	MILES	MIL EXPENSE	MOTEL	FOOD	PROFIT	MONTH PROFIT	SAT	RECAP NOTES
1											
2	$1563.70	$1250.96	$120.00	275	$90.75	$161.70	$75.82	$802.69		MAR 6	STEADY CROWD
3	$649.40	$519.52	$130.00	120	$39.60	$118.72	$85.00	$146.20		MAR13	
4	$983.70	$786.96	$105.00	360	$118.80	$0.00	$95.62	$467.54		MAR 20	SIGNED UP FOR BETTER LOCATION FOR 2000
5		$0.00			$0.00	$0.00	$0.00	$0.00	$1416.43	MAR 27	
6		$0.00			$0.00	$0.00	$0.00	$0.00		APRIL 3	
7		$0.00			$0.00	$0.00	$0.00	$0.00		APRIL 10	
8		$0.00			$0.00	$0.00	$0.00	$0.00		APRIL 17	
9		$0.00			$0.00	$0.00	$0.00	$0.00		APRIL 24	
10		$0.00			$0.00	$0.00	$0.00	$0.00		MAY 1	
11		$0.00			$0.00	$0.00	$0.00	$0.00			
12		$0.00			$0.00	$0.00	$0.00				
13		$0.00			$0.00	$0.00	$0.00				
14		$0.00			$0.00	$0.00	$0.00				
15		$0.00			$0.00	$0.00					
16		$0.00			$0.00						
17		$0.00									
18		$0.00									

CRAFT SHOWS 1999

	SATURDA DATES	TOWN	SHOW	ORGANIZER	PHONE	MOTEL	MOTEL PHONE	CONF #	DATES	SHOW HOURS
1	SATURDA DATES	MASON CITY	SOUTHBRIDGE MALL	TAMMY/4S	515-423-6888	COMFORT INN	515-423-4444	63606584	3/4,5,6	10-9,10-6,10-5
2	MAR 6 FRI 5,6,7	SIOUX CITY	SOUTHERN HILLS MALL	KATHY&ED DOVEL	402-330-3332	COMFORT INN	712-274-1300	63897440	12 & 13	10-9,10-9,12-6
3	MAR13 FRI 12,13,14	SIOUX CITY	CONVENTION CENTER		800-593-2228	DRIVING HOME AT NIGHT				10-6SAT11-5 SUN
4	MAR 20 SAT& SUN									
5	MAR 27									
6	APRIL 3		CARVER-HAWK ARENA	CALLAHAN PROM	319-652-4529	COMFORT INN	319.351.8144	63901273	SAT4/24	9am-4pm
7	APRIL 10				402-873-6654	OAK GROVE	660-744-5357	2499WS	4/30-5/1	?
8	APRIL 17		ARBOR DAY FEST/ARMORY	CHAMBER		OR ARBOR MANOR	402.274.3663		4/30-5/1	CANCEL IF NOT GOO
9	APRIL 24 SUN 4-25	IOWA CITY			816-792-6000	COMFORT INN	816.781.7273	64001763	14&15TH	8AM-4PM. SAT
10	MAY 1 SAT1&SUN 2	NEBRASKA CITY								
11	MAY 8		LIBERTY, MO(KC)	SPRING ON THE SQUARE	SHARON GRIMES					
12	MAY 15 SAT ONLY									
13	MAY 21									
14	MAY 28					COMFORT INN	605.624.8333	65217049	18&19TH	10-6SAT,11-5SUN
15	JUNE 5		POSSIBLE EDINA ART SHOW NEAR MINNEAPOLIS?			COMFORT INN	3192347411	65896212	26TH ONL	10AM-6PM. SUN
16	JUNE 12				POBOX 771 CF,IA					
17	JUNE 19 SAT&SUN	VERMILLION, SD	SUMMER ARTS FEST	CHAMBER						
18	JUNE 26 SUN ONLY	CEDAR FALLS,IA	STURGIS FALLS CEL. XXII							
19	JULY 3									
20	JULY 10		POSSIBLE BROOKINGS, SD SHOW							
21	JULY 17									
22	JULY 24		SHOW FORMS SENT FOR THIS WEEKEND-NOT SURE WHICH ONE WILL WORK OUT YET							
23	JULY 31									
24	AUG 7		PROBABLY TAKING AUGUST OFF AS FAR AS CRAFT SHOWS							
25	AUG14									
26	AUG 21									
27	AUG 28									
28	SEP 4				402-873-6654	DAYS INN	402-873-6656	PER ILLA	17-18	?
29	SEPT 11									
30	SEPT 18 SAT18-SUN19	NEBRASKA CITY	APPLE JACK FEST	CHAMBER						
31	SEPT 25									
32	OCT 2		MOST ALL OCTOBER WEEKENDS WILL BE BOOKED ON THE ROAD							
33	OCT 9		WAITING ON CONFIRMATIONS							
34	OCT 16									
35	OCT 23									
36	OCT 30		SANTAS N. POLE VILL.	ANK FR. OF ARTS	515-965-0940	SUPER 8	515-964-4503	58278090	5th&6th	9am-5pm
37	NOV 6 SAT 6 ONLY	ANKENY								
38	NOV 13		TWO OF THE 3 REMAINING NOV WEEKENDS WILL BE BOOKED. NOT SURE WHERE							
39	NOV 20									
40	NOV 27									
41	DEC 4		TAKING DECEMBER, JAN AND FEB OFF ON THE ROAD							
42	DEC 11					MOTEL	PHONE	CONF	DATES	HOURS
	DEC 18			CGS	PHONE					

Spreadsheets used by Deb Otto to monitor her costs and profits from craft shows. One includes all the contact information; the other, financial information.

the date of the last time that I spoke to the client and set a reminder for ninety days from that date. At that point, I touch base again."

Artist Deb Otto also uses spreadsheet software to monitor her costs and profit from each craft show she does. "My craft show travel spreadsheet has various column headings across the top. It includes all contact information for each show I do, travel reservation information and expenses, show fees, a record of sales with a cost of goods figure, and final profit. I enter formulas that calculate percentages and other figures into various cells in the spreadsheet. With the information on this spreadsheet, I can compare apples to apples per show (profitwise and travel, etc.) and I can look in one spot for all important information pertaining to my on-the-road business. I print a copy of the dates and motel columns for my husband so he can call me if needed, and I don't have to remember to leave the number every time. The best part of making your own record-keeping spreadsheets is that you determine what information is important to you, not some software company who may overkill on information until you don't understand it."

SOFTWARE BUYING TIPS

Selecting the right computer software is not easy, and many business owners end up frustrated with their purchase. Your first job is to decide what information you need to know to better manage your business, what you want your customer files to tell you when you study sales results, and what kind of mailings you plan to make.

Polymer clay artist Jacqueline Janes runs two businesses:

Banking on the Internet

The Internet is changing the way we do business and manage our money. Marsha Reed offers insight into something that may soon be standard operation for most business owners—banking online.

"All our banking is now done online over the Internet—no more having to wait for statements. I have four business accounts. In the past, when I wanted to check something—to see if a check had cleared, for example—I would have to pay a service fee. By doing my banking online, I can go in there anytime to see all the changes to my account as the bank is making them, and I can also transfer money from one account to another or make quarterly tax payments. The bank provided a simple computer program to accomplish this."

Keep Your Cat Off the Computer!

Cats and computers are great . . . but not together. What your cat wants most is attention, so when you're at the computer, that's likely where your cat will want to be, too. But giving your cat the run of your office could be expensive. If it loves to curl up on your computer monitor, that might block air vents and cause overheating. The static electricity from a cat's coat could discharge into the terminal and blow a computer chip. If cat hair is sucked into the computer through the floppy disk drive, it could cause overheating and loss of data. If you can't keep your cat out of the office, at least train it to stay away from the computer, perhaps by giving it a home on a shelf above the monitor.

Shown here is Dodie Eisenhauer's companion, Catbert, who looks as though he might be trying to hit CONTROL, ALT, DELETE.

Eggplant and Arizona Bead Company. When I asked what software she used, she said my question made her laugh and cringe at the same time. "You can get a simple mailing list or invoice program, or you can get the whole nine yards, but nothing in-between," she says. "I've learned that the most important part of buying software is making a list of what you will be using it for. It's a good idea to get a free trial version of software you're interested in. I almost bought M.Y.O.B. accounting, but when I tried it out, I hated it."

For her Eggplant business, which has a small customer base, Jacqueline uses My Advanced Invoices and the ClarisWorks database for mailings. "I've found it is sometimes less complicated to buy two programs to do what you need," she says. "Because my bead company needs more advanced features, however, I decided to buy QuickBooks for it."

Shopping for software, learning to use it, and then inputting all your customer data or prospect names will take a massive amount of time. I shudder when I recall the hundred hours it took me to learn my dBASE software back in the '80s, and the countless hours I spent putting thousands of names and addresses on computer, but that was the most important work I ever did for my business. It made all the difference between success and failure. No matter how long this job takes you, it's worth the effort because it will pay dividends for years to come.

MAIL LIST MANAGEMENT

You may not be planning to make regular mailings to your buyer list, but if you don't take the time to computerize your list of buyers, you will lose both sales and profits. As Dodie Eisenhauer explains, "It's essential to have your customer names, history, and record of purchases on computer. I pull reports regularly to learn how many of each item I've sold. I know what percentage of my income is generated by a particular item, what products to drop, and which ones to focus marketing attention on. By studying sales figures, I can tell how my business is changing from one year to the next. By doing annual comparisons, I can see how last year's gross sales compare to current sales. More specifically, I can study the buying habits of all my shops, looking at last year's sales vs. sales to date and see the difference between the two."

Many small business owners use the database features of accounting software to do their mailing list work. Peachtree, a user friendly I-con driven program, is good for those who want to structure a program to their own needs. Also check out Quicken's Home and Business Suite software or QuickBooks by Intuit.

Office management and accounting software programs will do your mailing lists for you, but if all you want are address labels so you can send postcards or brochures to prospects or customers, any database or mailing list program will do the job, including shareware you can get off the Internet. John Schulte, chairman of the National Mail Order Association, says the simplest database program he has found is Microsoft Access, which is usually bundled with Microsoft Word under the name of Microsoft Office.

"Some people have this software and don't know its capabilities, but it's easy to learn," he says. "It includes a Database Wizard that does all the work for you. Just click here and there to build an address book, order entry files, or a dozen other types of database files. If you need only labels, Microsoft Access is all you need, but if you want to send personalized letters to your customers, then you'll also want Microsoft Word."

In calling a couple of computer stores in my area, I learned which software programs are most popular with buyers today. Microsoft Office (pricey, around $500) is recommended for those who want a combination database/word-processing package that will handle most small business tasks. Other programs with similar capabilities in this same price range include Lotus Smart Suite and Corel Office Suite.

One store manager said that My Advanced Brochure and Mailer (by MySoftware Company) is a popular seller. "All the software manufactured by this company does exactly what it says it will do, and it's easy to learn," he said. "This particular program will also do a mail merge of addresses into correspondence for sellers who want to send personalized mailings." Another easy-to-use and less expensive mail list program for home business owners is FileMaker.

Renee Chase, Webmaster of Crafter.Com, uses Office Access, a relational database software program. "The difference between a regular database and a relational database is that you only put in your point of contact one time, and it is then assigned different relationships so you can pull up subscribers, media, friends, etc. Switching from my old software to the new will be easy," Renee adds, "because you can export your old database files in ASCII format and import it into the new."

Updating Your Mail List. Updating involves: (1) keeping addresses and buyer contact information current so your mailings don't go astray; (2) regularly adding information about purchases each customer has made; and (3) analyzing your database to decide when to cease mailings to certain names on your list.

"If someone hasn't turned in a card for a few years, we remove them from our active list," one seller says. But that's too long. Meg Sullivan has the right idea. She cleans her whole list once a year, weeding out all nonrespondents. "On the last couple of postcards we send to someone, we include a note saying they either need to purchase or communicate with us to stay on our list. Those who do not respond are dumped from the list. We usually end up dropping about half the list, but by the end of the next year, we're right back to where we started, with about 400 names on the list. We keep track of when people are first put on our mailing list. Then, as they make purchases or confirm that they want to remain on our list, we add a second date. This double date appears on the mailing label itself so we can see at a glance how long a customer has been with us and when they last ordered or responded to a mailing."

Bulk Mailings vs. First Class. If you plan to do a lot of mailings and want to save money, your address lists must be ZIP+4 compliant and mail must be sorted in specific ways (ask your post office for an instruction booklet). The post office will update your out-of-date mailings lists and add the extra four digits to Zip codes. (Again, contact the post office for details on how to do this.)

Eileen Heifner, who makes large mailings, has reached the point where all this bulk mail aggravation is not worth the time it takes, so she hires a local mailing service. She just gives them her address disk; they get it updated for her, and do the labeling and all the special presorts to get postal discounts. The money the presorting saves her nearly covers the cost of the outside service, but more important, Eileen says, is the stress this outside service saves her.

"Since we are a subscription-based publishing house, mail lists are important," says Bill Ronay. "Each day there are additions and purges from the master data list. But, as in any industry, ours even more so, people and/or their businesses move for the most simple as well as complex reasons. Many move, leaving no forwarding address. We do two mailings per year, at the same time of year and in the same way every year. We've found that bulk mail and first-class presort, in our situation, at least, was not worth the hassle. By the time we sorted, bundled, stamped, labeled, and did all of the post office work to prepare the mailings, we were much better off stamping with peel-off stamps and dedicating a specific time of day to get it all done at once."

I'm with Bill on this point. The small extra cost of first-class mail is insignificant when compared to the time and stress involved in doing all the preparation of a bulk or presorted mailing.

DESIGNING PRINTED MATERIALS

Thanks to computers, laser/inkjet printers, scanners, and colorful preprinted papers, you don't have to spend a lot of money to look like a professional today. Office and paper suppliers listed at the end of this chapter offer a wonderful variety of papers you can use to create matching stationery, cards, brochures, portfolios, presentation folders, and more.

"It's important to appear professional," says sculptor Robert Houghtaling. "I think many small businesses, and especially artists and crafters, either overlook the importance of this or try to be 'artsy.' When you are dealing with other businesses, galleries, wholesalers, suppliers, etc. you can't afford to project the image of someone operating out of a spare bedroom or their garage (even though you may be). If you project a professional image, you will be treated with respect and in a businesslike manner. Both your correspondence and Web presence should reflect that image."

After designing a new ornament, Robert took a picture of it with his digital camera, fed it into his computer, and printed it out for use

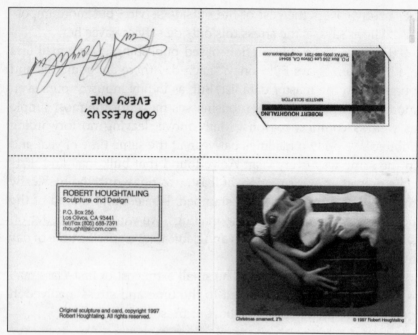

A promotional Christmas card designed on computer by Robert Houghtaling (it folds to 4 x 5 inches).

as a Christmas card that he sent to all his clients one year. "It served as a reminder of what I do," says Robert, "and my clients loved it." (See illustration.)

Being able to produce brochures and catalogs is a great time-and money-saver. Both can be updated periodically and printed in exact quantities needed. Often in the past, I've ordered a thousand copies of printed materials to get a better price, then ended up throwing out a third or more of them because they had gone out of date. It may cost more per piece to print your own brochures and other materials, but you have the luxury of being able to select from a vast array of fancy papers, can change copy or prices every day if you want to, and print exactly the amount you need.

"The MS Publisher program is fantastic for creating brochures," says Sue Johnson. "It's so exciting to be able to try something and to see the results immediately. When I think back to the days of working with a print shop on a brochure, it feels like going back to the horse and buggy days."

Rita O'Hara's business card and samples of hang tags. When buyers desire it, Rita preprices and barcodes her products for them.

Using Print Shop software, Rita O'Hara prints her own business cards, thousands of hang tags (see above), and all the gift cards and boxes she uses for her Stonewares products. (See Chapter Eight for information on how she makes and die-cuts gift boxes to match her products.) She also prints her hefty color catalog on order, sending it only to selected shops who want to order more products. "It costs about $20 to produce," she says, "but I have no waste of printed materials, and the first order pays for the catalog's cost."

"I do not need thousands of catalogs to sell my dough art creations," says Nancy Jaekel, "so I do most of my own design and catalogs now on computer. I tend to add so many new designs to my line that catalogs become obsolete fast. With the computer, however, I can delete, add new items, and print what I need. The quality isn't quite as good as professional, but I always send along a sample of my work to the shops."

Other printed materials are also easy to do, from press releases to artist statements and hang tags. "Now that I have a computer," says pattern designer Myra Hopkins, "I can design better-looking print-

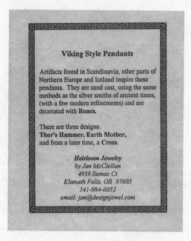

One of Jan McClellan's printed pieces. Inside this folded note (4¼ x 5½) is information about Runes and the three pendant designs available.

ed materials and press releases that are likely to increase both my orders and my press mentions."

Jewelry designer Jan McClellan uses her word-processing software to print her artist statement and informative notes about the gemstones she uses and the way her products are made (see above). "These I hand out at fairs and put with any jewelry that is sold."

Because scanners and color printers have become so affordable in recent years, many craftspeople now use them to create their own color printed materials and print them on demand, as needed for retail or wholesale customers. "I'm thrilled with the new software, more powerful computers, and other hardware," says Karen Combs, who presents quilt seminars. "It makes it easier to produce my own letterheads, patterns, business cards, etc. I rarely go to the print shop anymore. I just do it myself."

Woodturner Derek Andrews designs and print his own product tags, then cuts and punches them. "This allows me a lot of flexibility, instant changes, and the ability to print the wood type on the label," he says.

"Business cards are probably our smartest investment," says Meg Sullivan, who regularly sells at craft fairs. "My partners and I list our mail addresses, phones, e-mail, and Web site address on them. Do a lot get thrown out? Probably. Business cards are like any other cost of doing business—not everyone will net a sale, but can you determine which will?"

Sample product tags used
by Derek Andrews.

When Meg wants a bag stuffer, she finds it more cost effective to print fifty color copies at home (see below). "If we need several hundred business cards, however, we have them done commercially. In looking at the time and cost of printing large quantities at home, we found it was slightly more cost-effective and definitely more time-effective to have this kind of work done by a printer."

*Meg Sullivan
prints colorful
little bag
stuffers like
this (four to a
page, then cut)
to promote
upcoming
shows and her
Web site.*

BUYING OFFICE AND COMPUTER SUPPLIES

Do you buy whatever you need without checking first to see if someone else sells it for less? If so, you're probably pouring some of your profits down the drain. The only way to save money on supplies is to become unit-conscious about what you're paying for everything.

"It's important to keep records," says Kate Harper, "not just for the sake of keeping them, but so you know in your head approximately what everything is costing you."

I agree with Kate and Dodie Eisenhauer, too, who says, "Ordering supplies bogs me down. Looking for the best deal and making decisions on what to buy are a dreaded time stealer." That's true for most of us, but if we want to save money on office and computer supplies or printed materials, we have to shop around. This means taking the time to gather a collection of supplier catalogs or local supply sources, making a list of all your commonly ordered items, and comparing prices. Initially, this is a big job, but the time it takes will be worth the effort.

Keeping Track of Purchases. The system I've used for years is nothing more than a stack of 3 x 5 cards like the sample shown, one for each item I regularly order. When I ran a mail order business, I had dozens of cards because I used so many different printed items. Today, my supply needs are basically office and computer supplies. Even so, great savings can be realized by careful shopping. My biggest savings came the day I discovered I could get cartridges for my laser printer for $30 less than I had been paying a local supplier for the same item. Since I use many reams of paper each year, I've saved money buying it by the case. Only recently have I discovered the economy of becoming a member of Sam's Club, which (like Costco) offers a large selection of office supplies, equipment, and business services.

The benefits of my record-keeping system is that 3 x 5 cards are easy to handle and convenient to keep banded together at my bill-paying desk. By checking incoming invoices against my cards, I can quickly spot any billing errors that might occur or see when prices have increased. At that time, I may be prompted to look for a more

ITEM_____

Date	Order/Item #	Price Each	Purchased From

Sample of a card used by the author to monitor purchases and cost of office and printing supplies. (Shipping charges should be kept separate from the per-unit cost of items so you can compare apples to apples when checking the prices of one supplier vs. another. Some charge for shipping; others don't.)

economical supplier or ask if better prices are available with a larger order (particularly true when ordering printing of any kind). Reordering is faster because I've got a record of individual item/order numbers. And, when new catalogs come in, I can quickly compare prices of needed supplies, using my cards as a reference.

Money-Saving Tips. "Don't buy more printing than you need," says Pat Endicott. "It may sound like a good deal to order the larger quantity of catalog sheets, but it hurts worse to throw all those outdated sheets away."

"Order only from local stores that offer free delivery," Kate Harper suggests. "This is my policy for all vendors, from box makers and printers to my local photocopy service."

"Shop online," urges Gail Platts. "This can save the time it takes to buy locally and often the prices are just as good, even after shipping is added."

"Join a club such as Sam's or Costco," advises Bill and Camille Ronay. "This definitely pays off. Plan your supply-buying trips carefully. Buy two if you need only one. Remember the cost of having to get into the car and traveling back to the store . . . it does add up to much more than the price of the item you neglected to stock up on in the first place."

"Watch the Sunday paper advertisements from local office supply stores for special sales or rebate offers," says Susan Young. "If you see a good price on an item but it's not your preferred store, call them and tell them the competitor's price. My favorite store has always offered to match the competition's price, and I don't have to go to one store to save on one item, then go to mine for the rest of my purchases."

SETTING UP A BILL-PAYING SYSTEM

We all dread bill-paying, but it's an important part of business management and cash-flow planning. It's important to develop a good bill-paying system because it can be costly to pay bills after their due date, particularly where credit card companies are concerned. (Some now have late-payment fees of up to $29.) With the system I've developed, I am never late in paying a bill and I don't have the stress of wondering what's due when.

Based on when you receive income (weekly, the first of the month, the 15th, etc.) set up a regular schedule and stick to it. I used to pay bills every week out of habit, but this practice just kills a Saturday morning. When I began to schedule bill-paying every other week instead, I suddenly found myself with at least two whole Saturdays a month when I didn't have to think about money, and it was as if I'd given myself a gift.

As bills come in, I simply plot to my bill-paying calendar the particular Saturday they must be paid to arrive before their due date, allowing a minimum of ten days for delivery. I have two sets of 6 x 9 envelopes, one for each month; one set is for personal bills, one is for business bills (each paid from different checkbooks). These envelopes stand upright in a little plastic fileholder so bills can be easily added or removed. After figuring the due date of each bill and plotting it to my calendar, I drop it into the appropriate envelope and forget about it until my calendar note reminds me to pull it for payment.

The benefit of planning exactly what must be done when is a great stress reliever because you never have to think about anything except what you see on your calendar or list of things to be done.

A FEW WORDS ABOUT FILING

Dodie Eisenhauer has a good system for knowing when she needs to do deskwork or file things. "If the stacks of paper on my desk become too high, my cat knocks them over," she quips. "In a way, Catbert forces me to stay caught up."

If others criticize you because your desk or work area is always piled high with work and looks a mess, tell your critics this is one of your time-saving devices. (If you can manage to keep the entire surface of your desk covered with paper, you'll never have to dust it.)

Seriously, a small investment in new storage shelves, boxes, or organizers can make all the difference in getting your paperwork and files organized, which in turn will make it easier for you to manage your business more efficiently. Several craftspeople told me that their preferred method of organizing things (supplies, materials, files, envelopes, magazines, whatever) is to use boxes or Rubbermaid containers on shelves—with lids, so things don't fall out when they're accidentally knocked over. The fronts of boxes can be labeled as to contents.

Bill and Camille Ronay use a similar system. "We've found Rubbermaid containers to be the best method of storage for our paperwork after it has been processed," they say. "It is all in chronological order and can easily be found. Since we are in the events business, we found long ago that keeping logically stored documents is much preferred to indexing and generating needless cross-references. Information such as we use daily goes out of date almost immediately."

Freelance writer, artist and pattern designer Bobbi Chukran says she used to be so distracted by the piles and piles of papers and books around her desk that she couldn't concentrate on work. She solved that problem by asking her husband to build some floor-to-ceiling shelves with doors on them. "Now I can shove all the papers, books, and boxes in there, close the doors, and I don't have to look at them," she says. "Things are easy to find and the clutter is gone.

Also, the doors are large enough so that they make good surfaces for putting up design boards, large drawings, plot maps, etc.— essentially, they give me more wall space."

Prior to solving her clutter problem, Bobbi used to take her work into the living room or work on the dining room table. "It's easier to concentrate when you're in an uncluttered environment," she believes.

As you might expect, creative people tend to color-code their files. Jewelry maker Joyce Roark uses colored index cards to indicate the type of jewelry she has made. "Yellow is pendants, purple is earrings, pink is brooches, etc. I make a card for each piece with the item number, list of ingredients (parts), and the cost of the item. I have a second file for wholesale prices and a third one for retail prices. Each item is listed by item number but cross-filed by the stone in each piece."

Most of us can find things easier if cards, folders, or files are color-coded. Gail Platts's method is to file things related to expenses in a red folder; income in blue; brochures and tags in orange, etc. I like color, too, but instead of using the more expensive color folders, I use manila folders in hanging file folders that have tabs of different colors. I constantly recycle all my manila folders, too, first by turning them inside out, and later by sticking on new labels. (Who, me, cheap? Nah, I'm just *frugal.*)

Here's my best filing tip of all: When something must be filed, don't file it alphabetically or by subject category. Instead, consider the thing you thought of when you first encountered the information. This will tell you why you want to save it, how you plan to use it in the future, and where it should be filed for future retrieval.

MORE MONEY-SAVING TIPS

▸ **Banking.** Pay particular attention to the charges you are paying for your business checking account, as some financial institutions charge more than others for similar services. You can also save money on business checks and deposit stamps by ordering them from sources other than a bank, which always tacks on a hefty fee for this service.

▸ **Home Office/Workshop Insurance.** To protect all the equipment, tools, supplies, and other things in your home office, studio, or workshop against loss or damage, you must purchase either a business rider on your homeowner's or renter's insurance policy, or buy a separate business policy. (Your regular homeowner's insurance covers *nothing* that you normally use for business.) Several insurance companies now offer home office policies, and most small business organizations also offer premium-saving insurance packages for their members that include health insurance as well as personal and product liability insurance.

▸ **Health Insurance.** To save money on your health insurance, consider joining a national art, crafts, or home-business association that offers a group hospitalization/major medical plan. Also look into membership in your local Chamber of Commerce, whose low-cost group insurance plan has been the perfect answer for many home-based business owners.

▸ **Office Equipment.** Stay aware of new products. Marsha Reed found she could replace her manual postage meter ($45/month to rent, which had to be taken to the post office for refilling) with a new one that costs only $20/month to rent and can be refilled with a telephone call. Consider leasing, but be sure to read all the fine print in a leasing contract before you sign it and consider how fast technology is moving. Some things you might lease today for three years could be out of date long before your lease expires.

▸ **Tax Deductions.** Read tax guides and newsletters to make sure you're taking every available deduction to which your business is entitled. Then work with a good accountant or tax advisor to be sure all deductions are properly reflected on your annual tax return.

HELPFUL RESOURCES

Office and Computer Suppliers

Grayarc 1-800-243-5250
Office Depot 1-800-685-8800 (free delivery)
Office Max 1-800-788-8080 (free delivery on orders of $50 or more)

PaperDirect 1-800-A-PAPERS
Queblo 1-800-523-9080
Quill Corporation 1-800-789-1331 (free delivery on orders of $50 or more)
Viking 1-800-421-1222 (free delivery on orders of $25 or more)

Home-Business Organizations

The American Association of Home-Based Businesses, P. O. Box 10023, Rockville, MD 20849. This organization has chapters throughout the country. Members have access to merchant status, discounted business products and services, prepaid legal services, and more. Web site: www.aahbb.org.

Home Business Institute, Inc., P. O. Box 301, White Plains, NY 10605-0301. Offers merchant card services and a group health insurance plan. Web site: www.hbiweb.com.

National Craft Association, 1945 E. Ridge Rd., Suite 5178, Rochester, NY 14622-2647. NCA members have access to insurance programs, discounts on business services and products, merchant card services, a newsletter, and a variety of directories to help professional crafters find supplies and locate new marketing outlets. Web site: www.craftassoc.com.

Chapter Seven

Communicating Efficiently and Cost Effectively

||||||||||||||||||||||||||||||||||||||||||||||||||||||||

Convenience is the key to getting business today. Given the different time zones and the fact that people work around the clock in this country, we have to be available at their convenience and give them a variety of communications options.

—Barbara Arena, Managing Director,
National Craft Association

I sometimes feel very old when I look back and see that the main form of communication when I was a young woman were letters and telephone calls (or telegrams, if you didn't care how you wasted your money). Businesses, of course, also had teletype machines. In fact, my first job out of high school was as a teletype operator for the Pennsylvania Railroad in Chicago.

Although today's home-based business owners have a variety of affordable communications options to choose from, some are still locked into doing things the old-fashioned way. This chapter will be helpful to those who do not yet understand how the addition of a fax machine or use of e-mail could benefit their business. It also offers a revealing look at how different kinds of businesses communicate via phone, fax, and e-mail, with special emphasis on how to save money on your long-distance telephone service.

YOUR BUSINESS TELEPHONE

Most of the craftspeople I queried for this book do not have a business telephone number, but most found it necessary to add a second line to their home phone for the Internet. Individuals who sell by mail or on the Internet often have an 800 number as well. Since a business line always costs more than a home telephone number, most craftspeople who sell mainly at craft fairs or other retail outlets pass on this expense because they make few long distance calls to begin with and don't need a listing in the phone book.

"Long-distance is a thing of the past for me, thanks to e-mail," says Joann Haglund. I communicate almost solely by e-mail and have saved hundreds of dollars in telephone charges using an unlimited Internet service."

Having a separate business line is not important, either, to small mail order businesses who prefer the privacy a post office box address gives them. For years, I did not include my telephone number on my mail-order book brochure because I didn't want crafters calling to ask questions I didn't have time to answer. I started to do this only when I began to accept credit card orders. Pattern seller Vicky Stozich knows what I mean.

"I used to put my phone number on all the brochures I sent out, but I was getting calls all hours of the day and night from people who wanted me to walk them through a step in the pattern," she says. "Yes, people do sew at midnight, and they don't hesitate to call at that time. When we were gone, people would leave their number for me to call them. I don't mind answering questions for people if they don't understand something, but I don't appreciate someone leaving a long-distance number, with me having to pay for the callback. Since everything is done by mail, I finally decided there was no need to put my phone number on my brochures. I do have my e-mail address on my Web site, however, and I read and answer questions when it's convenient for me."

Those business owners who do have separate business lines feel they are invaluable. "I have a separate business line with a business listing in the phone book," says dough artist Nancy Jaekel, "and this has paid for itself a thousand-fold. My biggest sales are with customers I have personally contacted and visit with to make yearly sales."

The main disadvantage of trying to use your home telephone number as a business line is that you are currently limited in the amount you can legally deduct for telephone expenses on your Schedule C tax form. In addition, you may not be able to advertise a home number for a business without violating local telephone company regulations. This is something you need to check on if you haven't done so already.

NETWORKING SESSION #6: TELEPHONE COMMUNICATIONS

Once again, you are invited to sit in on an interesting networking session to learn how my book contributors handle their communications. This time around, I've included a mention of each individual's type of business so you can relate their use of communication methods to your own needs.

Do you have a separate telephone line for your business?

Shirley MacNulty (knitwear designer): "I have a separate phone line for my business, mainly to have a listing for advertising purposes and to have a business line for suppliers. It's an extra cost, but necessary."

Jacqueline Janes (bead business owner): "I don't have a separate line for business, but I do have a separate fax/modem line."

Kathy Wirth (freelance crafts designer): "Same here. I have a separate phone line for the fax and modem. By the way, a personal pet peeve is call waiting. I hate being interrupted when I'm speaking with someone on the phone, and then having to wait and see if the other call is more important than mine. I think this is rude."

Tori Hoggard (artist and teacher): "I did have a business line, which proved to be a waste. A voice mailbox that works when I'm online or on the phone is just dandy for me. The nature of my business, and the fact that I have e-mail, makes it unnecessary to have two separate lines now."

Joyce Birchler (glass artisan): "I have what's called a ring mate for my business number. For $4 a month, I have a separate number and a separate ring so I know to answer it as a business. I also have a sep-arate number for my fax/computer line, which helps a great deal."

Bill and Camille Ronay (publishers): "We have a separate phone line for our business that just rings into the office. It's also a fax line and rings nowhere else except the office. The other lines, one personal with 'ringdown,' the second as an alternate line, ring into the house with extensions into the office."

Do you find that your customers or clients prefer one method of communication over another?

Jacqueline Janes: "I'm finding that more and more of my customers like to communicate by e-mail."

Annie Lang (designer and author): "Because I deal with so many out-of-state (and sometimes out-of-country) clients, e-mail has been a terrific solution when wanting to communicate with any kind of speed. I send artwork files, photo scans, etc., via the Net and vice versa. It is the most preferred method of communication for me as well as my clients. Second is the fax machine. Third is the phone and last is 'snail mail.'"

Karen Combs (quilt seminar presenter): "I arrange most of my teaching jobs via e-mail but use a combination of e-mail, phone calls, and letters to manage my business."

Kathy Wirth: "Most of my business communication with clients and editors is done by phone and fax. Some use e-mail, but not too many. Mostly, my e-mail is with other designers and is more of a networking thing. The problem with e-mailing an editor is that she may or may not check for messages each day."

Lynn Smythe (bead and fiber artist): "I don't know what methods my customers prefer, but I like e-mail best. I can print out my e-mail and have a record of exactly what is expected—can't do that with phone calls. I also suffer from insomnia, so e-mail lets me talk to people at 3 A.M. without them hanging up on me."

Barbara Arena (director, NCA): "We've learned that convenience is a key to getting business, so we make ourselves available to our customers 24 hours a day, seven days a week. They appreciate having a variety of communication options, from mail and e-mail to a toll-free phone and fax number."

Tell me about your long-distance telephone service provider and how many times you've changed to get better rates.

Jacqueline Janes: "I've changed companies a few times, but if I see a better deal somewhere else, AT&T is happy to match it. Long distance is such a competitive business now that most companies will bend over backwards to keep you as a customer."

Kate Harper (greeting card publisher): "I use AT&T as well. I switched to them after a friend told me I was overpaying for long-distance, and this change saved me about $100 a month."

Shirley MacNulty: "Although I have a business line, I use the home phone for long distance calls as the cost is too great on the business line. We recently changed our home long-distance company from AT&T to Alltel, which is now my cell phone provider. They are doing what is called bundling, and we get better rates. AT&T was starting to charge $5 a month if we did not use enough long distance, and Alltel doesn't, and we get it at 9 cents a minute on the home line."

Annie Lang: "I've been using the same long-distance service provider for years. It has not been worth my time to seek out competitors, as my long-distance rates are extremely low for the amount of calling I do each month, and they have not increased since I signed with this service."

Derek Andrews (woodturner, Canada): "We swapped from our local company, MT&T to AT&T and finally to Sprint Canada. It was not so much for price, but because I got fed up with the plethora of different packages the others were offering. Sprint offered a no-nonsense, flat-rate 24 hours a day, no-minimum package that was easy to figure out and suited my low volume of long-distance calls."

Bill Ronay: "We belong to an international organization that makes services of its members available to each other. In this case, one of the members is a major long-distance carrier. Our rate with them, though not great, is consistent and dependable. After bad experiences with a couple of other carriers, we've found the savings realized by the dependability of the group carrier far outweighs any prestige of the brand-name carrier."

Is voice mail important to your business, or do you find an answering machine is sufficient for your needs? Personally, I haven't yet decided whether voice mail is a blessing or a curse, especially after I've spent a day playing phone tag with someone.

Leila Peltosaari (book publisher): "Voice mail is one of those things like the fax and microwave that, once you get it, you wonder how you ever did without. I love voice mail to the point that I wouldn't consider business or personal life without it."

Linda Beattie Inlow (writer/publisher): "Voice mail is too expensive. What's wrong with an answering machine or letting them call back?"

Nancy Jaekel (dough artist): "Voice mail is important. I think customers want to touch base with us, and I know how frustrated I get when I call someone and there is no answer and I can't leave a message."

Jacqueline Janes: "I don't use voice mail because I forward my phone calls to my cell phone when I go anywhere."

Bill Ronay: "Never had voice mail and don't intend to, either. Answering machines are bad enough. Now, with the ease of e-mail and faxing, we see no need to have any more of a network of complex telephony!"

Barbara Arena: "We receive a huge amount of inquiries from craftspeople during our off-hours, so a voice mail system is the perfect solution for handling these calls."

Sometimes the only way to have a productive day is to let the phone take messages all day while you work. Seems to me the small cost of returning calls will be more than offset by the quality or volume of work you can do if you are able to work uninterrupted.

Kate Harper: "I agree. Voice mail saves me a lot of time because everyone knows I rarely answer the phone, and they have been trained to leave a message if they want me to call them back. I started this habit when I started getting too many unsolicited telemarketing calls. No one has expressed any frustration at getting through to me, probably because most people get answering machines or voice mail messages these days and don't expect a real person to answer the phone."

Tori Hoggard: "I've trained my callers, too, making sure they know to leave a detailed message. Often, we get our business done through a series of messages. I am too much of a gabber to tempt myself with accepting every single phone call that comes in, so voice mail is an enormous timesaver for me."

I like this bit of Internet humor which found its way into my e-mail box as I was writing this chapter: "Only in America do we use answering machines to screen calls and then have call waiting so we won't miss a call from someone we didn't want to talk to in the first place."

Voice Mail/Answering Machine Messages

The advantages of voice mail over an answering machine are numerous. It's more professional. It's easier to change messages. When traveling, it's easier to retrieve messages, too. When you're talking on the phone, several people at a time can call and leave messages—which is particularly good if you've just gotten a blast of publicity or are getting a lot of response from an advertisement.

Whether you have voice mail or an answering machine, if you're trying to use your residential number for business purposes, at least leave a professional message for your callers. You cannot legally answer a residential phone number with a business name, but you can answer it with your full name. If two people share that number, answer with both names.

Nothing is more aggravating to me when I'm trying to reach a crafts business woman at the number she has put on her business card or stationery and get a message saying, "This is Tom, leave a message" or, worse, "You have reached 715-555-1234." That kind of message tells me nothing! That number may or may not be the number of the person I'm trying to reach. If I don't hear her name or the family's last name in the message, I don't know whether I've misdialed or if the woman I'm looking for still lives there or not. In such cases, I rarely leave a message at all.

A good message will tell callers exactly who they have reached (your full name or the names of both individuals sharing that number) and exactly what you want them to do (leave a message, request information, send a fax, or place an order with their credit card number).

HOW TO SAVE MONEY ON
LONG-DISTANCE CALLS

Like the companies who sell credit cards, long-distance sellers use all kinds of tricks to get people to switch. There seems to be a lot of deceptive selling practices out there—not deceptive enough to violate federal laws, of course, but definitely *sneaky*. If we aren't smart enough to ask certain questions, we'll end up paying more for telephone service than we ought.

For the past several years, we've all been getting an education in how to select the right long-distance service, but this area is still fraught with pitfalls and financial traps. In an attempt to get the lowest rates, individuals and businesses alike continue to change long-distance service providers on a regular basis. And when they're not switching voluntarily, they are often being switched without their permission ("slammed") by a competing service provider.

I have changed my long-distance service several times and encountered problems along the way. Companies I've discarded have slammed me in an attempt to take back my service, and it's always a battle getting refunds for charges once they're billed to you. (One business owner who was slammed was charged 50 cents a minute by the company that illegally took her service.) The last time I switched, I put a "pick freeze" on my account so I couldn't be slammed again. Although I was told the switchover was complete, I received minimum rate bills for three months from the previous carrier (MCI) and had a hard time getting them to disconnect me from their service. Other people have reported similar experiences with their carriers. "It's annoying to be charged for not making telephone calls," one business woman laments, "but all companies seem to do this today."

By asking questions each time I've been solicited to change my long-distance service, I've learned how various companies price their services. The following information will help you analyze your present service and determine whether you can save money by switching your long-distance service once again. Here are examples of how extra charges might show up on your telephone bill without you noticing it.

FCC Tariff Charges. The FCC mandates a minimum charge of $2.75 per line, but companies can legally charge more to increase their profits. I found I had been paying $2.90 per line—not a lot of extra money, to be sure, but if I owned a company with several phone or fax lines, the difference would add up over a year.

Toll-Free Numbers. Some long-distance companies tack on a "service charge" of $5 to $10 a month for an 800 line, even though 800 numbers are not actual lines at all, but merely phantom numbers. Many also charge more for calls to a toll-free number than what is normally charged for outgoing long-distance calls. Why pay a service charge on your toll-free number and a higher rate for your incoming calls if you don't have to?

Credit Card Calls. On checking, you may find you are not only paying a higher per- minute charge for credit card calls but a "bong fee" as well. That "bong" you hear when you make a call on your credit card could cost you up to $1.50 in addition to your per-minute charges, but you won't know it because it isn't broken down on your bill. So if a company tells you what your credit card calls will cost, ask if there are any surcharges on top of this.

Billing Method. Perhaps the worst offenders are the long-distance companies who charge for calls by the minute, instead of in 6-second increments. Even when you sign up with a company that bills in 6-second increments, however, there is yet another little financial trap you can fall into. There are only three national long-distance carriers: AT&T, Sprint, and WorldCom, which now owns MCI. When you sign with a regional (vs. national) long-distance carrier, it must "bounce" your long-distance calls from one server to another to get your call through. Each of these servers operate on a clock that may not be perfectly synchronized with other servers, and whenever this happens, you will pay for it at the rate of 3 or 4 cents per bounce.

To understand what I'm talking about here, take a look at a recent telephone bill and see if there are any calls to a single number that have two or three lines of billing. In addition to paying for the minutes you actually talk, you may also be paying two or three extra charges of three or four cents each because that particular call was "bounced" to servers whose clocks were off by half a minute or more. Although my former carrier offered 6-second billing and a rate of $.109 per minute, a check of recent phone bills revealed that, with all these extra "bounce charges," I was actually paying an extra three to eleven cents for each call I made. The company wasn't lying about the rate I was receiving because when they added up all the minutes vs. costs, it divided out to $.109/minute. What they didn't tell me (because I didn't ask) is that I was being charged extra money for minutes when I wasn't actually talking.

This kind of arithmetic is particularly important if you've signed with a company that is offering 7.9 or 8.9 cents a minute (two common rates being offered on the Internet). In actuality, you may be paying much more than this when you add in all the "hidden charges" previously mentioned.

Here are several questions you need to ask before you change your long-distance service provider:

▶▶ Find out if there are any special offers. Because of the competitiveness in the long-distance service industry, sellers often offer "sweet deals" to woo customers away from their existing provider. I switched to ANI because they offered me a special two-month introductory rate, extra minutes of free calls (based on the size of my last telephone bill), a lower rate for in-state calls than I had been paying, and a savings of 5 cents a minute on credit card calls. Together, these benefits add up to a nifty savings each month.

▶▶ Ask if the long-distance rate is a 24-hour/7-days a week rate, or if it is higher or lower on certain days or hours.

▶▶ If the rate seems especially good to you, ask if it's an "introductory rate" that will expire in a month or two. (Some companies may not alert you to this fact, figuring you won't check your bill after the first couple of months and will never notice when the rate increases.)

▶▶ Find out what the rate is for calls within your state. Because these rates are regulated at the state level, they vary from state to state and may be higher or lower than calls outside the state.

» Confirm that you will be billed in 6-second increments and *not* by the minute. Be sure to ask what the minimum billing charge is (ANI, for example, has an 18-second minimum charge) and exactly when charges begin. Avoid companies that charge for busy signals or rings, but no answer. Such charges can add up to several dollars a month.

» Ask if there are surcharges on either credit card calls (the "bong fee") or toll-free numbers. And check the rate for incoming toll-free calls. You should not pay more for incoming calls to your toll-free number than you pay to make long-distance calls yourself.

» Compare the cost of local long-distance calls (referred to as "Intralata" calls) billed through your local phone company versus the long-distance carrier. You have the choice of going with whomever offers the lowest rate.

Finally, a few words about the Federal Communications Commission (FCC) telephone slamming rules. If your telephone is slammed, the FCC advises that you: (1) notify your local telephone company to reinstate your original long-distance company and remove any "change charges" that were added to your bill; (2) call the company that slammed you and tell them you will pay only the charges your preferred carrier would have imposed; (3) call the company you were switched from and ask to be reconnected without charge. If you are unable to resolve your dispute with the company that switched your service, you can file a complaint with the FCC by writing to: FCC, Common Carrier Bureau, Consumer Complaints, Mail Stop Code 1600A2, Washington, DC 20554.

NETWORKING SESSION #7:
CORDLESS AND CELLULAR PHONES

We all need telephones to communicate, but what kind? Regular phones with cords are now viewed as archaic by many business owners who say they couldn't operate without a cordless or cellular phone. After learning the advantages of a cordless phone, I finally bought one for my business line. Although we have extension phones all over the house for our house phone, my business phone rings in only one room, and I was always missing business calls when I was in other parts of the house. (Have you ever noticed how many people call at lunch time or after 5 P.M., hoping you'll be gone so you'll have to call back on your nickel?)

The following networking session shows how some businesses use different types of phones to conduct business while saving both time and money.

How do you feel about cordless phones? Are they really important to a home business owner?

Morna McEver Golletz (magazine publisher): "I thought everyone with a home business had a cordless phone. I couldn't live without one because often what I need partway through a call is not within distance of my phone; plus, if I end up on hold, I can still work."

Barbara Arena: "I replaced all the handsets with cordless about four years ago. I feel they really save money on long-distance charges. If you get a call on a toll-free incoming line, rather than put them on hold while you get the information you need to answer their question, you can continue to talk to the person while you go to the spot to get what they need. This is a factor for us, as we often answer the phone away from our desks or computer stations. After discovering the convenience and freedom cordless phones offered my business, I also bought three phones for the home, one for each floor. (Do buy a quality phone if you plan to use it for business, however, so you get static-free, clear reception.)"

Dodie Eisenhauer (gift manufacturer): "I have one cordless in the house and two in my workshop. One stays there where someone is always working. The other I carry around with me all day. I can pick up my calls for some distance around, go to the mailbox, my retail shop (about the distance of a football field away), or back to the house. For my shop, I bought an additional cordless phone with dual rechargeable batteries. That means I never have to bring the phone back to put it on the cradle, but can simply switch batteries when one runs down as one is always recharging itself in the base unit. This has saved me the expense of running a separate phone line to my retail outlet. (If you want the phone to work a considerable distance away, get one that has at least 900 MHz of power. The higher the number, the greater the distance you can go from the phone's charger base.)"

Until you actually use a cordless phone, you don't realize how tethered to one spot you are with a regular telephone. I have a long cord on the phone in the kitchen so I can prepare dinner while talking on the phone, but I'm always knocking stuff off the counter as I move around the room.

Barbara Arena: "I know what you mean. A cordless phone has made my work less stressful because I don't have a cord dragging across my desk knocking papers on the floor when I reach for something else. The freedom a cordless phone offers makes it well worth the investment."

Dodie Eisenhauer: "A phone with a cord absolutely strangles me! I love the freedom—and privacy—a cordless phone gives me. I'm surrounded by people, so a cordless phone enables me to walk to a quiet place. I try never to allow background sounds to intrude on my business calls."

Liz Murad (calligrapher): "Cordless phones are indispensable to me. Not only can I be accessible to anyone who calls, I can walk away from my family when they're being rowdy and still have a good conversation. I can get to other areas of the house and access any information without needing to use that 'hold on' phrase."

Kate Harper: "Right! How many times has the teakettle started whistling while I was on the phone? A million. I need to be able to run from the kitchen (teakettle) to the porch (UPS guy) to the files (invoice questions). I also find I am on hold a lot for a few minutes. In that time, I can easily process or fill an order for my greeting cards. Cordless phones have also made my desk clear of messy wires. Space is also money, and cordless phones are essential for me."

Vicky Stozich (pattern designer): "When the phone rings, I always grab the cordless. If it's a customer, you can be walking to wherever you need to be while they are still talking to you. It sounds more professional to say, 'Yes, I have your file right here' instead of 'Wait a minute while I pull your file.'"

Kim Marie (potter): "One advantage of a cordless phone that some might overlook is the fact that you can have a phone in a place where there is no phone line hookup. My studio is in another building, but I can take my cordless with me every day without having to take messages on the answering machine. And when I get personal calls, I can chat with friends and family members without losing production time. (Now if I could just get this bend out of my neck!)"

Unless you're a secretary, you may not realize there is a gadget to solve this problem. It's called a "telephone shoulder rest" and you can get one from any office supply store, catalog, or store that sells telephones. Once stuck in place, the phone will rest comfortably on your shoulder without you holding it. Now if I could just offer a solution for another problem several of you reported—how to find a ringing cordless phone that's lost!

Gail Platts (doll designer): "Cordless phones are great for mobility, but I can't tell you how many times I've lost mine. It's ringing, and I have no idea where it is . . . in another room, or under that pile of fabric . . ."

Joyce Roark (jewelery designer and instructor): "Same here. I take the phone with me as I move from room to room to do my work, except when I forget to do this. If my short-term memory isn't up to par, I may not remember what I was doing earlier and where I was doing it, so when the phone rings, finding it is next to impossible. At times like this I'm glad I have my 'backup' phone hooked to the wall!"

Clearly the greatest benefit of a cordless phone is that it enables us to easily do two things at once.

Dodie Eisenhauer: "Right! If the phone rings when I'm in the house, I either head for the dirty dishes or the laundry so my time can count for mindless jobs and talk, too. When I'm in my workshop, I can keep my hands busy producing product while I talk."

Barbara Arena: "I like the cordless phone because I can talk on the phone while doing other things, like making a photocopy or running an order through the credit card machine."

Joyce Roark: "I use my cordless mostly in the summertime when I like to sneak outside and get some gardening work done. I carry a little container with my phone, notepad, and pencil with me. That way I can take orders or catalog requests no matter where I am. I often wonder what my customers would think if they knew that while taking their orders I was in the middle of my garden pulling weeds."

Chris Maher (artist and Webmaster): "Cordless phones are great, but wait till you get a cordless headset phone. It's the best of both worlds. They used to be expensive, but I got a 900 MHz cordless with a headset for $50 at Sam's Club. Now I can do yard work, pick up the house, or just enjoy nature and talk to clients at the same time."

Robert Houghtaling (sculptor): "Same here. I have a cordless phone with a headset so I can keep sculpting when the phone rings. I even answer the cordless while in the shower. And whenever I make or receive a call that I believe will last more than a few minutes, I get up from the workbench and walk. I can make a big circle through the house and even go outside if I don't go too far. The trick is to keep moving. It may sound strange to the person on the other end, but it is way too hard for me to actually set aside time to get off my duff and move around, so this is my solution."

Too bad the companies who are selling cordless phones don't know how to market the benefits of their products. They could

build a whole advertising campaign on this information! So let's explore cellular phones while we're at it. Harry and I have one we carry with us in the car, as insurance against a car break-down or medical emergency. Since we are getting older (along with our car), we like the feeling of security this phone gives us. We got our cellular phone for just a penny when Radio Shack was having one of its regular promotions, and our monthly cost is just $15. How do you folks feel about cellular phones?

Pat Endicott (crafts producer): "I don't have a cell phone now. It just killed me to pay $25 a month for something in the back seat of my car. At first it did give me peace of mind traveling alone, but it is also expensive. If I ever get another one, it will be one of the tiny ones that can fit into a purse, not a bag phone."

Jacqueline Janes: "Our cell phone has been a great help to us. We forward all of our calls when we go anywhere. We never have to wonder if we missed an important call, and we don't have dozens of messages on our answering machine when we get home from a show."

Kate Harper: "I refuse to use a cellular phone. When I leave the house, I leave the business behind. My biggest problem in even considering using cell phones is that when I get calls, I need to write everything down. Most of my calls are people wanting catalogs and there is no way I am going to take notes while walking around or in an elevator."

Susan Young (designer and artist): "A cellular phone is a nice security blanket while traveling if you're concerned about vehicle problems, getting lost, or delivering a product and needing to call the client for location directions. I support the peace of mind in case one should need help; otherwise, they are mostly a nuisance and a hazard. Statistics indicate that the number of auto accidents caused by people using cell phones is equal to the number of accidents caused by drunk drivers. And there are few things more irritating to me than to be in a nice restaurant and the jerk at the next table has his phone by his fork, and it's ringing off the tablecloth. I was in a long line at the post office the other day, and the woman behind me talked on her phone the entire length of the line, all the way through the service window, and all the way out to her car. Who on earth is *that* important?"

I guess being able to carry a phone around with them gives some people a feeling of importance.

Bobbi Chukran (freelance writer, and pattern designer): "Maybe so, but I hate it when somebody's phone rings in a grocery store or bookstore. I get away from home to avoid telephone noise, so it's

Surge Protectors and Storms

One way to save time and money is to make sure your computer and other electronic equipment doesn't get zapped during a storm. Lightning zaps nearly 100,000 computers every year, and computer losses are increasing because more people with a fax/modem now leave their systems on all the time. Since a surge protector will not save your equipment in the event of a direct lightning strike, the only sensible thing to do is unplug it during storms. And don't forget your cordless phones and fax machine, since they are equally at risk.

Simply turning things off during a storm isn't enough, particularly if there is a power failure. Unless protected by a surge protector, TVs, VCRs, computers, and cordless phones alike can be fried by a power surge when power is restored. As Shirley MacNulty confirms, "Our cordless phone, which is connected to our answering machine, burned up after Hurricane Fran. Although it was turned off before the storm, a power surge got it when the power came back on." (Because Shirley's phone was still under waranty at this time, it was repaired free of charge—a good point to remember.)

really irritating to hear ringing in those places. Thank goodness our library has banned the use of cell phones inside."

Perhaps this will serve as a reminder to not abuse the privacy of others when using cell phones. Besides their use at craft fairs to verify credit card purchases, the most practical place for a cellular phone seems to be in one's car. In addition to things mentioned in this networking session, some people use their cell phones to reschedule appointments, let their loved ones know when they're stuck in traffic and, most important of all, to order pizza on the way home from a crafts show!

The New Cellular Phones

We have used cellular phones at shows for credit card verification for about ten years now. But Analog cellular is the old way of doing things. We've just gotten a PCS (Personal Communications Service) phone, and it's great. The main differences are:

1) Cost—not only is it way cheaper per minute (just $30/month for 200 minutes), but your minutes are good anywhere in the U.S., not just in your home area;
2) No contract is needed;
3) It's super small, and loaded with features.

Here's an example of how it is a great asset for a working craft person who travels and has a Web site. When we leave for a show, we forward our phones (including the 800 number) to our PCS phone number. There is no charge for this, no matter where we are in the U.S. When people call the number on our web site, or call us for any reason, our PCS phone rings. The clarity is such that they never know they are being forwarded across the country. If we miss a call,

continued on following page

continued from previous page

the automatic caller ID lets us return it, or if the caller chooses, they can leave us voice mail. We can even have e-mail forwarded to it. And the phone (all 6.5 ounces of it) cost us just $150.

PCS has disadvantages, too. There is much less PCS coverage than Analog cellular, but our phone is dual band, so when we leave a PCS area it automatically switches to Analog. And the high frequency that PCS works on (1.9 gigahertz) doesn't go through buildings well. It's not unusual that I will walk into a building and hear my phone chirp the "I can't find PCS services, I'm switching to Analog" warning.

You might think that all the junk calls you get would be annoying and costly to forward, too. (Picture us sitting down for a typical meal on the road, at McDonald's, and the phone rings. It's some salesman trying to sell us replacement windows or another credit card.) But incoming calls lasting for less than a minute are free. So just say thanks but no thanks and hang up. Just like at home, but we don't have to get up from the table to answer it.

There are several competing plans offered by different companies, but I think the two best ones are AT&T OneRate and Sprint PCS. Check them out. It may change the way you do business on the road. Information about PCS technology is available on the Internet at http:/www.pscdata.com/whatspcs.htm.

by Chris Maher, Selling Your Art Online, http://www.1x.com/advisor

WHAT A FAX MACHINE CAN DO FOR YOU

The fax machine is a remarkable communications tool that you are sure you don't need until you get one and see what a great help it can be to both your personal and home business life. The benefits of a fax machine are much more than just speed and convenience, and any objections you may have to a fax machine now will quickly disappear once the machine is up and running.

"My husband had to drag me kicking and screaming to get a fax machine," recalls Sue Johnson. "I was firm that if folks couldn't wait several days for my answer, then I didn't want to deal with them. All I can say is thank heavens my husband was pushing me all the way to get involved with, and stay abreast of, technology."

Initially I resisted getting a fax because I didn't think I needed it, didn't have room for it, didn't have time to learn how to operate another technological "gadget," and didn't want the expense of an extra phone line. Of course I was wrong about not needing a fax. I solved my space problem by placing the fax on a board on top of a 12-inch square plastic storage box (open side out), on one corner of my desk. The mail basket that originally sat there now resides inside the plastic box so I haven't lost any desk space. Surprisingly, there wasn't a lot to learn to get the fax working, and I learned the finer points of punching in auto-dial numbers and doing broadcast faxes as time allowed.

Initially, I thought I couldn't afford a fax machine because I wanted a line dedicated to the fax, but didn't want the expense of two business lines. In checking, I found that my phone company could give me a dedicated line on a "flex line basis," where I would pay only for the actual time the machine was in use. On average, each fax I send costs me about 3 cents less than a first-class stamp, and my monthly cost has never been more than $10, even when I've sent or received dozens of faxes. The lesson here is that things are changing so quickly now that what you thought you knew yesterday probably isn't what is actually true today. Always check to see if new options are available to you.

"We've learned that a lot of things we thought were expensive turned out not to be costly at all," says periodical publisher Marsha Reed. "You should never assume something is too expensive until you ask a lot of questions and go directly to the source for accurate information on costs."

Like e-mail, faxing offers convenience and speed while enabling you to spend less time on the telephone, thus lowering your overhead costs. Many times I've faxed something, gotten a fax back, and then made a phone call. But I wasn't on the phone as long as I would have been without the earlier fax transmissions.

From the standpoint of your customers or clients, "fax" translates to "customer benefit." Many sellers thus see an increase in business when they begin to use a fax number in connection with charge card services. People who are too busy to write a check and send it by mail appreciate being able to fax an order along with their credit card number. (This kind of order is beneficial to the seller, too, who has documentation of the fax being sent from a traceable phone number.)

"I like faxes," says Kate Harper, "because there is always a paper trail and my memory is really only 24 hours long anyway. I never use the phone unless I'm willing to have a 15-minute conversation with someone. I normally communicate with sixty reps who phone and fax orders to me. I generally respond by fax because I can do it any hour of the day. I find a lot of vendors want to visit me, but I never meet with vendor reps since I've always found it a waste of time. Instead, I do all my ordering by fax. I send billing reminders via fax because my customers always want to see a copy of the bill if I call them about it. So I just stopped calling and now fax everything. The more you stay off the phone, the more time you will save."

"My wholesaling is done almost entirely over the fax machine," says folk artist Deb Otto, "with orders coming in from reps in twelve to fifteen states each month. My fax is on a designated line so I can receive messages at any time of day or night."

"Since voice mail messages often seem to be ignored by editors, I send faxes instead," says designer Kathy Wirth. "They are almost instantaneous, and the other party has a hard copy of my message to remind them of me. I file the original of my fax and follow up in a few days if I haven't received a reply. I also have a file for faxes I've sent requesting sample products from manufacturers and one for endorsement fee requests. When I receive the fee or product, I pitch the original fax request."

If you decide to purchase a fax, here are some things to consider:

▶ How do you plan to use your machine? Do you need a stand-alone fax or a fax/modem arrangement? If you want to be able to send a fax electronically while you're at the computer, a fax/modem arrangement is fine, but if you'd like to be able to send a fax at any time of day or night without having to turn on the computer, opt for a stand-alone machine.

▶ If you want people to be able to send you faxes at any time of day or night, avoid the arrangement where people have to call you first so you can turn on the computer. This is okay for friends, but it's a great annoyance to business people who expect your machine to be able to receive messages at any time.

▶ If you want to be able to receive faxes at any time of day or night without the phone on the machine ringing, the fax needs to be on a dedicated line. A publisher who sent a broadcast fax one night got a call the next morning from a woman who was upset when the phone/fax rang and woke her up. "If people are smart enough to be in business, they ought to be smart enough to have a separate line for the fax," she believes. (Many businesses send "broadcast fax" messages at night. They simply program numbers into the machine and press the SEND button. The machine then works for hours sending the same fax to everyone on the list.)

THE PLEASURES, BENEFITS, AND PROBLEMS OF E-MAIL

"E-mail is just dandy," says Leila Peltosaari. "No stamps, no mess—this is progress!" If you want to communicate regularly with family, friends, or business associates across the country or around the world, you can't beat e-mail for speed, cost, and efficiency. But not everyone believes that e-mail is important to their personal or business life.

I was slow to grasp the importance of e-mail communications to my business, thinking that, as a writer, I had all I needed with a telephone, fax, and Federal Express for overnight delivery of manuscripts. But once I was online and began to appreciate the *speed* with which I could communicate by e-mail—at no extra cost, mind you—I was hooked. As this book proves, my ability to do research for a book and communicate with nearly a hundred people every day has dramatically changed the way I now gather material for articles and books. Having access to the Internet and e-mail has also broadened the range of books I can now write because electronic research and communication is so easy.

Learning how to navigate the Internet has made a big change in Patricia Kutza's life, too. "Perhaps the biggest is my prodigious use of e-mail," she says. "While e-mail users can't quite qualify for being on the 'bleeding edge' of technology, they still hold a tremendous communication advantage. I do a substantial amount of freelance writing, and I know many editors who favor communicating by e-mail over snail mail. It has become an acceptable way of getting status from editors when a phone call (another type of interruption) would be considered unacceptable. Often, I find myself firing off a rapid exchange of ideas via e-mail. "

Chat Rooms and Mailing Lists. Crafters in general, and professional craftspeople in particular, have taken to e-mail like a bear to honey. Those who also have Internet access are finding the World Wide Web a gold mine of information and ideas. Here, through chat rooms, bulletin boards, and discussion groups (called "mailing lists"), individuals can network with countless others who share their interests and concerns. There are hundreds of special-interest mailing lists for craftspeople on the Internet, each one addressing a particular topic or audience. These lists are managed by individuals who collect messages and e-mail them to members once a day. (To find some of them, visit www.onelist.com or www.liszt.com on the Internet and click on the "Arts" category.)

Be careful about signing up for several lists, though, because this kind of communication can become not only addictive but terribly time-consuming. Busy professionals must be very selective in which lists they decide to join since it is common for just one list to produce as many as twenty-five to fifty e-mail messages a day. (You can elect either to receive these messages individually or in digest form, the latter of which makes it much easier to delete if you find the content not relative to your specific needs).

If a list is one that is helping you successfully manage or market your business, the time spent on it may be worth its weight in gold.

If you subscribe to a discussion list merely because you're curious to see what others have to say on a particular topic, you may find yourself wasting a couple of hours a day that could be spent more profitably in producing goods for sale.

While on one of the mailing lists for professional craftspeople, I found evidence of how stressful e-mail can be when it piles up. An individual posted a message saying she had had surgery, and after recuperating for a week, came down with a cold. Christmas day found both her and her husband with violent sinus infections and on their way to bronchitis. "I am now over 1,000 messages behind on reading my e-mail," she wrote. "I have no hopes of ever catching up. I can't face all that e-mail. Each day the problem gets worse. I have finally made the painful decision to just delete everything and start over from scratch in January."

Like surfing the Internet, sending and reading e-mail communications can become addictive. Unless you are happy being chained to your computer, you should set up a schedule that gives you some time away from the Internet so you can have a life, at least on weekends. The fact that e-mail is an instantaneous communications method doesn't mean you have to instantaneously respond to it.

"My problem is the vast numbers of e-mail that need response," says Morna McEver Golletz. "People who tend to send e-mail seem to believe their method of communication requires a priority response over regular mail. But when you get a lot of both types of mail, it is hard to keep up. Also, I find that with my background as editor, I tend to take too much time to structure my answers. I don't find e-mail an acceptable excuse for sloppy grammar, spelling, etc."

"I check my e-mail only one or two times a week," says Lynn Smythe, "but it's hard. Some weeks I want to sign online every day. Unless I'm expecting something from one of my publishers, the rest of my e-mail can wait—it's usually just other bead-addicted friends saying hello."

Too much e-mail causes not only stress but wasted time. One kind in particular—jokes, funny stories, or motivational messages forwarded to you by well-meaning friends—can eat up an hour a day if you try to read it all. When I'm particularly busy, I don't even have time to pull up such messages and delete them, let alone read them. Just because we all have the capability of sharing with dozens of others every little thing we personally find interesting to read is no reason to do it. We should first get permission from our individual correspondents before loading up their mailboxes with unwanted messages.

Help for Nontypists. As a speed typist, I tend to forget that many people who are now sending e-mail messages are not typists, per se, but trying to get by with their own hunt-and-peck system. "This two-finger approach gets tiresome," moans Carol Carlson. "I thought only people who were going to be secretaries had to learn *that* stuff." Sculptor Robert Houghtaling can do intricate work, but says his big fingers often hit more than one letter on a keyboard. "Although I'm not dyslexic, my fingers seem to be. I don't transpose letters when I read but sometimes do when I type." Gail Platts says her dyslexic tendencies come out in her keyboarding, too.

One of my book contributors told me her mother made her take typing in school; another said her father made her spend a summer's break from junior high learning to type because he thought it would be a good skill. (Ah, how smart our parents were! And they didn't have a clue as to just how valuable typing skills would later become.) If you are only now trying to acquire typing skills, take heart. You will improve with time and practice.

If you don't want to learn how to type, or if you have a disability that makes typing difficult or impossible, there is help in the form of affordable voice recognition software. Howard Broman, who moderates a discussion list on the Internet, uses a program called DragonDictate and recommends another one as well called Naturally Speaking. (On the Internet go to http://www.dragonsys.com/index.html or http:/www.voicerecognition.com/.)

"After installing the program, you just talk distinctly into the speaker and it types what you say," he explains. "You can program it to do standard phrases you use a lot, such as an address or standard letter closing by selecting a code word you can say, and you can program in a list of names. You need to watch as it types, however, to correct errors in common words such as 'two,' which may come out as 'too' or 'patience' which may come out as 'patients.' Due to this kind of error, my correspondents sometimes get a good laugh, but it's worth it."

For those of you who have carpel tunnel problems (strain from doing the same repetitive movements all the time), Linda Beattie Inlow suggests you try the split keyboard. "It's fantastic," she says. "I can type longer without getting tired. Can't wait for the day when they put the mouse tracking onto the keyboard—this will greatly help my right wrist."

A COMMUNICATIONS CHECKLIST

In summary, your ability to communicate in various ways will enhance your professional image and open the door to profitable opportunities you might miss otherwise. Keep these things in mind as you analyze your communications needs:

▸ A separate business line adds to your professional image and gives you a good tax deduction, but may not be necessary if you sell mostly at craft fairs or in local shops and don't need to advertise your phone number to get business.

▸ Whether you make long-distance calls on your personal or business phone, ask a lot of questions and learn exactly how charges are calculated. Change carriers anytime you can find a better rate.

▸ Enhance your professional image by leaving a good message on your answering machine or voice mail that tells callers exactly who they have reached and what you want them to do.

▸ Consider the purchase of a cordless phone if you don't have one now, as this could be one of the greatest time-savers you'll ever find.

▸ If you regularly communicate with a growing number of customers or clients, the addition of a fax machine will save you time, money, and stress.

▸ Protect your electronic equipment with surge protectors and avoid communicating on the telephone or via e-mail during a storm. If power fails, unplug everything to prevent damage from power surges when power is restored.

▸ If you have a computer and modem, you can communicate by e-mail and connect with people all over the world. Once you get a taste of the pleasures and benefits of networking by e-mail, you'll be hooked for life. In addition to the mailing list sites mentioned earlier in this chapter, here are two more connections you can explore:

Deja News (http://www.dejanews.com/). Search over 15,000 Usenet groups by topic, with results returned chronologically arranged.

Forum One (http://www.ForumOne.com/). A guide to online discussion forums on the World Wide Web. This site catalogues over 37,000 separate discussion forum topics, or "threads."

Chapter Eight

Time Management, Organization, and Work Places

|||||||||||||||||||||||||||||||||||||||||||||||||||

When a race is run round a track, sometimes there is one guy who lags way behind all the others. Eventually he is so far behind that he actually looks like he's ahead.
—DODIE EISENHAUER

I think the niftiest and best time saving tip is short term memory loss. If you can't remember what you need to be doing, it doesn't get done, so therefore you have saved the time that you would have used for that task.
—NANCY JAEKEL

Business revolves around Father Time and his first cousin, Organization. If you have disorganized work habits, you automatically waste time—and you know what they say about time being money. To help you see where you might be wasting time, this chapter illustrates how various business owners structure their working hours and maximize the time they have each day.

In addition to saving time, the main benefit of becoming more organized is a reduction of stress, a topic discussed at greater length in the last chapter of this book. Have you ever stopped to reflect on how stressed you feel when you're looking for something you can't find? Or when you're trying to work around a pile of stuff that shouldn't be there but is because you didn't take time earlier to put it in its rightful place? I certainly have. It takes discipline to keep your work area organized at all times, but the time you take to do this each day will automatically save you time later on.

It may seem unimportant to try to save only a few minutes here and there each day, but if you could save just half an hour a day through better time management and more organized work habits, you could gain an extra 182.5 hours a year, or more than a week's worth of time. And that would be enough for a nice vacation, something most crafts business owners say they never have time for.

HOW TIME FLIES

"I'm so far behind most of the time I should have a skinned nose from keeping it on the grindstone," quips gift manufacturer Dodie Eisenhauer. NCA director Barbara Arena probably feels the same way. "I made time management my big goal this year," she says. "I call it my T-Thing. I work with priority and subpriority lists, but the truth is, no matter how well you plan, things seem to crop up every day. These unplanned items are usually things that require you to drop everything else and deal with to keep things running. So it seems no matter how good my intentions are, the T-Thing is still a blister on my toe of progress."

Woodturner Derek Andrews says the biggest problem he faces is finding enough workshop time amongst all the other work and nonwork activities that demand his attention. "I am currently helping with a community project (as a volunteer), which is taking up quite a lot of time and involves meetings during my normal working day. I think that when you work from home, people don't realize that you are at work, and they expect you to be able to go and do things at times when an employed person couldn't. Not that I mind doing this (perhaps I should), but it does make time management very difficult."

Newsletter publisher Betty Chypre likens herself to a monkey that puts its hand in the pipe to grab the apple, but now has a fist too large to pull it out—and yet it doesn't want to let go of the apple. "High-tech living makes demands on my time in many ways," she says. "I wanted to know more about desktop publishing and Web-page development, so I joined a Special Interest Group (SIG) and signed up for classes in HTML. Since my life is already full, these activities throw another level of time-related stress into my life, but I won't open my fist to let go of the apple! Although my ego delights in knowing how to do all these geeky things, it does-n't add to my bottom line, it just sucks up time. Since play is an important part of life, I've relegated these fun things to 'playtime' and set limits to the amount of time they can take. Periodically, when things get too hectic, playtime gets cancelled."

Hmmm . . . see how we creative people try to ease our business stress by calling some jobs "work" and other things "play?" Interesting how we can so easily justify certain things in our mind. I'm the same way, only to me, my "business play" is reading busi-ness magazines and books. Somehow, when I do "work" in a room different from my office, it doesn't seem as much like work to me and can actually be relaxing. (Which is why I sometimes do editing and proofreading at the kitchen table or in the living room.)

NETWORKING SESSION #8:
A TYPICAL DAY IN THE LIFE OF . . .

Creative people structure their work days and manage their time in different ways, depending on their personality, lifestyle, and demands of their family. Many of you tend to get up early in the morning to get certain jobs out of the way before the rest of the household gets moving, right?

Tori Hoggard (artist/teacher): "I get up at least an hour earlier than everyone in the house. Working at home with a house full of kids and a busy spouse makes this the best thing I can do. I usually begin with exercise of some sort for maximum energy through the day. Since I can't add more hours, I maximize the ones I do have."

Joann Haglund (artist): "My day starts around 5 A.M. I get on the Internet and Web when it's the quietest so I can zip around quick-ly. I check e-mail, my eBay auctions, do my online banking, and get off around 8 A.M. I do production work for three hours, then leave at 11 A.M. for shipping and shopping. I always take 12:30 to 2:30 P.M. for a nap."

Pat Endicott (crafts producer): "I'm most productive first thing in the morning. If I have a heavy load, I'll set the alarm and start earlier; otherwise, I can usually get in about two hours work before the house starts moving. I usually do e-mail and correspondence later in the day or in the evening when I can relax. I try to plan one day a week for most of my errands."

Do you do certain work at certain times or play each day by ear?

Dodie Eisenhauer (gift manufacturer: "I begin my day with meditation. My office activities are then grouped. First I pet Catbert so he doesn't jump on the keyboard. He's not very good at invoicing, but he purrs very well when being stroked. Next, I make sure my coffee cup is full, with adequate cream. (Catbert is also happier with the leftover coffee if it's pretty white.) Bills are paid once a week; payroll, every other week. I do most office work in the morning after the kids go to school. Some days I do all production work if deadlines are approaching. (I love production work! If I finish on time, I reward myself with design time.) Invoices are done early to midafternoon in time for packing and shipping preparation. Statements of past-dues are done once a month."

Bill and Camille Ronay (publishers): "Our office is a remodeled boat storage garage about thirty yards from our home on a lake. We have definite hours during which we work in the office, just as if we were in a downtown high-rise office complex. We've found that we save a great deal of time and misdirected energy by having a work plan and daily regimen. We seldom waiver from it."

Chris Noah (printmaker): "I organize tasks according to my daily energy fluctuations. I do detailed, difficult painting early in the day, more routine work later in the day, touch-up work and getting ready for the next day in the evening."

Bob Gerdts (artisan): "I do what I feel like doing at the time. But that means that at the end of the year I have a really big job getting ready for taxes."

Leila Peltosaari working on Halloween costumes she has designed for publication in one of her self-published pattern books.

Leila Peltosaari (book publisher): "It's important to respect your mood. When I don't feel like working, I do something else and wait for 'the mood' to arrive. It always does, since I expect it subconsciously and even coax it by closing my eyes and talking to myself about the things I will do when I'm good and ready and I start feeling more positive. I don't have regular hours and this is the beauty of a home office for me. I break the rules, never carry a watch, and often work in the middle of the night in my nightgown when inspiration comes my way. As Pindar said, 'Learn what you are and be such.'"

Annie Lang (designer): "I tend to select one day for 'bookwork' (updating records, filing, bill paying, etc.), and this day, usually Saturday or Sunday, is by far my most dreaded—right up there with laundry day. But designating it at the end of the week makes my Monday mornings go much smoother. Since my design work schedule is erratic and unpredictable, I prioritize jobs according to deadline, then complexity. I rarely work on two design projects at the same time because this breaks my concentration on the task at hand. I do, however, keep a notebook handy to write down other project ideas or solutions that come into my head as I'm working."

Bobbi Chukran (writer/designer): "After fighting with myself for years, I finally realized that the best way to manage my time was to work during my peak hours. I have a strange schedule. I'm at the computer by 8:00 A.M. or so, sometimes a little earlier. I work until noon or so, get a snack and eat at the desk or take a short walk outside. I read for a few hours, then take a nap. I work a few more hours before making dinner, and then I may work after dinner until 1 or 2 A.M. This may seem strange to 9-to-5 people, but this is what works best for me. I tend to do my fiction writing late at night, and the other stuff during the day."

Do you tend to clump work of a similar nature together, or do a little of everything every day?

Nancy Jaekel (dough artist): "I try to do a little every day. I do most of my marketing work (talking to customers) during the day, but most of my office work is done in the evening. I guess you could say that I work a split shift—production from 7 A.M. to 2 P.M. and another hour or so in the evening."

Tori Hoggard: "My main focus now are my workshops and production for galleries and commission work, so my plan is to do a little of everything every day, breaking up the day into chunks for production, preparing for workshops, bookkeeping, Internet work, etc. I do selling and shipping once a week and need to spend one day a week just for marketing. What good will all this production and promotion do me if I don't have customers and students?"

Chris Noah: "Too much bouncing around from one thing to another makes me anxious. I much prefer to group similar activities."

Lynn Smythe (bead/fiber artist): "Clumping work is best for me, too. If I do a little of everything every day, it doesn't seem as though I've really accomplished anything."

Derek Andrews (woodturner): "I try to clump work together, but in blocks measured in hours rather than days. I get bored with repetitive tasks, so it's a trade-off between efficiency and motivation. I try to save quiet jobs (no noisy machinery) for the evening so I can listen to favorite radio programs."

Joann Haglund: "To keep from getting bored, I tend to mix tasks at the same work stations."

Gail Platts (doll designer): "You do need to learn how to balance your work day. To avoid repetitive stress injury and also keep from getting bored, I need to break up my day. But breaking it up too much can cause distractions and make me feel I haven't gotten anything done."

Robert Houghtaling (sculptor): "I tend to do a variety of things each day, kind of sandwiching them in together as I think they will fit. I usually do my first e-mail and Internet stuff in the morning over breakfast. Then do sculpting. When I break for lunch I may do more computer stuff, then back to sculpting."

Bill Mason (jewelry artist): "I spend fifty hours a week on design and fabrication. Concurrently I am also online (eighteen or more hours a day), doing Web design, uploading new products, reading, surfing for contacts, or soliciting link and banner exchanges. My life is set up to allow me to seamlessly go from one medium to another as this is how my brain works, and it is the best way for me to use my own personality to best advantage."

Isn't it interesting to see the different ways creative people work? It's clear that there are no set rules here, and we must all find our own way of blending business into our personal lifestyle.

KEEPING TRACK OF TIME

"Time is like a sunset," says Dodie Eisenhauer. "You can either capture the beauty and make it a part of you forever or lament its passing."

To successfully manage time, you must first know how you're spending it. If you feel like you have too much to do and not enough time, you may be able to solve your problem by doing a time study of your life.

Years ago, I decided to record how I spent time for an entire year—not just my working hours as a writer and publisher, but my out-of-office time as well. First I made a list of basic categories I could use to code each entry, based on how I normally spent each day. Then I logged how I spent each hour or fraction of an hour. At the end of each week and month, I tallied the various time categories. Interesting patterns emerged quickly, and I began to see what I needed to do to become more efficient in my work habits. By year's end, I was astonished to learn that I had spent 30 percent of my office time manually maintaining my growing mailing list. I suddenly realized that the purchase of a computer would give me hundreds of extra hours each year that could be spent on other activities.

If your business is not yet computerized, a time log of your activities might confirm that you need a computer, too. More important, however, may be a picture of how your life is actually divided. If you need more time for one thing in particular, you must first discover how you are actually spending all of your waking hours. How much time is given to running your business vs. housework, family, community work, social activities, and so on? What things could you eliminate, or where could you cut corners to gain an extra hour or two? In analyzing the time spent on your business, consider how much time you normally spend on such things as designing products, producing goods for sale, marketing your business, dealing with customers or clients, purchasing supplies and materials, running errands, preparing for and doing craft shows, handling paperwork, correspondence, and record keeping and time on the Internet (research, Web site maintenance, and e-mail).

As Bill Ronay confirms, "A regular and serious review of schedules and actual work accomplished over a given period of time will help to put your efforts into perspective."

DOING TWO THINGS AT ONCE

Doing two things at once is as natural to a creative person as it is unnatural to one who lacks a creative mindset. I rarely go anywhere

Business Owners' Timesaving Tips

▸ Use the Internet to save time in both your personal and business life. Before leaving for a new store, I always use a search engine to see if the store has a page on the Web. If I find one, I use a map-it service to set up a driving route. This takes only a moment at home, yet often saves me a great deal of time on the road since I don't have to hunt for the location of the place I am driving to. —Wendy Van Camp
▸ Cook ahead and build a stash of precooked foods. This is great to have on-hand for unexpected guests, who will think you've worked a kitchen miracle when you put a great meal on the table with a minimum of effort. —Susan Young
▸ When cleaning up an area, have two sacks or boxes, one for trash and the other for stuff that goes elsewhere than where you are. That way you don't keep leaving and getting sidetracked. —Linda Beattie Inlow
▸ To save both steps and time, have a spot at both the top and bottom of the stairs to collect things that have to go up and down. —Sue Johnson
▸ Do the task you hate most first thing in the day. Otherwise, you waste time dreading and thinking about it all day. —Michelle Temares
▸ Stay off the phone. Stay off the computer. Stay out of your car. —Kate Harper

in the house for one purpose without also doing something else on the way or at the spot where I stop. Maybe that's why I found this bit of time-management humor from Bill Ronay particularly funny:

You know you are getting older when you start looking for several things to do while you are bent over doing something else—just so you don't have to waste time bending over again to do it.

If I have to go to the basement to get something from my pantry, I'll stick a load of laundry in the machine (and then write a note on the kitchen counter to remind me to put it in the dryer; otherwise it could mildew before I think of it again). I make most of my personal calls in the kitchen so I can prepare a meal at the same time. I always have reading material and a notepad in the bathroom as well as in the kitchen, because I can read a little, make lists, or capture good ideas while watching dinner cook. And some of my best times for talking to God (my CEO) about my life and business are when I'm communing with nature or taking a shower (one of the few times of the day when I'm totally removed from all distractions).

"The best timesaving tip I ever got was to group activities and eliminate wasteful movements," says Joyce Roark. "One way I do this is to clean house in the areas where I am working. If I'm in my studio, for example, while waiting for the computer to download, I'll empty wastebaskets, organize my desk, and do other odd jobs."

I completely understand Pat Endicott, who wouldn't think of leaving home without a book or project in her purse. "I always carry a kit in the car because busy hands ward off nervous tension for me," she says. And I can relate to Dodie Eisenhauer, who totes a little canvas bag with her everywhere she goes, just in case she gets stuck somewhere for thirty minutes with nothing to do, like at an airport or a doctor's office. It contains pliers and the special wire she uses to make her gift items. "I always have orders waiting for small items I can make in a few minutes time," she says. "I'd be doing more of this at meetings and social gatherings if I wasn't afraid of offending people. Few understand my almost eccentric need to always be doing something."

Shirley MacNulty really has her craft projects down to a science. She not only keeps knitting by the phone and never goes out in the car without her knitting bag (which she calls her 'car breakdown insurance'), but also has 'power failure projects' at hand, things she can work on just by feel. "I've used this several times in recent years," she says. "We had three hurricanes in two years, with lengthy power failures, and it was great to have something to work on."

"I have difficulty relaxing," admits Kathy Wirth. "I always feel like

I should be doing something constructive with my time. Lately, I've been reading and answering my e-mail while I eat lunch. If I don't have a crossword puzzle, reading material, or stitching to do while I watch TV in the evening, I fall asleep."

Like Kathy, I enjoy good television, but I have to be absolutely exhausted to just sit and watch it. Most of the time, I "watch" television with my ears because my eyes are fully occupied by my needlework, mending, or other evening project. Although I and others recommend doing two things at once to save time, for some, this practice may be too stressful. As I was writing this chapter, I happened to read an article on how to lessen the stress in your life and chuckled when I got to the point that said, "Try to accomplish one thing at a time. If you are waiting for someone on the phone, don't attempt to look through the mail or a magazine. Instead, look at a restful picture or do some relaxation exercises."

Sorry—that just doesn't work for me and most other creative people because our "curse" is that we can't just sit or stand and *do nothing.* Is it just women who feel they must always be doing something day or night, or do creative men have the same kind of compulsion? I asked my male book contributors to comment on this question, but got only two responses. Artist Chris Maher thinks this is a personality trait, not one related to creative nature. The question, he says, is "What is relaxation? I personally find it a treat to relax and read trade magazines like *Infoworld, PC Week, InternetWorld, Boardwatch,* etc. I can't see 'doing nothing' as relaxation."

Robert Houghtaling would agree, I'm sure, inasmuch as he often does *three* things at once while relaxing in the evening. "My wife gets on my case because I always have to be doing something," he says. "Late night finds me online while I sculpt and watch TV. I have the computer set up so I can watch TV in one corner of the monitor and listen with earphones so I don't wake her up. The bathroom is the library (and sometimes the phone booth), I do e-mail and newsgroups with breakfast, and listen to books on tape while I sculpt."

While it's a blessing to feel you have a mission in life, it's a curse to be so propelled that it's almost impossible to ever slow down, let alone stop. If this describes you, here's a tip for you: Instead of facing your full day with the thought that you can't possibly get it all done, think positively, since this attitude will automatically lower your stress level. As one woman put it, "I tell myself each day that there's always enough time for the things that are important to me. Curiously, when I believe I have time, I get more done."

Laptop Computers: Good Helpers

Annie Lang says she has added several hours of time to her work day with the help of a laptop computer she now thinks of as her second helper. "Because graphic work files and printing take up a lot of time, I've found I can work on the laptop while the main computer is busy."

And here's how calligrapher Michael Noyes uses a PowerBook computer to advance his business: "I take a laptop computer to shows with me because this greatly increases my productivity. In slow periods at a show, I can do all kinds of work, including designing, entering orders, updating my mailing list and e-mail database, correspondence, and working on my Web site."

Now there's an idea for how to attract attention at a crafts show! Just pull up your Web site on your computer and invite browsers to take a look.

A promotional postcard used by Michael Noyes to announce his upcoming craft shows and advertise his Web site.

NETWORKING SESSION #9: HOME AS WORKPLACE

Our workspace is ultimately dictated by the nature of our art, craft, or home-based business, but few people who work at home can run their business out of a single room or area. In fact, most home-based businesses naturally overflow into all areas of the home until people jokingly say, "I don't have a business in my home; I have a home in my business."

It's amusing how zoning ordinances across the country stipulate that home-based businesses are legal, provided they occupy no more than ten or twenty percent of a home's square footage. Of course no one ever checks on this sort of thing, and local zoning officials have no way of knowing what percentage of "home office space" one reports on their annual Schedule C report. No one pays much attention to these ridiculous laws—which is good news when you consider that the average business at home probably occupies a third or more of the home's living space.

The following networking session offers a fascinating behind-the-scenes look into how and where creative people do all the work related to their home-based business.

A growing product-oriented business simply cannot be run from a single room at home, and even simple writing businesses like mine need more than just the space of a single room. Harry has his own office and our basement holds additional filing cabinets, boxes of old tax files and records, my book inventory, shipping materials, and overflow of office supplies. How about you?

Rochelle Beach (dollmaker): "I thought a four-bedroom house would accommodate all of our work stations, but somehow everything overlaps in the heat of production, especially around the holiday season when it literally takes over our whole house."

Pamela Spinazzola (artist): "Somehow I thought I was the only one whose home life is affected by work-storage areas being in the living quarters. I have filled a few rooms in another location for storage, but getting organized seems to be an ongoing process."

So tell me . . . how many rooms of your house are actually used for business, and what kind of activities do you normally do in each of them?

Sue Cloutman (stuffed toy manufacturer): "My business takes up two rooms of an eight-room house, plus a finished garage. My sewing room and office are housed together in a 15 x 18 room we had added on for a family room. The kids gradually got kicked out of there as my tailoring business grew, so we added on a 20 x 22 family room to the back of the house that is now used for packaging. Goods packed for shipment are stored in the garage, which we insulated and sheetrocked three years ago. The car got kicked out, too."

Sue Cloutman at work (a posed photo used for promotional purposes).

Derek Andrews (woodturner): "My workshop is a small room at the back of the house that used to be the summer kitchen. During winter, our living room is used for storage, wood drying, finishing, and packing; in summer, it transforms into our retail craft shop. My wife makes brooches, and the hand sanding, painting, gluing, and finishing is done at the dining room table, but she is currently fixing up a small bedroom to use as her workshop. Our main problems are having somewhere dry and warm to store wood, and also the wood dust and chips that spread effortlessly through the house. We have wood stored in the mudroom, basement, loft, veranda, barn, and in the solar kiln. All in all, this does not make for comfortable living, and we dream of being able to build a workshop and craft shop separate from the house."

Jean Belknap (soft dolls and toys): "A spare bedroom is my computer/work area. I store most of my materials in plastic containers and basket. A small closet holds seasonal items and small accessories used in my products. A guest room serves as a showroom for people who come to my home to see finished products. Show materials (backdrops, tables, benches, etc.) are stored in the garage. I feel I always want to push the walls out to make more room. My dream is to turn our large garage into a shop and work area."

Joyce Roark (gold filled jewelry): "My business is located in the sunroom in my house, where I have my office area and computer and store raw materials and finished products. My jewelry polishing equipment is in the laundry room. When I am making the jewelry, I set up a station in the family room so I'm near both the door and phone. All shipping is done in the dining room because I have a table big enough to hold all the supplies needed."

Rochelle Beach: "We use the kitchen to manufacture our Cinna-Minnie doll blanks, which are then dried in the laundry room. Each batch of dough takes up to a week or more to cure. We package and ship from the dining room, where the table usually holds the products waiting to be oiled and priced—a job actually done in the family room. This work often spills over into the formal living room as well."

Joann Haglund: "I paint in the kitchen near the sink because I need water to paint, and sometimes my husband finds paint on his dinner plate. (If I run out of the little meat trays I use for pallets, I might reach up into the cupboard and grab a dinner plate. 'No, that's not egg on the plate, dear, just paint. Acrylic is not poisonous; it just doesn't taste good.') I'm thankful I have a husband with more patience than sense, and no taste buds left."

Phillippa Lack (painting on silk and gourds): I have a 13 x 30 room for my painting studio, but it always looks like it's been hit with a bomb, what with my silk frame (two sawhorses and 1 x 2" lumber sides); my table for gourds and cards; my sewing table; boxes of designs for silk, dyes, and fabric; and my computer desk. Scarves awaiting packaging are on a rack in the laundry room, where the washing machine serves as packing table."

Jan McClellan (jewelrymaking): "I do my jewelry making in my back yard shop, but my computer desk is in the house, where I do all my office jobs and work pertaining to my Web site. Packing and shipping, a very small part of my operation, are usually done on the dining room table."

Annie Lang (designer): My 13 x 13 studio contains everything I need for my design work except a drafting table, which sits outside the room next to the kitchen table. My storage area (for all the free supplies I regularly receive from manufacturers) is in clear shoeboxes on shelves in the furnace room."

A digital photo of Annie Lang's studio. (The camera is plugged into an adapter which allows the picture to go directly from the camera into the computer and into the software program that comes with the camera. At this point, Annie transferred the image to her Adobe Photo Shop program to crop the picture, change it to gray scale, and print in on glossy paper.)

Chris Noah (printmaker): "My setup has taken several years to optimize, and I am still in the process. Much of our home is given over to the business. All of the downstairs (450 square feet) and smaller areas upstairs are being utilized all or most of the time. I do all my etching and printmaking downstairs. Painting is done in the dining room since it is the most comfortable spot and has the best light, (not to mention the refrigerator and telephone nearby). In the laundry area, I have my light table and drafting equipment, as well as some storage and several large Rubbermaid containers used to transport artwork to shows. Tom rules the woodworking area—formerly an old screened-in porch we rebuilt as a patio enclosure for all sawdust-producing woodworking. Of course the garage has been pressed into service for wet-frame processing, spraying (with special spray box), and framing. *This* is how you turn a typical two-story tract house into a place of business!"

Robert Houghtaling (sculpture and design): "My studio is a glassed-in deck with a view that is always inspiring. Our A-frame in the mountains north of Santa Barbara overlooks the beautiful Santa Ynez Valley from an elevation of 3,300 feet, where we get a little dusting of snow a couple times a year. We are thirty minutes from the nearest village, and the ranch is surrounded by National Forest. I do all my work here while enjoying the abundant wildlife in the area, which includes mountain lions and bears. (I once had a bear try to come in the screen door while I was working, and a California Condor cracked a window.)"

Sculptor Robert Houghtaling at work in his glassed-in studio. This picture was taken with his video camera and then run through a converter program for display online before printing it out as a gray-scale picture for this book. Admittedly, the print quality isn't as sharp as a photograph, but this technology is perfect for Robert when he wants to e-mail a client a picture of a sculpture in progress.

Wow, what a setup, Robert! I'm envious of your location. Others of you also work in only one room, too, but you have to cram more activities into that area. How do you set up your work space to maximize productivity and efficiency?

Kate Harper (greeting card publisher): "People think I'm super-organized, but I'm simply forced to deal with zero space because rent in the Bay area is so expensive. My work area is a 10 x 11 spare room with an L-shaped desk/table that covers two walls, with shelves of stock covering the other two. Hand-built wall shelves above the tables hold unmade card stock. Every square inch is utilized. I do everything here, from designing and shipping to packing. Everything has to be put away once completed as there is no room. Most of the time, shipments coming and going end up sitting in the living room. Supplies, such as decorative art paper, are filed in skinny, upright portfolios stashed behind freestanding shelves. I try to have most supplies delivered directly to my home pieceworkers so I don't have to store it before I give it to them."

Gail Platts (cloth dolls): "Along one wall of my business room is a work table with two sewing machines, a small desk with computer, and a file cabinet. Above the sewing machine/computer area is a pegboard where I hang my work orders and schedules, to keep my eye on the goal. Along the next wall there are three shelving units for supplies and stock, another small filing cabinet for my pattern stuff and, on the next wall, a work station/cutting table that I bought when a local So-Fro was going out of business. This little gem is a good height for working standing up, and it has lots of storage space for shipping supplies and bolts of fabric and a large surface area for work-in-progress. On the shelving units I also have baskets for each product in varying degrees of finish. I like this; if I'm ever stuck and unsure of what to do next, I have work already started, so I just pick up a basket and work. Work is always available in many different stages, so I can always just go in the studio and 'make stuff.'"

Sue Johnson (Sun Print Kits/sewn items/book sale): "My office has an L-shaped desk with computer, scanner, and two printers; underneath, there are three big file drawers. Above the desk are, cupboards and a bookshelf that houses books, extra paper, envelopes, etc. To the right of my computer, on my desk, is a two-shelf bookcase that holds tape, a three-hole punch, computer disks, and business reference books. Across the room, there is another large desktop with sewing machine, paper cutter, electric stapler, and copier. Underneath are drawers that hold sewing supplies. Kit supplies are stored in my basement shop, which is where I assemble Sun Print Kits and pack *Grandloving* books for shipment."

Chris Noah: "In my etching/printmaking area, there is one table for drying prints and another for holding damp paper waiting to be printed. There are also five storage cabinets of varying sizes for supplies and for finished goods. One of these cabinets contains my unlimited edition prints and another one has office supplies, reference materials, and the lighting for inside shows. I also have a desk and the credit card terminal. There is a four-foot diameter round table on the office side of the space that is used for mat cutting and mounting and, at other times, a catch-all spot."

Most of us have space somewhere—the trick is to use it efficiently. Each person must develop a system that works for his or her particular business, work habits, and personality. If I were giving awards for the most creative use of space, however, Elizabeth Bishop would win the prize. Tell them your secret, Elizabeth.

Elizabeth Bishop (doll designer): "I work in a large room off the kitchen and bedroom that can be closed off completely when I have guests. I do everything here, and there isn't a square inch of free space. Even the windows have shelving and books in front of them (my claustrophobia being weaker than my desperation for space). I own every organizer system imaginable, from clear plastic cases, hanging baskets, shoebags, stackable units, and roll carts. When I had to have more room, there was nowhere to go but up, so I purchased netting to hold big bulky items such as batting and stuffing and hung it from the ceiling (see photo). I can easily see it all, and retrieve it with a toteable ladder."

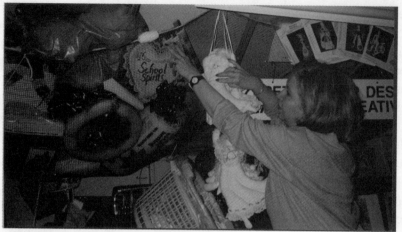

Elizabeth Bishop retrieving an item from her ceiling-hung netting—a creative space-saving/storage idea for anyone who is desperate for space.

Eileen Heifner (doll designer): "One of the biggest challenges new business people face is getting organized in a state of constant growth. It's much more difficult than going into a job where all you have to do is learn to do your little section of the job and how it fits into the company as a whole. When you open your own business, you sometimes don't have any idea where you are going or where you will end up. This makes planning difficult. One thing you can do, however, is be discerning about what you keep in your office. The more stuff you keep because you think you may need it someday, the more stuff and clutter you will have to eventually sort through and clean out to get things done."

HOW TO FIND MORE SPACE

If business is booming and you feel cramped for space, it may be necessary to find studio space outside the home, put some outbuildings on your property, or simply move to larger quarters. As I was finishing this book, Meg Sullivan was moving her business from an apartment to a three-level townhouse so she could devote an entire floor to the business. "I can hardly wait," she said. "I will now have a planning/production area, a sewing area, an area for finished goods, and an entire room for storage."

Until Joann Haglund and her husband moved into a new 3,000 square-foot house with two craft rooms, a sunroom, and five bedrooms, she was literally working all over their three-story 1,400 square-foot townhouse. "One whole floor of the townhouse was filled with paint, stock, and storage, including stacks of shipping boxes and dozens of birdhouses waiting to be painted," she told me. "But the rest of the downstairs was also filled with walls of stock and stuff. Our master bedroom closet contained 1,000 feet of bubble wrap I won on eBay because it wouldn't fit in the craft room. (My wardrobe is small, so hiding the bubble wrap in the closet seemed logical at the time, especially since my dresser drawers were half full of hangers and smaller birdhouses.)"

Studio Space. The solution for some artisans has been to rent studio space outside their home. Artist and teacher Tori Hoggard has a small studio away from home that has classroom space, a small gallery area, and storage space in the attic for supplies too bulky to keep at home. "Since I have small children, I work at home about 70 percent of the time," she says. "My workspace is in the kitchen, which has shelves for immediate supplies and a table large enough to work on. But that means we have to eat meals in the living room much of the time, which I don't like."

Lynn Smythe was looking for space to rent as I was writing this book. "I've been running my bead business out of our very small house for five years," she told me, "and I've finally decided to move the business out of the house because my productivity has been going down the tubes with everything spread all over the place. My current setup leaves no room for me or my family, who are beginning to get annoyed by all this. I also have a problem of not knowing when to quit because the beads and paperwork are always here. I'm currently looking at a store with two rooms that are air-conditioned. The front room would be set up as a bead and fiber art supply store where I could teach classes or have other artists come in and teach. I also plan to have some of my finished bead jewelry for sale. The back room would function as my studio, holding my workbench, kiln, and glass supplies as well as my computer equipment and shipping area. There's also a storage closet, which means I can reclaim the laundry room and bedroom closet at the house.

"Deciding to open a retail store has been a difficult decision," Lynn concludes, "but after five years, I see no other way to maintain productivity and have any kind of home life. I plan to be open five days a week, which will force me to take off two days a week."

Exterior Buildings. Artist and designer Susan Young designed a 12 x 16 wood structure to be built in her backyard. "Because I live outside city limits, there were no zoning problems," she says. "I didn't need a building permit because the structure was not considered permanent (as it would have been if built on a concrete slab). I added a tile floor, baseboard heaters, and a window air-conditioning unit and laid a cable from the house for electricity. It has all the comforts of home." Later Susan added a second building to house her stash of supplies of materials, furniture, and other wood awaiting decoration.

Susan Young's backyard Peach Kitty Studio has all the comforts of home. A companion building houses her stash of painting supplies and products awaiting decoration.

Jan McClellan also has a shop in her backyard where she creates heirloom gemstone jewelry. "What does it look like? Very messy! Once a month or so I clean it up, but it is a mess again within a day," she moans. "Jewelry making is dirty, and it is my nature to have things laying all over—stones, works in progress, etc. I keep all my jewelry—making supplies and raw materials in the shop. Another area is devoted to lapidary work, but it doesn't get used as much, so I keep my booth and display things in this part of the shop."

Calligrapher Michael Noyes has three exterior buildings on his property, one for his studio, another for production, and a third for shipping. "I like working in them because they offer privacy and

Mail Handling Tips

According to Liza Kanarek, author of *Organizing Your Home Office for Success*, it's a myth that you should handle a piece of paper only once. The rule, she says, is not to handle paper once, but *to do something with the paper* each time it hits your desk.

It's great when you can process, file, or throw out a piece of paper the first time you touch it, but more than likely, you'll have too much of your mail in a holding file because you won't have time to deal with it the first time you encounter it. The "to-do-later-jobs" typically include things like bills that must be paid, correspondence and catalog requests that must be answered, orders that must be processed, things that must be read later, phone calls to be made, things to check out on the Internet, and so on. The following tips reinforce this message.

- ▶▶ "Don't feel as if you have to go through the mail each and every day. Quickly scan it to see if there is anything that needs immediate attention, and handle the rest later when you're not so rushed."—Lynn Smythe
- ▶▶ "Do mail once a week. That leaves the rest of the week to work on other things."—Myra Hopkins
- ▶▶ "If you must let the mail stack up for a few days, place it into categories for easier response when you have time." —Camille Ronay
- ▶▶ "Create folders for the various categories of mail you normally receive, and as you open each piece, place it in the appropriate folder for processing."—Anita Means
- ▶▶ "In reading mail about a future event that interests you (such as a trade show), mark it on your calendar, then file the info in a file folder named Events so you can go back and look at the details if you choose."—Eileen Heifner
- ▶▶ "As you get your daily mail, open it over the garbage can— in the garage, if it isn't too cold—so you don't bring any unnecessary stuff into the house."—Sue Johnson

quiet," he says. "Since they're portable, I can also take them with me when I move. I got my last 10 x 14 building from an Amish manufacturer (in another state, so no sales tax). It cost $2,000 delivered and setup. I ran electricity out from the house for lights, heat, and air-conditioning."

For others who may be considering this idea, it would be wise to check with local zoning officials to see what the size limitations are for exterior building, and also to ask if a builder's permit is needed for this kind of structure. Suppliers of exterior buildings and sheds can be located by checking the Yellow Pages.

A TIME MANAGEMENT/ORGANIZATION CHECKLIST

Your time is worth as much to you as it is to the wealthiest person in the world. Each day, God credits your "Time Bank Account" with a total of 86,000 seconds you can spend any way you wish. Since you can't retrieve lost time or draw against tomorrow's account, you should learn to value the time you have and use it well; or, as Kipling put it, "Fill every unforgiving minute with 60 seconds worth of distance run." As this chapter has illustrated, it's important to make time management and organization a goal. Use this reminder checklist as a plan of action.

▸ Don't let family and friends steal your time. Be firm about having some private time for yourself, and set specific times for family activities or visits with friends.
▸ Create quiet time in which to work. You can do a lot of work in a less-than-quiet atmosphere, but your best work will be produced in those blocks of time that are truly your own. If you have young children, consider paying an older child to entertain them for a couple of hours each afternoon so you'll have a couple of quiet, "golden hours."
▸ Save time by having office and computer supplies delivered. If you don't have a local supplier who delivers, order from major catalog houses that do. Most office suppliers ship the same or next day by UPS, and many offer free shipping on larger orders.

▶ Buy a calendar or notebook and begin recording how you spend every hour of your day. Do this for as long as possible or until interesting patterns emerge.

▶ If you're on the Internet, sign up for the free "Memo to Me" service (offered by Joel Johnstone at http://www.MemoToMe.com) that lets you set up a customized reminder list of everything you need to remember—from appointments, birthdays, and anniversaries to things you need to do on a regular basis. Then, each day you need a reminder sent, it will appear in your e-mail box.

▶ Make a list of all the things you do each day and see how many of them you can "match up" to one another so you can learn to do two things at once without any added stress.

▶ Set up a daily work schedule for yourself that is right for your personality, lifestyle, and family responsibilities, and try to develop a routine that is normal for you (even if others think it's weird).

▶ Absolutely can't meet that deadline date? Ask for an extension. If that doesn't work, do your best to finish when you can, but forgive yourself if you fail to meet the original deadline date. Never make yourself ill trying to meet someone else's deadline. Sometimes the only way to get it all done without going to pieces is to get it done late.

▶ Obtain some office supply catalogs and look for shelving, boxes and other organizers that would make your work areas more efficient, thus enabling you to become a more organized worker.

▶ At least once a year go through all your file folders, drawers, storage shelves, and other "holes" in your home office, workshop, or studio where clutter naturally occurs. Reorganizing such areas will make your life easier and give you a sense of accomplishment. Knowing where everything is, and having everything in its place—even for a little while each year—might even lower your blood pressure.

▶ Give yourself a larger working area. Buy a couple of inexpensive two-drawer filing cabinets and lay a piece of vinyl laminated board over the top. Voila—a desk that is both efficient and attractive.

Even with sufficient space in which to work, some people tend to be disorganized no matter how hard they try. If this describes you, don't fret about it. You may actually be a right-brained individual who functions better in "controlled chaos" than in an organized environment. In fact, research has shown that right-brained people can actually sabotage their creativity by attempting to follow the suggestions of well-meaning left-brain people who can't resist trying to physically organize them. (Tell that to the next person who calls you a disorganized slob!)

RECOMMENDED READING

Taming the Paper Tiger at Home, Barbara Hemphill (Kiplinger's).
Home Office Know-How, Jeffery D. Zbar (Upstart Pub. Co.).
Tips for Your Home Office, Meredith Gould (Storey Publishing).
Getting Organized, Stephanie Winston (Warner Books).
Organizing Your Home Office for Success, Lisa Kanarek (Dutton/Plume)

Chapter Nine

Product Design and Packaging

||||||||||||||||||||||||||||||||||||||||||||||

In designing, having the ability to impart emotional aspects to products or services is crucial for success. The most emotional and striking parameters of products are first the color, then the form, feel, structure, and material.
—KATHY LAMANCUSA, TREND ANALYST,
PROFESSIONAL COMMUNICATOR, AND AUTHOR

To make a part or full-time living from their work, professional artisans must constantly come up with new products or at least variations on a theme. But where do all their ideas come from, and what things need to be considered in the design process? This chapter answers those questions and others related to the design process, including how to:

▶▶ brainstorm for new product ideas,
▶▶ design for a niche market,
▶▶ redesign an existing product,
▶▶ develop a successful widget, and
▶▶ design packaging that will sell your products.

BRAINSTORMING FOR NEW IDEAS

"But I can't create my own original designs," a beginning crafter moans. "I have to use the patterns and designs of others."

Really? Thousands of craftspeople who once thought like that are now designing all their own products. I believe you *can* come up with your own original ideas if you put your mind to it and, if your goal is to have a profitable part- or full-time business, you *must* create originally designed products to successfully compete with the thousands of other people now selling handmade or handcrafted products. If designing is difficult for you, take heart. With time and practice in your art or craft, you will automatically develop design ability. This chapter will encourage your natural creativity and help you develop your design skills by giving examples of how other creative people get their ideas and turn them into salable products.

To get you started, here are some things to consider as you try to think up new products you might sell:

Think "Leisure." Consider making products that will help people fill leisure hours, such as games, puzzles, or humorous playthings for adults. Patterns or kits for toys, dolls, teddy bears, and other things people enjoy making for themselves or as gifts are always in demand, too.

Think "Scraps." Do you have odds and ends of supplies left over from other products? Lay them all out together and see if the combination of materials, colors, textures, etc., suggests new product ideas. Play with them for awhile until an idea suggests itself. Consider doing small versions of larger products for dollhouse or miniatures collectors . . . novelty or souvenir items. . . or a promotional item or freebie you could give to children as a device for drawing adults in to your craft booth.

Think "Busy Women's Needs." Look at your local marketing opportunities and try to create products to fit available outlets. Think of things that would solve a specific gift need facing busy women, such as an upcoming graduation, birthday, anniversary, wedding, or baby shower.

Think "Tourists." Do you live in a tourist area? If so, consider making products in the following categories commonly purchased by tourists (in addition to antiques and crafts in general): postcards and booklets about sites visited; T-shirts and other clothing with the name or picture of a location or attraction; local food products; items that can be added to a collection; and mementos (novelty items) of a location or attraction.

Think "Hot Colors." Pay attention to the colors used in new products each year. Stay up on color trends by reading newsletters and magazines for professional crafters. You can get a good idea of what's hot simply by spending a day in a shopping center and browsing clothing racks. Notice the colors of new cars, too.

Think "Collectors." Collectors are less concerned with price than the average consumer and tend to buy on impulse when something strikes a nostalgic chord or satisfies a longing of the heart (both marketable benefits). If you do not already produce items for collectors, brainstorm product ideas for such buyer categories as animal lovers, sporting enthusiasts, musicians, circus fans, carousel buffs, people who love dolls, teddy bears, miniatures, woodcarvings, etc.

Think "Size." One way to quickly expand your product line is to offer basically the same products and designs, but to do them in different sizes or change the way they might be used. For example, a design now used as a plaque for the wall might become the design on the top of a box; a line of rag dolls for children might be done in miniature as adult collectibles.

Using Findings and Parts

At what point does buying findings or parts compromise one's craft, a seller asked on Howard Broman's online discussion group. He responded:

"We artists have always held a tremendous amount of pride in the fact that we make what we sell. For years, a vast majority of arts and craft shows made this a necessary requirement of entry. But I'm afraid those times have gone, with the exception of the fine art and crafts sold at ACC shows to the top one percent of the population—the privileged and wealthy.

"Nowadays most promoters will let you have other craft items in your booth if they're less than 10 percent of your total display and handcrafted by an otherwise qualified artisan. And, many promoters are having a difficult time filling up their shows with 100 percent qualified artisans, so their choice is either go broke or bend. I think it's a change many of us will have to get used to."

Think "Feel-Good Benefits." In designing handmade garments, designer jewelry, or related accessories, try to come up with products that will make people feel good when they wear them. People naturally want to feel more attractive, and they enjoy wearing clothing and accessories that make them stand out in a crowd. (This, of course, is a marketable benefit you should emphasize in your advertising.)

Think Backwards. When brainstorming for new product ideas, try thinking backwards. Think first about the problems, special needs, or personal desires people have that you might be able to solve with a particular product. Then think how you might market it by imagining typical buyers in terms of the publications they read, the organizations they belong to, and the places where they are likely to gather. (This is the method I've always used in deciding what kind of book to write next.)

After you have filled your mind with ideas and impressions, think about how you can combine those ideas in a way that is different from what everyone else is doing. That is creativity!

NETWORKING SESSION #10: BRAINSTORMING

As this networking session illustrates, creative people get ideas for new products in a variety of ways.

How do you brainstorm for new product ideas or product lines?

Bob Gerdts (decorated eggs): "I don't really brainstorm; I just keep thinking . . ."

Joann Haglund (whimsical tole painting): "My brain is in a constant state of 'storming.' Sometimes it's hard to turn it off. I bounce ideas off my wood-wizard (the fellow who makes the birdhouses I paint). He prototypes the impossible and produces the best sellers consistently on time."

Tori Hoggard (painted murals, furniture, and hand-bound journals): "I stimulate my mind by going on scavenger hunts through secondhand stores, bookstores, craft stores, galleries, and boutique shops. Then I silence my mind and let whatever comes in happen."

Eileen Heifner (porcelain doll kits): "New product ideas just come to me. I think it is because of information I have gathered on a subliminal level that I'm not even aware of."

Deb Otto (art prints): "I always start my brainstorming by looking at the environment in which products are intended for. With my print line, I am trying to appeal to folk-art-savvy customers who decorate in casual country to early American and primitive styles."

Dodie Eisenhauer (screen wire gift items): "I'm constantly looking and thinking of ways to change what we do or new things I could try. I jot ideas down on small pieces of paper and shove them in a wooden bucket under my desk."

Kate Harper (greeting cards): "I listen to people and learn about their lifestyle, always looking for words to address their experiences. I watch mothers with children at playgrounds, I talk to people who work in cubicles all day. I listen to computer programmers to see what they think is funny. People and their stories have always interested me. I hear their struggles, hopes, and fears and am always looking for words to address their experiences. I look for those things that relieve unhappiness in some small, simple way." (See also sidebar, "How a Greeting Card Designer Designs.")

Pat Endicott (quilted creations): "I stimulate my mind by keeping my ears and eyes open. I'm always window shopping, inviting feedback from customers and friends, and reading magazines."

Obviously, you all get ideas from magazines, catalogs, and other printed materials, but how do you use them for design inspiration?

Phillippa Lack (silk painting): "I study the fashion magazines and newspapers to see current trends. I look at haute couture publications and use their colors as well as tried-and-true combos (jewel tones are always popular)."

Deb Otto: "Magazines help me watch for general color trends, whether they are lighter or darker this year, whether there are more of certain colors (blues, greens, etc). In using magazines, however, be sure you are identifying trends only, not copying a motif directly. This will backfire as you will lose your own artistic identity and not be identified for your own style. You also need to be aware of 'overdo' in a design or color scheme that limits an item's use in a wide variety of homes."

Friends and customers are often a good source of design inspiration, aren't they?

Steve Appel (bolt people sculptures): "I have a friend in the same business I'm in, and we talk over breakfast."

Vicky Stozich (clothing patterns for cement geese): "On my mail order form, I ask my customers to submit ideas for new patterns they would like."

Tabitha Haggie (primitive folk art): "I show the product to my 'research committee' of diehard craftaholics and can usually judge the popularity of the item by their enthusiasm or lack thereof."

Phillippa Lack: "I listen to those who sell my products in their boutiques and galleries. They tell me what colors or designs are moving best, and I paint to that goal."

Jan McClellan (gemstone jewelry): "I listen to my customers at shows, see what they want, then try to make something along that line. I've noticed that people in different areas like different styles. For example, they like 'big' jewelry in San Francisco, but more conservative things in Oregon. I pay attention to fashion trends as well. A few years ago, big and dangling earrings were in style; today, many people want small earrings. I try to make things I hope will appeal to the particular market I'm traveling to."

Kim Marie (pottery): "If I get special requests from more than one customer, I feel it may be a direction to try. I like to make things that have some kind of function, like kitchenware, cooking ware, candleholders, and the like. So if people tell me they'd like to see some turtles in my line, I first try to think of something the turtle can do. For example, I've got a turtle with a removable shell that is a cone incense burner, and

my Kandle Kats hold tea candles that twinkle and glow from the cat's eyes, mouth, ears, and design at the neck. These items appeal to my younger customers for dorm rooms."

In my own craft work, I find my most creative design ideas come while I have my hands on the project. It's as if my hands know the way better than my mind.

Jan McClellan: "I can relate to that. My jewelry is mostly one-of-a-kind, and I brainstorm by looking at stones, moving them around, and combining them with other stones until inspiration hits. I often draw or cut out shapes from paper to see how a stone will look on it."

Jacqueline Janes (jewelry from handmade beads): "I look for trends in other markets, malls, galleries, and magazines, but I don't really brainstorm or plan ahead too much. I just let the pieces come together bit by bit as I play around with beads to find a pleasing combination of color and design."

Do you design products hoping they will appeal to everyone, or do you find it more profitable always to design with a specific buyer or niche market in mind?

Bob Gerdts: "I don't try to target anyone in particular. That doesn't work for me."

Gail Platts (whimsical cloth figures): "I do not design for others, but to express myself. If it sells, good; if it doesn't I move on to another design. Trying to design for others is too complicated and tangles up my self-esteem. I just do my own thing."

Joyce Birchler (stained glass jewelry): "I design what I like and hope the world agrees. My jewelry makes people smile, so I never have to convince someone to buy."

Chris Noah (contemporary art prints): "My designing is a balancing act between what I like and what, in my experience, has done well. I have been wrong, of course, but more often I am right."

Pat Endicott: "I design quilted items with function and practicality in mind. (See right.) Over the years I've learned that my buyer is most likely to be a middle-age woman."

Steve Appel: "My product is designed for people who have everything, and I design for all occupations and sports. If buyers don't fall into one of these two categories, they have friends that do."

Patricia Kutza (neckware and jewelry): "I design for women between the ages of twenty to sixty-five who need to 'dress' for work (suits, tailored pantsuits, or dresses). My customers value knowing that they (or their gift recipient) will be wearing something unique. My Whatknots were created to fill the vacuum in the late 1980s for a classy looking accessory business women could

A watercolor illustration Patricia Kutza created to display her Whatknots neckwear accessories in galleries.

wear instead of the floppy ties then flooding the market. Today they're an excellent compromise for 'dress-down Fridays' when my clients (often lawyers) still need to attend meetings but want to dress a bit more relaxed."

Jacqueline Janes: "Trying to guess the public's taste sometimes makes me want to pull my hair out! I have a particular necklace I love and wear all the time. When I go out, I get a lot of positive comments about it. So I made a bunch of them, and I think I've sold maybe two or three in the last two years. This has taught me that there is a big difference between what the public *likes* and what they *buy*."

Kim Marie: "I once heard that people part with their money for two reasons: either they absolutely *need* what is in front of them, or they absolutely *love* what is in front of them. I always try to design for the latter. When designing products, I keep several things in mind. Will the price be what a customer would be comfortable paying? Will there be a market? If there is a great market, will I mind or be able to make great quantities? Can I make it faster and maintain quality? Will it make people smile? Many people make pottery, so I have to find a way to have my work look different from other potters and attractive to potential customers. I can't make everyone happy, but I try to be versatile and fresh. If I have the right form, they might not see their color, so if I have a good design, I try to have it in many colors. I have colors available like purples, crimsons, and pinks that are not always seen in functional pottery but seem to be good sellers."

It's one thing to design a product; another to design and develop a line. Sales reps emphasize the importance of developing a line with a cohesive look, but what else should sellers keep in mind here?

Pat Endicott: "There is more to the development of a successful line than the beginner might imagine. Previously we had listened to new product suggestions and came out with many products that weren't quilted (our usual line). Many stores complained, as these weren't what they were expecting from us. You see, we had worked years to educate people about our string-quilted products, and it was a mistake to offer a different type of product. I've learned that once you develop a certain trait, reputation, and priorities, you must not let yourself get distracted."

Deb Otto: "Crafters often limit their items for sale because they think one type of item or one type of motif will be hot and they want to have enough. But what happens if you're known as 'the snowman booth' or 'the sunflower lady' and the one motif fades in popularity? One solution is to pick a wider topic. In my Cricket in My Closet printed shirt line that I sold for years, the only requirement in each design was the hidden cricket (like a secret signature). Within the line, I chose many popular motifs through the years, but in time the whole line was looking too 'country' and as that style started to get overworked, I closed down the Cricket line entirely and started my newer From the Hand of Hannah line, which appeals more to the growing number of folk art enthusiasts. The switch not only involved subject matter but my product itself, as I switched from clothing to framed prints of my designs—mainly because that was what the majority of folk art collectors look for."

Meg Sullivan (cross-stitch, knitted, crocheted and sewn items for babies and children): "We do about thirty-five craft shows a year and I try to have something new at every show, so we frequently add new items to our line. 'New' can be defined as an entirely new product or line, or an established product in a new color or fabric. We often retire products for a season or more. Sometimes sales are declining, sometimes we can't stand the thought of making one more of an item. When we bring them back, they're new again. To increase profits and productivity, we take the time every year to evaluate which products are not selling well and which of those products are most profitable. (Just because it's fun doesn't mean it's profitable.) We weed out the products that are less profitable so we can concentrate on our profit centers."

What happens if you fail to update your designs or product lines on a regular basis?

Jacqueline Janes: "At one point, I realized I had not updated my product lines for a couple of years and my sales at shows suffered as a result. The following year, I introduced some new products and styles. Currently, I'm planning on scrapping most of my products and concentrating on limited-edition and one-of-a-kind pieces."

Meg Sullivan: "The worst thing a crafter can do is make the exact same things year after year, then set up their display the exact same way every time. We have a friend who makes wood signs (doctor, nurse, engineer). Very clever, but after you have one, you don't buy another. His sales were sinking into the sunset until he started doing signs with sports team names. He took twenty Buffalo Bills signs to a show in New York, sold them all, and left the show with over forty more orders."

That sounds like a winning idea, but before you start making and selling items that incorporate the name or logo of any sports team, avoid legal and financial problems by first contacting the sports organization for permission. Most likely you will have to pay some kind of licensing fee and a percentage of your sales for the use of any team's name.

Protect Your Creativity with Copyrights

Ideas themselves cannot be protected by a copyright, but you may protect your *expression of an idea* by copyright if it is in tangible form, such as a design, pattern, or other written or drawn material. Some creativity and originality must be incorporated into a work for it to be copyrightable, however. For example, you cannot copyright a common form, shape, or object such as a circle, triangle, heart, rose, or butterfly, but you *can* create original designs that incorporate such common forms, shapes, and objects. You cannot stop anyone else from using the same common forms, shapes, or objects in their own designs, however. For example, six artists could paint a picture of a butterfly sitting on a rose, and each artist could copyright his or her own original picture.

To further illustrate, you can copyright the design on a craft object when that design can be identified separately from the object itself, but you cannot copyright an ordinary object such as a ring, a plate, a coffee mug, or a box. You cannot copyright anything that has fallen into public domain, but you can make and copyright your own adaptation. Names, titles, and short phrases may not be copyrighted, but may qualify for trademark protection. Although inventions are protected by patents, the written description or drawing of an invention can also be protected by copyright.

from The Crafts Business Answer Book & Resource Guide, Barbara Brabec (M. Evans).

DESIGNING FOR NICHE MARKETS

It's difficult to sell something to a mass market, so to increase sales, think "niche market." Such markets will quickly come to mind if you think in terms of how your products benefit specific groups of people—brides-to-be, nurses, grandmothers, nostalgia buffs, or pet lovers, for example. Once you've focused on a particular market, get more specific in your thinking. Take the baby market, for example. Crocheted or knitted items naturally come to mind, but such products are often difficult to sell at a good profit. More profitable items might include: (1) novelty gifts for baby showers; (2) items that could be personalized with a child's name; or (3) higher-priced decorative accessories or furniture for a nursery or child's room.

Here are examples of niche markets my book contributors regularly design for:

- ▶▶ "My niche market is contemporary galleries or funky little gift stores," says Gail Platts, who sells whimsical little cloth figures—things that catch people's attention and make them smile. "My things are often bright, not cute, but loud."
- ▶▶ "We sell best to a niche market that could be described as upper-middle class, well-educated professionals," says printmaker Chris Noah. "This is the niche market we ourselves fit into. We seem to sell best to people we communicate with best."
- ▶▶ "A local arts and crafts co-op moved their store to a vineyard, which prompted me to start making bottle stoppers," says woodturner Derek Andrews. "They now sell well at most of my outlets, and I don't know why I didn't start making  them sooner. Recently, after a customer saw my bottle stoppers on my Web site, I got a substantial order for customized bottle stoppers to be used as wedding favors (with name of the bride and groom and the date of the wedding inscribed on the stopper using pyrography techniques). I think this idea has a lot of potential for future marketing of a very simple product."
- ▶▶ "My products also appeal to people I know and understand who are like me," says greeting card manufacturer Kate Harper. "Instead of trying to reach out to people I don't understand or know much about, I try to really listen to friends and hear what their fears, dreams, and needs are. I generally sell to baby

boomers with demanding jobs. They have children but feel they never get enough time with them. They are everything from teachers to stockbrokers, and they live in urban environments. They like the outdoors and have a spiritual interest. Most are Democrats."

▸▸ "Teachers and children are my market for one of my most popular sellers—a spool necklace decorated for different holidays," says Jana Gallagher. "The necklaces are inexpensive, cute, holiday-related, and a conversation piece. They make perfect teacher gifts."

▸▸ My newest niche market is designing custom earrings for hand-screened shirts created by other artists," says Jacqueline Janes. "I'm finding that custom work can be profitable. If you have a product that you can do custom work with, I say exploit it. It's the only way to create something truly unique. My other niche market is selling my beads wholesale to other artists and bead stores. I used to do more of this, but find that selling my finished products at the retail level is more profitable."

▸▸ "American tole painting is a niche market to begin with," says Joann Haglund, "so my work does not appeal to everyone. But the upscale buyer who is beginning to collect a particular artist is always a good source for repeat sales for me—the gift-giver looking for something original but cheap."

▸▸ "Since jewelry is not a necessity or something a customer can justify buying for their home, I must find prospective buyers with disposable income," says Jan McClellan. "Thus, my market is the more upscale neighborhoods and professional people."

▸▸ "To the New Age/personal/spiritual-growth market, I sell cards, wall and floor cloths, journals, and treasure trunks," says Tori Hoggard. "I recently developed a game to be used by mental health-care professionals that will hopefully do well. To the juvenile market, I sell wall and floor cloths, baby books and albums, and handpainted furniture."

You must constantly be on the alert for new niche markets and be prepared to design for them when you find one. Dodie Eisenhauer offers a good illustration. "I sold my new Wine Carry to a cou-

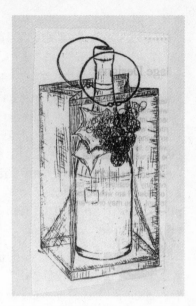

A new product called "The Wine Carry," designed by Dodie Eisenhauer for a niche market.

ple of wineries at market in January, and now plan to promote to more wineries," she says. "I plan to send a free Wine Carry to a select list of wineries. If the mailing proves successful, I'll expand. This new product comes in different sizes and is selling well to a high-end market. It could also fit the corporate gift market since it can double as a flower container after the wine is gone."

In addition to the previous tips and ideas, here some additional things to keep in mind when designing new products.

Custom Design Options. Potter Kim Marie says she looks at her work as "functional pieces with a dash of elegance. The Harlequin Series is some of my upper-end work. With it, I can work with a customer and design patterns to be put on place settings. I have a return customer who originally wanted some plates and bowls. So I worked up some designs and sent them to him. He now adds to his girlfriend's set any time there's a holiday. So what started with plates and bowls has grown to include mugs, serving platters, teapots—and who know what he will want next!"

Supplier Problems. When designing a new product, make sure your supply source is reliable; and always have a back-up supplier waiting in the wings. Many craftspeople have launched new product lines assuming that the special supplies or materials needed for them would be available indefinitely. But companies go out of business, get overworked, or have their own supply problems. (For more on this topic, see Chapter Twelve.)

Consumer Safety Laws. If you are developing new products for children, be careful to comply with consumer safety laws. A wealth of

How a Greeting Card Designer Designs

Kate Harper's greeting cards are printed using soy ink on recycled paper. Each includes a swatch of Chiyogami paper imported from Japan; they are packaged in biodegradable cellophane wrappers. Kate combines the design/market-research process in an interesting manner. Whenever she adds new quotation cards (more routine than new products such as gift items) to her line, she uses the following five-step process:

1. Review quotes by freelance writers and pick the best ones.
2. Write up a "best ones" list and have a "Quote Vote." ("This means I have the sales reps and top-selling retail stores vote on the best quotes, and they fax back their picks to me.")
3. Design cards based on winning quotes. ("Winners have to get at least 50 percent of the votes. In other words, about half the people who voted should have chosen that quote.")
4. Print 750 of each greeting card with the top winning quotes on it. ("Depending on how many quotes were winners, this could be four cards or a dozen.")
5. Put the cards on the market and see if they are going to sell. ("If the sales of a particular card are too slow for my taste, I don't reprint it in the future and it's dropped from the line. New ones, hopefully more exciting, will replace the dogs.")

Quotation by Shirl Ransley; Artwork by Kate Harper
© Kate Harper Designs. Used by permission.

consumer product information is available from the Consumer Product Safety Commission's toll-free hotline. Call 1-800-638-2772 to get a menu of several extensions you can punch to order publications related to the manufacture of toys and children's products.

Limited Editions. Many states now have laws that impose strict disclosure and warranty requirements on sellers who offer limited editions of art or craftwork that include certificates. Before offering any kind of limited edition, check with an attorney who can answer questions about your state's law and, if necessary, help you draft the necessary certificate forms.

Designing for Collectors

There are many different kinds of collectors out there who regularly buy handmade or handcrafted items. The following tips from two dollmakers are applicable to everyone who is creating products aimed at the collector market.

Says Bobbi Chukran, "In the doll world, you have one-of-a-kind dolls, limited editions of twenty-five, one-of-a-kind dolls with different clothing, etc., to designate how unique each doll is. Couldn't other craftspeople use some of the same designations? I think we all are going to have to get really smart about selling, designing, and manufacturing to compete in the present economic climate and come up with ways of letting the public know why our products are priced higher than imported items."

"Even with a product line as broad as dolls, most people still have a preference," notes Eileen Heifner. "My own staff offers a perfect example of this. One dollmaker loved antiques while another liked them but loved Indian dolls. One loved babies, while another loved dolls that were like eight-year-old girls. The popularity of the time-out dolls with no faces gives an indication of buyers' unusual tastes in dolls. Dolls cross every ethnic and social group and, because they frequently resemble children or people, they have an emotional tug as well. I try to make or design my dolls to be both pretty and interesting."

REDESIGNING EXISTING PRODUCTS

As you've already learned, it's important to keep offering new products and designs every year, but old products can often be redesigned to make them look new or to make them appeal to a different market. Sometimes they must to be changed when supplies or materials become too costly or are no longer available. Products are also redesigned because of production factors.

Potter Emily Pearlman stopped making candlesticks for the simple reason that they took up too much room in the kiln, making her fall behind on other items. "The same thing was true for teacups with saucers," she said. "The saucers are impossible to fit in, so I'm thinking of redesigning the teacup so it doesn't need a saucer—or raising the price of the cup and saucer a lot."

For printmaker Chris Noah, the redesign process is almost always an aesthetic consideration, rather than an attempt to reach a different market or even sell more. "Often, though, that is the upshot," she says. "I give some considerations to current color trends, but have found that color trends are not really as significant as the design world cutting edge would have you think."

In any case, *change* is the key word here, and the following examples offer more insight into how you might change your products to increase sales and profits.

Change Colors. "A lot of good products can be marketed anew with just a minor change of design," says Eileen Heifner. "I've found that updating a color scheme can do wonders."

"Taking a basic product and using updated colors, I'm constantly redesigning my entire line, adding more upscale items like jewelry boxes in the shape of birdhouses," says tole painter Joann Haglund. "As the collectibles market opens up to my work, I need to keep designing new items for the collectors."

"I redesigned my entire card line many years ago," says Kate Harper. "My cards looked good at home, but after seeing them in a shop, I found they looked dark and drab in comparison to others. Now I hang up other people's cards in my office as a test to see whether my cards will stand out on a store shelf."

Change Size, Finish, or Design. "Jewelry trends are tough to work with," says Jacqueline Janes. "What do you do when the trend of the moment is to wear a single piece on a cord that looks invisible? (I will never understand this concept.) At a certain point, you have to go against the trend and hope that you still have a big enough market for your style. I have, however, reduced the size of my beads, and I've been using smaller accent beads to design my pieces."

For some time, Pamela Spinazzola has offered a standard-size floor standing quilt and blanket rack. She still sells that item, but she created a new product by redesigning it for childrens' bedrooms. "I simply changed the size, softened the lines, and finished it in a different way," she says. "The scaled-down version is just the right height for a child. The hand-painted finish either has stencil art or original paintings of childhood themes."

"I made a dragon oil lamp about ten inches high," says Kim Marie. "Though quite popular at $25, many of the people who wanted the dragons for themselves either couldn't (or wouldn't) spend that much on themselves. So I redesigned the piece to be smaller and changed how I made the dragons. This way I could sell them for $16. It has made a tremendous difference, and now the  baby dragons are one of my hot sellers."

Change Materials. I'm getting away from the complete steel look of my bolt people by mounting them on wood," says Steve Appel. "My scuba diver, for example, is now being placed on driftwood, with a few steel strands of seaweed."

Change Construction Method. "It's funny how redesigning a product can make sales soar," says Joyce Birchler. "My dragonfly pin (which I loved) wasn't selling, so I redesigned it by changing the colors, making the wings iridescent, and soldering them on at an angle instead of flat. Giving the pin 3D treatment brought it to life. Now I can't keep it in stock."

Change Product's Function. "What started as a potholder," Pat Endicott says, "has evolved into our popular three-pocket fabric hanging. This organizer (with removable hanger) appeals to all ages because it is both practical and decorative."

After one of Dodie Eisenhauer's wire angels was a big success as a Christmas decoration, she painted it a verdigris color, added a hat, basket of flowers, and a tripod to push down in the ground for the angel to fit over. "Now I have a new creation called The Gardening Angel," she says.

WHY YOU NEED A WIDGET

Technically speaking, a widget is a small mechanical device, especially one whose name is not known or cannot be recalled. Craftspeople, however, have now claimed this word, applying it to their "bread-and-butter" items—products they can always count on to sell.

"This is the era of the widget," says Susan Gearing, whose friends call her The Widget Queen. "A trend we're seeing now is a decline in sales for high-ticket crafts. I've been selling for twenty-two years, making home-dec items, small quilts, afghans, and ornaments, but my line today consists of over fifty widgets because I've found I can sell fifty $2 products a lot faster than I can sell one item for $100. Widgets sell consistently, but to make money here you have to keep thinking of new widgets all the time."

Susan's line includes pins of all kinds; painted cups and pots; magnets and keychains; potholders and granny crafts in contemporary designs and colors; fabric gift bags and comfort bags. Each of her products costs between 12 to 20 cents to make, and she retails them for $2.50 to $4 and sells thousands of items a year.

ICED TEA... HOUSEWINE OF THE SOUTH !

SHE WHO IS LOOKING FOR A HUSBAND... NEVER HAD ONE!

Pictured here are samples of her "Tile Magnets with Sassy Sayings" ($2.50). She buys tiles in sheets, a case at a time, decorates them thirty-six at a time with Sharpie markers, gives them a finishing coat, and glues on a magnet.

Her newest widget is a $3 Booboo Bag for kids that sells itself. "It's nothing more than a five-inch-square fabric bag double-stitched on the outside, filled with rice, and tied with a ribbon and laminated instruction tag that says 'Best when used with a hug.' Kids can store it in the freezer and apply it to their little boo-boos."

Even the high-end artists are selling widgets these days because the return on investment of widgets is such that they can afford to continue making their high-end pieces. As Joann Haglund confirms, "Widgets support my higher-end work, which includes products such as a tole-painted gazebo garden ornament ($300) and a fireside box ($500). People who will not or cannot buy the larger pieces or commissions still like the signed smaller items, especially those under $20. I usually sell a minimum of 250 of my $7.50 rolling pin recipe card-holders at a show, and my next best item is a Chalet Birdhouse. Available in four sizes from a two-inch mini to one that's twelve inches tall, the seven-inch-tall units, painted to the max, are still the staple of my line, retailing for $34." (See sidebar, "Finding Help on the Internet.")

By the way, Susan and Joann are friends who banter back and forth about the topic of widgets and whether it's the price point or the quantity sold that makes a product a true widget. Susan says a good widget is any kind of product that is cheap to make, can be sold at a low price, and is easy to produce in volume. Joann says price has nothing to do with it, but agrees a widget is definitely something you must be able to make in quantity. "And it should be so easy to make that you can do it in your sleep," she adds.

"While it gets monotonous to mass-produce things like greeting cards and small wall hangings, my customers don't think about this when they buy one," says Tori Hoggard. "They just seem glad they can afford something handpainted, albeit small. I am just as delighted to know a recipient of one of my greetings has the card stuck to her fridge as I am knowing a wall hanging is gracing someone's office. I mean . . . how many times do you go to the fridge every day? I have made some of my canvas wall hangings into oversized refrigerator magnets, giving them versatility as well as giving the buyer

something unusual to add to their decor. These handpainted magnets, which I call Signs of Life, range from small (2 x 3) to large (8 x 10) and sell for $2 to $3. I think they sell well for the same reason bumper stickers and posters sell: everyone wants to make a statement or remind themselves of certain things."

A widget is a good gimmick, as Derek Andrews has learned. His widget is a "Fidget Kit" that retails for $3.50 Canadian. "It's just a small piece of wood, cut out and slightly sanded, packed in a zipper bag with sandpaper and instructions," he says. "Yes, it's a gimmick, but it extracts a few bucks from visitors to my shop who might otherwise leave no poorer than when they came in."

Pocket Fidget Kit

Keep it in your pocket and fidget with it whenever you need.

Sandpaper and instructions included.

One of Dodie Eisenhauer's widgets is a Marble Angel she wholesales for $2.50. "It's a little wire mesh figure with a marble for the head that can be used as a Christmas ornament or sun catcher," she says. "Put a magnet on the back, and it sticks to the refrigerator or file cabinet. Put a pin on the back, and it becomes jewelry. It's appealing to almost everyone and makes a great gift item for employees, teachers, club members, etc."

Kim Marie's widgets—the dragon oil lamps and Kandle Kats mentioned earlier—sell well, she thinks, because they are different. "I don't limit myself to making just what some might construe as art. These are fun little critters I enjoy making, but sometimes I push myself too hard. I often tell people that when working on cats, if I start chatting with them and expecting them to answer, I've been in the studio alone too long and it's time to do a show and see real people."

"My widget is a little pellet-filled whimsical shelf doll ($15)," says Gail Platts. "It's a good impulse item that does well as a computer sitter and also makes a good cheer-up gift. The product is simple to make and I can comfortably hire help with its construction, so I can produce it in quantity."

"I used to have some widgets," says Jacqueline Janes, "but I made the mistake of selling low-priced items like keychains and shoe charms. People were buying the low-priced items and staying away from everything else. The next widget I create will be more about the item, and less about the selling price."

After years of relatively unsuccessful selling, weaver Bobbie Irwin says she has finally found one item she can weave that actually gives her a decent return for her time. "I weave earrings—tiny inkle-woven pendants from fine yarn—which I call Inklings. It costs me 4 to 6 cents per pair in materials, including the mountings, and I'm retailing them at $6.50 a pair. Since it takes me less than fifteen minutes to complete a pair, including preparing the loom, weaving, and finishing, I can get more than $20 an

hour for my time on this product. So sometimes smaller is better—and smarter. I do these in limited production style, weaving six pairs at a time in a huge variety of patterns and colors (although each 'production line' of six pairs is the same). This is just a sideline activity, and I could make considerably more money at it if I wanted to devote more time to it. I am considering upgrading the mountings to gold or sterling (instead of steel) and possibly using finer threads or silk. This would probably increase my cost to about 25 cents a pair, but it would also enable me to raise the price. What's interesting is that most of my customers are other weavers who could easily make similar earrings themselves."

Finding Help on the Internet

Here's a good example of how having an online network can help solve a design or production problem. Howard Broman moderates one of the best online discussion groups on the Internet for professional artists and craftspeople. People in this group will bend over backwards to help another person in the group who has a problem, no matter how busy they may be.

When Howard needed a metal cap for his "Rose of the Titanic" vial necklace, he presented his problem to the group, and sculptor Robert Houghtaling said, "Send me some vials, and I'll sculpt a cap for you." When Howard got the sculpture, he sent it to a jeweler in his online group for casting.

Joann Haglund sells thousands of originally designed handpainted birdhouses and other wood items, thanks in part to the help she gets from her "wood wizard," a fellow named Gene Rix. "We've never met personally, but we have a great working relationship," she says. "We met on the Internet through a bulletin board when I put out a request for a wood craftsman who could take my written description of a product I envisioned, interpret it in an artistic way, then produce it for me in quantity. Eighteen craftsmen responded by sending me drawings of a birdhouse I envisioned and described verbally. I chose Gene's design, and I've been working successfully with him ever since. He produces all the wood products I hand paint. I just send him a description of what I have in mind, and he makes it for me in any quantity desired."

Si', the smallest rose (blossom about ¼-inch in diameter) was hybridized by Pedro Dot in Barcelona, Spain, in 1948. Howard Broman is now one of the largest growers of Si' in the world. The miniature roses he used in his vial necklaces are suspended in baby oil. Other roses used in pins are protected with a special coating called Craft-Flex that Howard invented to waterproof and protect the flowers.

Howard Broman's hot widget in 1999—his sales gimmick to get people to seriously look at his rose jewelry—was a rose vial necklace that played on the popularity of the award-winning movie, Titanic. Priced at $5 wholesale, it was advertised as "The Rose of the Titanic," and it included a small printed piece with this copy:

> *Captured in the crystal clarity of glass, a single rose, the symbol of everlasting love. Frozen in time, a real miniature rose, perfectly preserved. When others slip beneath the waves of time, your precious remembrance lies suspended forever "Between the Ice and the Sea."*

Now *that's* clever marketing, folks! Howard says teenage girls simply *swooned* over this item, often buying several for friends. He sold thousands of his Titanic necklace before this particular craze died out, but his rose vial necklace lives on with a different hangtag and a higher $6.90 wholesale price, and it remains Howard's greatest widget to date.

A Few Words About Packaging

Good packaging is important, and it should be considered part of the design process whether you're selling at craft fairs or wholesaling to shops and stores. The cost to package a product must also be included in your pricing formula, a topic discussed in Chapter Eleven.

If you sell only at craft fairs, good packaging can be as simple as putting buyers' purchases in a nice-looking bag or, better yet, one that has been imprinted with your business name (so you get free advertising as shoppers walk around a fair with it in hand).

Howard Broman displays his jewelry on specially designed display cards (gold ink on black card stock), while Bob Gerdts uses gift boxes. "Most people buy our Egg-Art as a gift," he says, "so we package pieces in white boxes with a gold seal identifying our firm. We also place a flyer in the box for the gift (which explains egg art, its history, and our business), and include an extra one in the bag for the buyer to encourage reorders."

If you plan to wholesale a line of products to classy stores, you may need to offer point-of-purchase displays (POPs) to help stores sell them. Here is more information on packaging from three professionals who have learned from experience.

Point-of-Purchase Displays (POPs). "Point-of-purchase displays sell products," says Howard Broman, "and using them in the

arts and crafts industry will put you one step above the competition. In fact, many gift stores are now beginning to insist that manufacturers supply POPs with their initial wholesale orders, and they understand the display will cost extra. Ideally, you will be able to find suitable displays you can buy at wholesale; if not, you may need to make them yourself or pay for custom manufacturing."

Howard couldn't find what he needed, so he devised a clever spinner for his real rose jewelry products

A display of Howard Broman's real rose jewelry on his handmade Velcro-covered "spinners."

using an eight-inch square box about eighteen inches high. The box is attached to a ½-inch plywood base and "lazy Susan" swivel hardware. It's completely covered with dark hunter green Velcro loop fabric (available wholesale by the roll from Velcro USA, Inc.).

"I simply stick Velcro tab hooks to the back of the display cards to which my jewelry is attached and arrange them on the box. The display costs me about $12 to make (plus labor) and is included free with any order for $250."

Note: Howard adds that Velcro loop fabric is absolutely the best covering for craft fair display boards of any kind because it's spongy on the back, doesn't wrinkle, and is easily cleaned off with Scotch tape.

Good Packaging Translates to More Sales. Rita O'Hara is a savvy marketer who understands the relationship between good packaging and good sales. The secret to selling more, she says, is to give buyers more service. "We can't just sit around and create—we have to *sell* as well. Price is not as important as quality and service."

Rita sells her Stonewares products and accessory items separately, giving consumers the option of buying a matching gift-wrap package (unfolded box, tissue paper, gift card) and bottle of scent refresher if desired. She designs and makes her own small boxes using an Ellison die-cut machine (about $300). Using a variety of die-cutting tools, she first designs the box on computer (using Print Shop software), prints it out on card stock, and then cuts the boxes. "It takes a lot of fiddling to get the type to fit in the right areas on each of the special die-cut boxes I now use, but once I've done it, I have it forever," she says. "I write most of the verses and poems for my cards, but I use decal patterns on all my products. I simply scan these designs into the computer to create matching boxes, hang tags, and gift tags."

One of several small boxes Rita O'Hara makes using an Ellison die-cut machine.

Example of the kind of promotional flyer Rita O'Hara designs and prints for stores when she makes in-store appearances to promote her products.

Grand Opening
March 12-14, 1999
Mulberry Lane Floral & Gifts

Personal Appearance by
Rita Lynn O'Hara
Creator and Designer of
STONEWARES

Handcast and kiln-fired bisque hearts, ovals and tiles which are delicately decorated and then adorned with colorful cords and ribbons. Scented with pure essence oils. ♥♥♥♥♥
Perfect gift for All Occasions!

Saturday, March 13, 1999
11:00 AM - 4:00 PM
Mulberry Lane Floral & Gifts
511 West Main
Greenwood, MO 64034
(816) 537-6661
Signing & Personalizing Free With Purchases
Register-to-win Special Door Prizes !

To make it even easier for retailers to sell her products, Rita offers to help them display her products by offering special displays on which to hang her Stonewares products, or referring the store to a place where they can buy them directly. "I also offer to do an artist signing in their store (just like authors do in bookstores when they're promoting a new book). This is called 'event merchandising,' and retail stores are thrilled with this idea. I provide them with free bag stuffers they can use to announce the event and a stand-up frame to hold one of my flyers in the product display area (see illustration). I do all this because I've learned that buyers like to know the artist, and because this helps the shop set up a special area for a large display of my products. Hallmark produces only a small portion of the gifts they sell (all kinds of collectibles), so I am a 'department' in their stores and they 'romance' my products accordingly. Whenever I do a signing, people flock to the store because of the bag stuffer they got with an earlier purchase. I give free gift packages with purchases made that day. I also take a door prize that customers might win simply by registering. (They're happy to register, and these names and addresses add to both my and the store's mailing list.) I don't know of another artist who does what I do, but I think many could increase their sales dramatically by making artist appearances in some of their best retail outlets."

Expensive Lesson Learned. Sue Cloutman wishes she could have found a less expensive way to package her toys when she started her Color Me Creations business. "I started with plastic bags and cardboard headers, which was fine for craft shows but not good enough for wholesale buyers. My reps convinced me that toy stores wanted boxes so they could stack them on shelves or in the warehouse, so I eventually spent $10,000 for 10,000 boxes (see photo). At this time, I was in

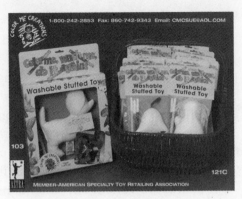

A promotional color flyer used by Sue Cloutman to sell her line of "Color Me Creations," white stuffed toys children can color with water-based markers, then wash and color all over again. Depending on the design (thirty in the line), these toys wholesale for $2.50 to $7.50 each.

my 'grandiose stage' with sales reps in thirty states and dreams of starting a small factory, but things didn't work out that way, and it's going to take me a long time to use up all these fancy boxes."

Sue worked with an art director who pulled together a focus group of individuals (store managers, parents, and grandparents) who voted on eight different box designs. "I made up a questionnaire for each person, and the first question asked which box caught their eye when they walked in. 'You have virtually two seconds to catch the customer's eye,' a store manager had told me, so we went with the bright yellow box that most people in the focus group said caught their eye first."

If she were doing it over again, Sue would not go this route. "I anticipated volumes of business that didn't materialize. Don't worry about fancy packaging until you're certain the product is going to sell," she advises. "I envisioned getting large orders from major toy stores, but I later learned I could never deliver the volume of merchandise they wanted, nor give them the discounts they demanded."

Sue no longer sells through sales reps, but does wholesale to shops by mail and on the Internet. Her POP display (a red basket) helps move small toys that wholesale for $2.50 each. "Stores buy these items by the basketful," she says. "I buy the baskets at wholesale and charge stores 30 percent more than I paid for them—less than $20."

Donate What You Can't Sell

As you design one new product after another, what will you do with all those imperfect prototypes you've created in the process?

Elizabeth Bishop offers the perfect solution to this problem.

"I normally do not have time to donate to charities or become involved in our town's fundraisers or benevolences," she explains. "What I do instead is donate things I cannot sell. Since I design original soft sculpture and sewing projects, it is necessary for me to go through a lot of experimentation and prototypes before I make *the* one I have in mind. I was frustrated that so much of that effort was wasted, and these preliminary projects were taking up so much space. Yet they did have some charm, were 'almost right,' and I just couldn't throw them out. One night the dream lightbulb came on, and I knew the perfect solution. I would add a quick bauble, flower, or accessory to change or fix the project and put it in my 'Giving Box.' Here's how it works.

"I have a list of worthwhile causes I've read about and match them to a project I have. When I become stressed or overwhelmed, I close up shop and deliver goodies to various people and charities around town. For example, our local hospice hosts a Chili Challenge each year and asks for donations to the silent auction. Last year, I fixed a doll that had a bad hair day by gluing silk dogwood blossoms all over her head and naming her Springtime. She brought a nice sum, I was told. I also jot down names and addresses of people I'd like to remember in a small way, like the lady at my credit union who is so helpful and always comments on articles about my dolls and activities. During my last 'Delivery Week,' I gave her a small doll with a wardrobe, a project I had published several years ago. And my mailperson has surpris-

Elizabeth Bishop with two of her life-size cloth dolls, Rufus and Minerva. (Notice that Minerva has a touch of phlebitis in her legs and is always springing runs in her panty hose.)

es galore; she rings the doorbell to thank me, and we carve out a little visit to catch up on each other's news.

"In my small town, they trust me to bring safe dolls or animals for the nursery or children's ward in the hospital. For the nursing home, I recently delivered to one of my elderly Sunday school members an elaborate soft-sculpted hat I had experimented with. She loved both the hat and my visit.

"Doing for others is a balm to the soul and body. By the time I have matched projects with names and made my deliveries, I am refreshed and ready to get back to crafting. By the way, this also gives me a ready answer for all those solicitations for donations from very worthy causes. I tell them I have a predeveloped system for donations—much better than a guilt-panged, cold NO."

What a wonderful idea! Isn't it fascinating to see how professional artisans weave their work into the fabric of their daily lives? Now that you've gained insight into how creative people develop new designs and package new products, it's time to take a closer look at the production process and some things you can do to work smarter instead of harder.

HELPFUL RESOURCES

Die-Cut Machines. Ellison Craft and Design, 25862 Commerce Centre Drive, Lake Forest, CA 92630-8804. 949-598-8822. E-mail info@ellison.com

Velcro Loop Fabric. Manufactured by Velcro USA, Inc. 406 Brown Ave., Manchester, NH, 03108. 603-669-4892.

Point of Purchase Displays. Check out this company on the Internet for POP displays at reasonable prices: www.art-phyl.com/

Free E-mail Newsletter. Trend analyst Kathy Lamancusa publishes *Tuesday's Trend Talk to Transform Tomorrow*, which you can receive free by e-mail by visiting Kathy's Web site at www.lamancusa.com.

Chapter Ten

Production Methods and Strategies

||||||||||||||||||||||||||||||||||||||||||||||||||||

Is it "handcrafted" or "manufactured?" It's a waste of time to debate whether something is art or craft, where handcrafted leaves off and manufacturing begins, or whether a one-of-a-kind artisan is better than a production artisan. The usefulness of this kind of discussion is universally questionable, and has nothing to do with solving marketing problems.

—HOWARD BROMAN, REAL ROSE JEWELRY

The debate about art vs. craft that began back in the '60s continues on the Internet today, but now we have a new twist to the discussion: At what point does *craft* turn into *manufacturing*? Today's Internet discussions sound much like those of the craftsmen and women I used to network with back in the '70s when I was publishing a magazine for craft professionals. Funny how everyone is still arguing about what constitutes art or craft and forgetting that the most important thing should be finding work you love to do that generates the level of income you want or need.

My respect goes to anyone who can figure out how to use their hands and mind to make a living, and I couldn't care less whether they make things totally from scratch, use findings or imported supplies, or have an assembly line going to mass-produce products. The purists in the crafts community are always going to look down their noses at craft sellers who don't make everything from scratch, but I know this: a lot of "crafters" are making more money than a lot of "artists," and they are benefitting not only themselves and their families, but often whole communities by providing work for others.

Dough artist Nancy Jaekel, who has five employees and makes a six-figure income, expresses it this way: "If I were a painter and had my original paintings printed, signed and numbered and could get $200 each for those reproductions of my original art, would that make me less of an artist because someone else helped me reproduce my product? If so, I guess I would rather be a rich 'lesser artist,' than a *poor* artist. If some people would let go of their artistic idealism, they could do the same. I may not have the title of "artist," but I'm building a retirement fund for myself and living pretty well in the process."

In truth, anyone who makes anything is manufacturing it. Craftspeople are certainly manufacturers in the eyes of the law (rules, regulations, taxes, etc.) whether they make one-of-a-kind originals or turn out thousands of widgets. My hackles rise when someone says products can't be called handmade if they're being manufactured assembly-line style. The fact that several people contribute to the making of a product as it goes through the assembly-line process doesn't make it any the less handmade.

"Nobody really cares whether products are actually handmade," says Bill Mason, a former gallery owner whose art is eclectic gemstone jewelry. "Artists and craftspeople may operate under the premise that handmade means "better," but the market will always dictate the reality. If you don't make a profit, you'll go out of business."

Now that we've got *that* topic out of the way, the rest of this chapter will focus on how one-of-a-kind artisans and production artisans alike can improve their production strategies through

- smarter working habits,
- the use of written production plans,
- production-line techniques,
- the use of special tools and equipment, and
- hiring help.

Working Smarter Strategies

Since the amount of products that can be sold is directly related to the amount of time it takes to make them, it is natural for creative people to think that they harder they work—the more hours they put into making products, that is—the greater their profits. But as this book proves, time devoted to production is just one part of the profit puzzle. In the end, profit is directly related to every topic under discussion in this book, and even a minor adjustment in any of these areas could increase the profits you earn from your business this year.

Craftspeople have some interesting ideas on how to manage a business—ideas not learned from books, but developed as a result of their natural creativity. Consider the way Ruthann Broman divides her work in the jewelry business she operates with husband Howard: "*Futzy work* is stuff like cleaning, filing, organizing, idea generating, etc., while *nitty-gritty work* is anything that will make the business bring in a physical dollar bill. Futzy work does not do this, but shipping an order does," she explains. "If I have a great idea, I'll write it down, but I can't work on it when the need is to generate income. Ideas are great, but they do not generate money, and it can be a real cop-out to lay income-generating work aside to play around with an idea. You have to make time for this kind of work apart from your income-generating work."

If you're the key individual in a business that is labor intensive, the real trick to growth and increased profits has to lie not in working harder, but in working *smarter*. As discussed in earlier chapters, some of the ways this can be done is by making changes where necessary, maximizing the use of computer software, making business plans, developing better work habits, getting organized, and managing time more efficiently.

To learn what your true production capabilities are, you must keep a record of the time you spend making products for sale—not just all products in general, but each product individually. This will aid you not only in setting prices, but in planning for craft fairs and wholesale shows where orders are commonly taken for delivery weeks or months down the road. If you don't know exactly how long it's going to take to fill each order taken at a show, you may find yourself in a state of panic, wondering if you've taken more orders than you can possibly deliver. Knowing your production capabilities before going to a wholesale show, however, will enable you to plot delivery dates of each order to a production calendar while you're at a show. If you get more orders than anticipated, you'll be able to see at what point you might have to stop taking orders. (Promising delivery dates that can't be met is a sure way to lose future business from wholesale buyers.)

"I have a good idea when I go to market how long it's going to take me to deliver orders," says gift wholesaler Dodie Eisenhauer. "We're usually caught up to begin with, so I may start a show by saying we can ship orders in two weeks. If it's a four day show, however, on day two and three the lead time will change depending on how many orders I have by then. But getting the orders out is never a big problem for me because, unlike the craftsperson who works alone, I can always call in extra help."

Kate Harper recalls the day she came home to an order so huge it was like a year's worth of sales. "My first reaction was panic," she says. "How could I make all these cards in the allotted time? I rallied all my friends to help me out, but funniest of all was my boyfriend, who had just had eye surgery and had a big patch over his eye. I still remember seeing poor Peter making cards for me on the coffee table, in pain, with one eyeball."

Production Schedules

Knowing how much product you've got to turn out to fill an order is only part of the job, of course. Whether you're preparing for a big retail show or trying to fill all the orders you've just brought home from your last wholesale show, you need a production plan to keep you on schedule.

"I've had to make very concise, detailed written plans for each show or risk going stark, raving mad," says printmaker Chris Noah. "My highest anxiety always hits at the beginning of a work cycle for a show when all of it lies before me. Not knowing is always worse than knowing. To allay this state, I write out all my lists and my schedule for myself and for my husband. I'm terrible about underestimating the amount of time a given task will take. I keep a daily production record in my calendar/date book. Mileage and purchases and other notations are also recorded there. I've been lax about this in the past and always suffered for it, so I'm trying to mend my ways."

Woodturner Derek Andrews says his discipline is maintained by setting a production schedule and monitoring progress on a daily basis. "Last year it was based on retail value, but this year we have changed to reflect only the labor content of the finished product— a better way to indicate my income for the year," he says. "'Senior Management' produces a monthly chart that shows what my cumulative total-to-date should be, and alongside this I pencil in my daily production and actual total-to-date. This way I can see at a glance if I am ahead or behind schedule. My work is all very labor-intensive, and if I get too far behind I might never be able to catch up, so this system is vital if I am to make a living from my craft."

Potter Kim Marie finds that she accomplishes more in a day if she makes a daily production plan. "I've been keeping spreadsheet records of the dollar amount produced per day, and on the month I went out with specific throwing plans, the dollar amount for that month was approximately 40 percent higher than when I didn't," she says. "There were other factors, but I believe the written lists were a definite advantage."

Let the Computer Figure It Out

"While sitting with the calculator and the orders from the last gift show, figuring out the time needed for each, I had the epiphany that I could give each item a time value in my FileMaker program and let the program tally the hours needed for each order. If I see that my next order in queue will take sixteen hours to finish, I might block out four days (planning to spend four hours a day working toward that order), which would still give me time each of those days for working on other stuff coming up so I don't have tunnel vision on that one order. Sort of like driving a car— focused on what's in front of me, but still looking at what's coming ahead."

—*Gail Platts, InCalico*

Because Kim keeps a record of the pottery she throws each week, she can compute a wholesale and retail dollar value for each week and use those figures to project her annual income. "If I want to make $45,000 per year," she says, "this helps me see that I've got to make a certain amount of product to accomplish that goal."

NETWORKING SESSION #11:
PRODUCTION-BOOSTING STRATEGIES

Everyone wants to know how to increase production without working themselves to death in the process. In this networking session, you'll learn how various artisans do this.

If your goal is to produce more products in a shorter period of time, how do you begin to do this without working longer hours?

Chris Noah (printmaker): "We learned a lot about increasing productivity by doing a detailed flow chart of the process for making a picture. We then could see areas where improvement could be done. In this way, we've been able to make art better, faster, and cheaper."

Meg Sullivan (needlework): "We took the time to look at how we make our products, which are cross-stitched, knit, crocheted, and sewn gifts for babies and children. I talked to others, and we all found that when we're making something—a quilt, for example—the first one takes about four times as long to make as the tenth. So instead of making one of these and one of those, we now make ten (or twenty or thirty) of something using an assembly-line type of production. The rhythm takes over, and what previously took an hour to do now takes only thirty to forty-five minutes. So when someone asks me how long it takes to make a particular item, I never have a clear answer. I just know how long it takes to make ten or twenty and can divide the time."

Derek Andrews (woodturning): "I started by identifying production tasks that would be more efficient in larger batch sizes. These are mainly jobs that take a long time to set up relative to the time it takes to do the work. For example, the preparation of bottle stopper blanks involves cutting the wood to size, drilling a hole in the center, cutting dowels to length, and gluing the dowels into the holes. The first three operations require machines to be set up and can take quite a while. So now I usually do one or two hundred at a time. Then, when I need to make bottle stoppers, I have blanks that are ready to go straight onto the lathe."

Michael Noyes (calligrapher): "I've increased production through standardization. I once created a different mat and frame treatment for each design. Now I have just a handful of standards that fit most of what I make. This way I can produce in numbers (saving money and time) and have fewer variations I need to keep in stock."

Kate Harper (greeting cards): "That's my strategy, too. If there's anything I've learned about manufacturing greeting cards, it's simplification. For example, if I used a different colored envelope for each of my card designs, not only would I have to store a variety of colors of envelopes, but I would have to predict my usage of each color. I would have to ship different quantities of each color to my card-makers, and I can just imagine the nightmare of trying to keep track of something so insignificant. That's why I design all my cards around just one color of envelope."

Isn't it true that, if you plan to sell in any quantity—and especially if you plan to wholesale your work—you have to streamline your designs and eliminate unnecessary embellishments?

Dodie Eisenhauer (gift wholesaler): "Right! Production must begin with the design itself. I always think first about how a new product will be constructed, how it can be broken down into production steps, and which of my employees can do this work."

Susan Gearing (production artisan): "I'm an advocate of the "good enough" school, which means I can decide when a product is good enough to sell, as opposed to when it's perfect. So many arti-

Dodie Eisenhauer (back, right) with three of her employees, Angie, Jan, and Terressa (left to right).

sans just keep adding one more flourish or bauble to a product until it becomes too costly to make a profit or too time-consuming to produce profitably."

Sue Cloutman (stuffed toys): "I have thirty fabric toy designs in my line. Rather than design out the details on all of them, I sell the harder-to-make ones at retail craft shows and wholesale only the less labor-intensive toys."

Joyce Roark (jewelry): "When I placed an advertisement in a wholesale catalog to be sent to 50,000 retailers, I had to plan for an increase in orders. Since it takes me a full week to make chains for all the pendants I normally produce each month, for these orders,

Some of the paint-and-wash toy designs in Sue Cloutman's line.

my solution for this particular production problem was to order chains ready made."

Howard Broman (real rose jewelry): "Craftspeople create a lot of their own pricing and production problems when they embellish their products with needless extra touches. It may satisfy their artistic nature to do this, but many of these embellishments are lost on buyers. If we want to make a living from our art or craft, we should never give customers more than they want or are willing to pay for. For example, if you told a buyer that it would cost a dollar more to finish the back of a picture, they'd probably ask you to forget the finish and deduct the dollar since they aren't ever going to see the back anyway. Craftspeople are notorious for blaming the customer for their ineptness in business, but we must always remember that the customer is never, ever wrong."

Describe your production process or the assembly-line methods you use.

Joyce Roark: "I've increased production by doing all of one type of piece at the same time; i.e., all the earrings, pendants, and pins of one size at a time. I work the same way when I'm working with wire because the same amount of wire is used on the same size stones. I cut all the wire, then twist all the pieces that need to be twisted, then I construct the pieces. This is much faster than doing the cutting and twisting as needed for each piece. When all pieces are made, I polish them. Then I photograph and package everything. My inventory is then edited to reflect the new pieces, which are stored for shipment. Then it's on to the next batch."

Jan McClellan (jewelry): "I layer two sheets of metal together so I can cut (saw) two pieces at a time."

Sue Cloutman: "All of my fabric for toys is cut by professional cutters in a nearby town where they can be cut twenty-five pieces at a time. I sew a lot of the same pattern animal at one time, stuff a lot at once (often in front of the TV at night), and then everything goes back to the sewing room to have the stuffing hole stitched up before packing the toys in window boxes. To do this, I set myself up assembly-line style on two card tables so I can reach all the items that need packing without having to get out of my chair."

Gail Platts (cloth figures): "I cut all the pieces of a certain workable number of one design; next step is to sew and trim them; then I might put them in a basket. Later, I can stuff as many or as few as I need (or can stand to do). Once the figures are stuffed and assembled, I put them on the work surface and do the fine-finishing (faces, hair, etc.), then tag and place on the storage shelf."

Liz Murad (calligraphy): "My production-line system is simple: I have outlines of my mat shapes drawn in heavy marker (two sizes of oval and square openings). A selected size gets taped to the light box. Next, my guideline page gets taped on top of that; and last, my piece of parchment. Light box on, I see the shape and parameter of my work area and don't need to rule lines for the calligraphy. I get quite a rhythm going, first doing the calligraphy saying and then embellishing with artwork. Sometimes I do a lot of calligraphy and then go back with the art; sometimes I do each individually. When that's done, I scan the image into my computer. When I'm ready for a show or sale, I print the image out onto parchment paper and color with markers. I can now create the design once and keep it always, reproducing the big sellers in quantity for a show and keeping track of what doesn't sell, or what colors were hot. Sayings about moms are big sellers, followed by Bible verses and funny sayings, such as "Sometimes I wake up grouchy, sometimes I let him sleep.""

Pat Endicott (quilted products): "When sewing, I look at the whole project and work on several steps at the same time. I pin everything that needs to be pinned, then I sew everything, then I press and repeat the process."

Chris Noah: "It's impossible for me to do anything approaching a real production line, but I can do a modified version. Because table space is limited and my arm reach is only so far, usually I can only do about four of anything at one time. The painting paraphernalia takes up a lot of room and, with frames, I can sometimes do only two or three at a time. Still, production is the name of the game for me because I spend about 90 percent of my workdays painting on either paper or wood. Some general painting rules that help my production flow are to always paint from the known to the lesser known, the easier to the harder. In other words, get as much surface area covered as quickly as possible. Then zero in on the questionable or difficult areas. Usually I do the tricky linear work separately. I also make color photocopies of my painted pieces to serve as a guide for less frequently done pieces. Even though they aren't quite color true, they are an invaluable memory refresher."

Products usually go through several different production stages, often requiring a waiting period before work can be completed. How do you avoid wasting time while you're waiting for things to "happen" in your production process?

Tori Hoggard (painted items): "I always have several products I plan to do, so I'll prep them all in one big swoop, as well as put a finish on them all at once. I also do some of the design work all at once, which is faster than working on one individual piece and waiting for parts to dry before I can move on. For instance, while working on painting a trunk, I'll paint some and while waiting for that section to dry, I'll work on painting cards or other small items that require less concentration since I'm painting similar designs on each. Not only is this efficient timewise, but it taxes my creative energy less by giving me breaks in between."

Jan McClellan: "Like other jewelry designers, I work on several pieces at once so I can always work on something while waiting for a piece to finish pickling or to cool off before going to the next step; or, if I have to set up a special soldering rig, I can do several pieces while it is there before going on to another step. This method also works for one-of-a-kind pieces. I always work on three or four at once so I have no waiting between procedures."

Jan McClellan, working with a Foredom flex-shaft machine commonly used by jewelers for grinding, polishing, and texturing of metals.

What other things can be done to save time or maximize productivity as you work?

Pat Endicott: "I work on several projects at the same time using the same color thread. This may sound like a no-brainer, but once you calculate the one minute it takes every time you change thread, you realize how much time you can save by doing as much as possible with a single color at a time. To cut down thread changing even more, I use neutral colors that blend with the fabric, particularly beige and gray for construction."

Pat Endicott, House of Threads & Woods, Inc., working on one of her quilted products.

Sue Cloutman: "I know what you mean. My computerized sewing machine has sped production because it cuts the thread, changes the stitch with a push of a button, and threads easily. It's amazing how much faster that makes things go. I wind a dozen or more bobbins at a time and use an industrial size spool of thread so I don't have to keep stopping to replace thread all the time."

Sylvia Landman (writer): "As an arthritis patient, I must watch the many hours of repetitive hand and body movements. Recently when I was working on two books at the same time, I worked on book #1 while sitting at the computer using an ergonomic wrist pad. After lunch, I turned the monitor slightly and stood up to work in the afternoon using an entirely different keyboard with gliding hand rests. Thus, working on book #2 was different in every way, which relieved the tedium, kept me feeling refreshed, and enabled me to keep the material separate as well."

Jana Gallagher (various crafts): "When completing items for a boutique, I tag and box them for delivery as soon as they're finished instead of handling them again right before the show. In addition to saving time, I've found my prices are more accurate because I have the supply list handy as each project is created and completed."

Meg Sullivan: "My best production tip has nothing to do with manufacturing. It's Caller ID and voice mail/answering machines. When I'm on a tight production schedule, I ignore the phone until I have time to return calls, and the Caller ID box is next to my sewing table so I can monitor who is calling, especially if I'm waiting for someone."

Derek Andrews: "To become better at your art or craft, teach it to others. This has helped me identify and focus on techniques that I didn't fully understand myself. As a result, I am faster and make fewer mistakes."'

The reason some people don't produce products in quantity is that they get bored doing the same thing over and over. What can one-of-a-kind artisans do to increase their production output?

Gail Platts: "When I first started wholesaling my dolls, the hardest thing for me was to get over the six-hump: I could not seem to do more than six of one item without getting terribly bored. My big 'work-smart breakthrough' came with the realization that I could make better time if I didn't stop and change work stations so often.

For example, there is one sewing/trimming/turning task I had timed out at fifteen minutes each when I was doing just one; but when I do twenty-four at a time and divide it, that time goes down to just ten minutes each. This may seem self-evident, but to get into the wholesale mood, I had to change my way of thinking. I changed from thinking I had to completely *finish* a certain number of dolls in one day—which was actually limiting, because each day I had to start all over again. When I wasn't working at my craft full-time, I used to practically take January to March off; to start anew and get into a routine again was so much work. Now, with baskets of work always in progress, I always have work to do and am less likely to get bored."

You might think that you could increase your production if only you had more space, but that's not necessarily true, is it?

Phillippa Lack (silk painter): "I could produce more painted scarves if I had room to set up more silk frames, but my time is never wasted. While two or three painted scarves are drying on my silk frame, I simply paint gourds or do paperwork or computer work."

Phillippa Lack working on a silk painting in a workspace she wishes were larger; with one of her finished scarves.

Elizabeth Bishop (doll designer): "Even though I have a guest suite that could be commandeered to double for business use, I find it easier to have everything in one area close to my other living space. I can put a load of clothes into the dryer without missing a lick on designing doll patterns, or take something out to thaw with just a pause at the computer. In one-fell-swoop style, I can draft and cut out a doll body pattern, roll in my chair to the sewing machine to stitch and stuff it, then roll right over to my computer to write the instructions and do the how-to illustrations. In a previous house, I had the luxury of two large rooms plus a storage shed for my business, and I really like this compact mayhem a lot better."

As one who spends a lot of time cooking, I understand Elizabeth's reasoning. I would hate a large, spacious kitchen if there was too much space between the sink, refrigerator, stove or countertop. I like my tight little office, too, because while

Take Care of Your Eyes

Do you do a lot of detail work? The wrong lighting not only causes visual discomfort, but can also lower productivity, so for minimum eye strain, vary the intensity and type of lighting used while you work. Try fluorescent or halogen lamps, which produce a light that is brighter and whiter than that of incandescent bulbs. They reduce glare and, subsequently, eye strain.

Also, have two different light intensities because your eyes will get tired if lighting remains at the same intensity level all day long. For example, you might use your overhead light for general office work, and a task light source for specific work areas.

Literary agent Barbara Doyen does a lot of computer work and fine-print reading on contracts—a heavy load for her eyes, she says. "Two things have helped me immensely: (1) full- spectrum lights—I have eight, four-foot tubes above my large desk (not only do they light better without distorting colors, but they are healthier to work under); and (2) eyeglasses with nonglare lenses from a prescription made especially for my computer work by measuring the distance from my eyeballs to my preferred monitor position and to my desktop."

sitting at the computer, I can lean back and place (toss, actually) things to my other two work areas without having to get up. (I know; the exercise would be good for me, but at least I'm reaching and stretching all the time!)

Clever Tools, Equipment, and Production Aids

Having the right tools and equipment makes all the difference in being able to produce goods in quantity. The following examples show how various artisans have increased their production using both common tools or machinery and industrial machines and equipment. You may not see your particular art or craft represented here, but perhaps these examples will spark your creativity and help you "invent" a useful tool or device that will improve your production capabilities.

MIXING, ROLLING, SHAPING, TWISTING

» Dodie Eisenhauer says men try to think how to industrialize her business, but she does just fine using ordinary tools. She makes gifts using both screen wire and regular wire that is first curled by placing one end in an electric drill, then shaped into various sculptures, such as Christmas trees, cats, and display props for retail shops. "We also size wire by wrapping it around different things such as pizza rollers, soda bottles, or PVC pipe to get uniform sizes," she says.

» Rochelle Beach's Cinna-Minnies are made from a specially formulated cinnamon dough that used to be mixed by hand, but is now mixed in a pasta maker. Hair for her dolls is curled by securing jute to a metal knitting needle inserted into an electric drill.

» When Nancy Jaekel decided to increase her wholesale business, Anything Doughs LLC, she increased her production by purchasing two commercial convection ovens and a pizza roll machine to roll out the dough. "The ovens are like those used by bakeries," she says, "bigger than a refrigerator, one on top, one on the bottom. It was a challenge to get them through the doors of our workshop, but we can now do 400 to 500 pieces a day in them."

ART PRODUCTION AIDS

▸▸ Chris Noah says she usually takes to a show anywhere from one to two hundred framed prints, plus shrink-wrapped work. "This amount of work demands precise organization or chaos will rein. Every phase has its stack-up area as it is completed. Incompatible phases (e.g., painted etchings and frames with varnish drying) are kept segregated. To store picture frames as they are processed, I bought a great big bun stacker apparatus like those used in the food service industry. It's about six feet tall with removable shelves about two feet square each."

▸▸ Wendy Van Camp recommends a tabletop screen printer called the Gocco. "It can screen everything from greeting cards to invitations or patterns on fabric," she says. "If you need to make limited editions of a print, such as calligraphy, this might be a quality production device to check out. They cost around $150 and are therefore quite reasonable."

CUTTING, SEWING, AND STUFFING

▸▸ Sue Cloutman's favorite tool for stuffing her fabric toys is a simple wooden spoon handle.

▸▸ Jean Belknap has saved hours of production time by purchasing an embroidery machine that does the most popular embroidery stitches wanted by the public. "Previously," she says, "I would spend hours doing hand embroidery on a doll's jacket or dress to give it that extra special touch."

▸▸ Meg Sullivan, who uses a rotary cutter to speed the cutting process, says her serger is her best friend because it cuts down sewing time as it sews and trims. "Plus it runs at a faster speed than a standard machine," she says, "so projects are completed faster."

» Connie Colton, a craftswoman featured in one of my other books, started her home sewing business cutting fabric with the kind of cutters quilters use. As her business grew, however, she found it necessary to buy an industrial sewing machine and serger, plus an industrial strength cutter that could cut through forty layers of flannel at a time. "The trick lies in how the material is folded after it comes off the bolt," she told me. Connie is out of this business now, but her story reminds me to emphasize here that commercial sewing machines are not designed for industrial output and will not hold up long if used in this manner. More important, commercial use of a regular sewing machine invalidates the terms of the warranty. Be sure to read the fine print in your instruction booklet.

MISCELLANEOUS TOOLS AND DEVICES

» Jewelry maker Jan McClellan says she has often jerry-rigged a tool from something else, such as her late husband's carpenter tools. "For example, I use an ordinary piece of wood as a dappling block for shaping metal; nail punches for chasing tools; drill bits for mandrels to make jump rings on; etc."

» Rita O'Hara sells tiny vials of essence oil to refreshen the scented bisque gift items she sells. The production challenge here was how to fill all those little vials with oil. "I made a holding board by drilling it full of holes all the little vials could be set into," Rita says. "I hire a kid who comes in with a squirt bottle and fills them up and puts them in a little bag. Later, another worker attaches them to the cards."

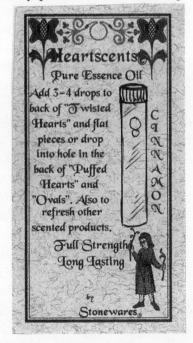

Heartscents
Pure Essence Oil
Add 3–4 drops to back of "Twisted Hearts" and flat pieces or drop into hole in the back of "Puffed Hearts" and "Ovals". Also to refresh other scented products.
Full Strength
Long Lasting
by
Stonewares

Employees and Other Workers

When your business begins to grow to the point where you cannot do all the work alone, you have to make an important decision: Will you stop the growth of your business at that point, or will you expand your production or sales capabilities by hiring outside help?

"The first thing I did when I started my greeting card business was factor in the cost of labor," says Kate Harper. "If you want to grow a self-supporting, profitable business, you cannot run it and make the product, too. I did it all wrong until a professional pointed this out to me. At first it's easy to make a few cards and fill a few orders, but if you ever want the business to take off, you need to look realistically at what is the most important, better utilized way to spend your time."

Home business owners generally begin by hiring family members or independent contractors or by using the services of disabled individuals in sheltered workshops. But if you have an art or crafts production business, ultimately the only way for you to expand production is to hire employees. Because of the IRS's and Labor Department's position on independent contractors, however, it is not legally or financially safe to use them in your business *unless you hire people who work for companies and businesses other than your own.* It's beyond the scope of this book to get into a lengthy discussion of the tax and legal problems you could incur by hiring Mrs. Jones down the street and calling her an independent contractor, but I have discussed this topic at length in both *The Crafts Business Answer Book* and *Homemade Money*.

Here, I merely want to give you perspective on how production artists and craftspeople have increased their production capabilities by working with family and friends and how they feel about hiring and working with employees.

Help from the Family. When we need help, most of us turn to first to our family. If you have a supportive partner who is willing to help you in your business and who shares your dreams and goals, count yourself blessed. Two people working together can do four times as much as one person working alone in a constrictive atmosphere. I am certainly grateful to have a cheerful spouse who has always been willing to do grunt work for my writing and publishing business. So is Jean Belknap.

"It's a godsend to have a husband like mine who will help with buying materials, doing bookkeeping, stuffing, or whatever else you need," she says. "But unless you're a miracle worker, you must bring others in or find a factory to help you produce products in quantity. To further our sales, our daughter has now come into the business."

"My four daughters and one son work with me daily," says Joyce Birchler. "Dawn does all my shipping and organizing. Dena helps in production and keeps new ideas flowing into the business with designs and such. Sandra works for me part-time while going to college, while Matthew is my computer whiz. He built my Web site and maintains it plus other related computer work. Sarah, my youngest, foils for me a couple of hours a week when she is not in soccer, track, or other acivities. My husband and I do most of the shows; sometimes Dawn and her husband do a few. I sit at the computer and check e-mail once a day early in the morning."

"When the time comes that you need to recruit family, friends, or hire employees, the hardest part is learning how and what to delegate and be comfortable with it," says Pat Endicott. "I think that as long as you are in control of the design and quality, you can hold the amount of business to the level you're comfortable with. Many crafters have recently expanded to a warehouse and have lost it due to the high labor costs and lost vision of their dream. Other crafters have tried some high-tech methods and have lost valuable customers in the process."

Hiring Regular Employees. "It took me a long time to realize that hiring employees does not cost, *it pays*," says dough artist Nancy Jaekel. "It seemed like a lot of money to shell out at the time, but in looking back, there is no way I could have grown my business without them. A little quality was lost, but it didn't seem to affect the business. I also learned this about doing volume business: *Sell more for less rather than less for more.* Now I am not only making more money, but also helping others to provide an income for their families."

When Nancy's business grew to the point that she needed employees, she incorporated as an LLC. "An attorney suggested this form of incorporation," she said, "because it was easy and inexpensive to set up, is simpler to operate than a regular corporation (no corporate board meetings, less bookwork, paperwork, stress, etc.). You do have to be a partnership, however, so my husband is named as my partner."

Nancy works five days a week in her shop and has three employees who work in the shop on four of those days plus another one who works at home. "Delegating is not something I do well," she says, "but I need employees to help me make my product."

If she were doing it over again, NCA managing director Barbara Arena says she would have learned to delegate jobs earlier. "It is still hard for me, but to grow you have to learn to let go," she emphasizes. "Turn over work to others and do what you do best. Focus your time on the parts of the business that need your expertise and let others handle the other work, even if this means hiring others. If you're great at creating but find it a struggle to do the paperwork, hire someone to do what you know you won't or don't have time to do. For a business to grow, you need to have everything in balance."

Some artists worry about losing control of the quality of their products when they hire employees, but this has not been a problem for Nancy Jaekel (although she admits she's always in the shop supervising everything). Nor it is a problem for potter Emily Pearlman, who has the equivalent of one full-time employee in the form of two part-time assistants, one of whom works two days a week, the other three. "They do all the work I don't want to do, like mixing glazes and doing some glazing, packing, sweeping, reconditioning clay, etc. I've increased my production by working out a method where my assistants can do my slab work. I make a thrown mold (a platter, for example), and then use it as a press mold. Because I've thrown the original piece myself, anything pressed into the mold looks like the original. I give these pieces my own special touch, however, by carving in a special design."

Independent Contractors. "My business is becoming more profitable because I have raised my prices to include production costs, which in turn allowed me room to afford to hire a subcontractor to assist me in sewing," says Gail Platts. "It was hard for me to hire out work at first. I didn't know if I could handle not being in control of everything, but it has worked great. It allows me time to

work on more detailed and expensive items and keeps me from getting bogged down with the easy, and sometimes boring, work."

"I've had difficulty supervising or being boss," says Kate Harper.
"I solved that by having everyone work at home. This creates hap-
piness all around, and I have a waiting list of people who want to
work with me. Initially I used sheltered workshop employees (job
training programs for the disabled) to make my cards until I no
longer had time to pick up and deliver. Now I use contract piece
workers to manufacture my line of greeting cards and gifts. (I went
to see two tax people and a lawyer to make sure I was doing it
right.) It has taken me about four years to get my business 'down to
a science.' I simply show my cardmakers efficient ways to make the
cards, but once they work at home, I have no idea whether they follow my lead or not. I also try to set up situations for everyone to succeed, not to be tempted to be irresponsible. I'm glad I can't see them
working because I would probably be hanging over them making
suggestions and driving them nuts."

Susie Little has a true cottage industry business called So Susie
Spins. Although she spins novelty yarns and yarn for doll hair,
mostly she oversees the production of a variety of products made by
other women she works with. "I buy raw wool in quantity, from 500
to 1000 pounds at a time, send it to mills for washing and carding,
then hire others to spin it into yarn," she says. "The yarn is used to
make a variety of products, including teddy bear fabric, baby diapers, wool soakers, and blankets. I work with professional seam-
stresses, weavers, and spinners on a piece basis, paying at least minimum wage. All these people have businesses at home and work for
other people, and I've checked with a legal adviser to make sure I've
got all my ducks in a row."

Cautionary note: The independent contractors you hire may *say*
they have their own businesses and work for other people, but if I
were hiring this kind of help, I would get a statement from them to
this effect, on their business stationery, with the names and
addresses of other customers or clients for whom they work. My
research indicates that if you hire someone the IRS or Department
of Labor says is *not* an independent contractor but an *employee,*
you're the one who will pay mightily for the error in back taxes and

penalties—not the individual you've hired. If you have any questions about whether you are on safe legal ground or not, consult the Department of Labor, read IRS's legal guidelines for independent contractors (Form SS-8), and/or seek advice from an attorney who specializes in labor law.

Independent Contractors vs. Statutory Employees. As Dodie Eisenhauer has learned, hiring *statutory* employees is the perfect solution for small manufacturers who want to operate legally. They cost more than independent contractors because you must pay social security and Medicare taxes, but they are less expensive to hire than regular employees because there are no unemployment taxes involved with them. (For more information on this topic, obtain the IRS booklet, *Tax Guide for Small Businesses.*)

"I encourage people who are still using independent contractors to reclassify their workers as soon as possible," says Dodie. "You immediately gain peace of mind from knowing you're operating on a 100 percent legal basis, and you no longer have to worry about the IRS or Department of Labor putting you out of business."

Leasing Employees. Until I wrote this book, I had never met anyone who had experience in leasing employees, so I was glad to connect with Howard Broman of Real Rose Jewelry. At one time, Howard had nine employees and was grossing $350,000 a year—and experiencing all the problems that come with this kind of business volume. In time, he and his wife, Ruthann, decided they would be much happier with just one employee and a lower gross income.

"If you need employees," says Howard, "never hire one—*lease* one instead. And never hire a relative because you can't fire an incompetent relative. Leasing employees was absolutely the smartest thing I ever did. It enabled me to fire without emotional problems and took all the tax and paperwork problems off my back. JobPower and ManPower have good leasing services. The way it works is you hire the employee you want and use the service to manage them. In return for 20 percent of the employee's gross wages, they'll do a drug test, offer the employee medical insurance, and take care of workman's compensation and FICA."

Sheltered Workshops. Don't have enough time to produce all the products you can sell? Consider farming out piecework to sheltered workshops that hire disabled workers. They commonly do such routine production work as cutting, painting, sewing, gluing, assembly work, packaging, collating, sorting, labeling, price marking, etc.

As Kate Harper mentioned earlier, she has had experience in working with disabled people who put the finishing touches on her products (gluing paper onto cards, putting envelopes and cards together, and sliding them into cellophane covers). "Such workers are extremely dependable, but the quality of work isn't always consistent," she says. "Still, for many craftspeople who need extra help, this could be the perfect solution."

Sue Cloutman also uses disabled workers who were placed in her business with a job coach and given forty hours of training at no cost to her. "They package, stuff, assemble catalogs, even do faxing occasionally," she says. "One functions on a higher level than the other, and I can pay her hourly. The other only stuffs toys, and I pay her by the piece."

Other Kinds of Help. Folk artist Deb Otto is proof that you do not have to have employees to wholesale, but she emphasizes that the only way to do this successfully is to use outside sources of help.

"When I had a retail shop, I had to have employees, but now that my retail shop is closed, I no longer need them. I'm happier as a result because I feel like I have greater control of my business now. As long as you're the artist or designer, you don't have to make everything yourself or do all the work to make a living. I create the original art for the line of framed prints I sell. Instead of making my own frames, I purchase them from a supplier who offers the sizes and finishes I need. A commercial print house does my prints. All I have to do is frame them and sell them."

Deb creates her original folk art paintings on acid-free Bristol paper, using a combination of acrylics, watercolors, ink, and colored pencils. The print house makes the necessary color separations and prints them on glossy paper. "My prints look almost identical to my originals," she says, "but fine artists who want even better reproduction for limited edition/signed prints should investigate art printers who specialize in this type of printing."

When Deb does craft shows, she always takes some of her original paintings with her to show that she is an artist, and the back of each framed print has a personalized backing that she can sign if the customer wants this personal touch. Prints sell for $49.95 framed, but buyers can purchase original unframed paintings for $250 if they wish. Deb points out that it's nice to be able to sell original art only, but she couldn't make a living doing this because she doesn't live in a major metropolitan area and can't afford to travel extensively to do high-end art shows. And why should she when she can sell $50,000 worth of art prints a year through a combination of wholesaling and craft shows?

Eileen Heifner offers yet another solution for the production problem, which many "craft purists" won't like. To increase production without increasing the number of employees or buying more equipment to mass-produce dolls, she decided to do the designing of the dolls and have the work done overseas. "But I have to warn anyone who thinks this is easy," she says. "Importing/exporting is scary stuff, and you must acquire a tremendous amount of knowledge about what you're doing before you even attempt it. You can get burned very badly, and you don't have the recourse that you have in the U.S. You have to deal with foreign exchange, Letters of Credit, and have enough collateral to back up a loan of $20,000 to $50,000. It's true that you can get things made overseas at a better price than you can get here, but you will have to make a concentrated effort to sell the thousands and thousands of items that they require for a minimum order."

I've included Eileen's comments here for those who may think overseas production is the answer to their production problems. I know very little about importing and exporting and don't care to learn. I understand why Eileen has gone this route; her business has grown so large that it can no longer be based at home. I commend her for her business expertise and entrepreneurial spirit, but I would not encourage the average artist or craftsperson to go this route.

Finding Good Employees

"I'm having a hard time breaking into the employee scene," says Michael Noyes. "Unemployment must be really low, because there's no one available to work at the wages I can afford. Dependability is

OSHA Laws

"Employees know all they have to do is call OSHA and you could be out of business, so always call OSHA before you hire employees," advises Howard Broman. "They will send people to your workshop and give you a report on any chemicals, paints, or other potentially hazardous situations they see and help you solve problems before they occur. If you suspect you have a problem and call OSHA to check it out, they cannot press charges against you.

"I just took a chance one time because we'd put in some exhaust fans and employees were complaining about the smell. I said 'I don't know if I'm getting myself in trouble here, or not, but I'm concerned. . .' and OSHA said I'd just gotten myself *out* of trouble because I'd called them. 'Trouble occurs only when an employee calls OSHA to complain about your workplace,' they told me."

Howard emphasizes that OSHA laws are changing all the time and employers are not notified when they do. Thus, something in your work place that passes inspection one year may not pass it the next, so it's always wise to invite OSHA in to verify that you have a safe working place or learn what you need to do to comply with current laws. To verify this information, simply call your nearest OSHA office.

---

really low, too. Twice in one week, I arranged to interview someone responding to my ad and they didn't show up or call or anything. I couldn't believe it. I'll be happy to share the wealth (if it ever comes) with valuable employees."

Even when you can find employees, the experience is not always positive. One year in October as Deb Otto left to do two week-long craft shows, she left employees running her retail store in Iowa. When she got back into the office after the shows, she got a call from the local bank asking if it was unusual that one of her employees had been passing large checks from her company account to "reimburse herself for CODs she paid" while Deb was gone.

"I was expecting about $500 worth of CODs," Deb told me, "so I left signed blank checks to pay for them. I learned that one of my employees had made out the checks to herself for over $11,000. When confronted, she fled to Wyoming. After doing a thorough search through the retail books she worked on, I found she had cashed other checks for cash, and when my inventory was counted, I was $14,000 short. A search warrant found many of my items in her home, but there was no proof (according to the local police) that the items were in fact mine since no one saw her take them. It was then I learned that my theft insurance policy would not cover this type of theft since I did not have a special "Employee Theft" rider.

"By mid-December, the SBA, which had financed my business, decided to foreclose on my retail shop, saddling my smaller whole-sale-craft show business with this $25,000 debt. As a sole proprietor, I was informed that if I didn't stay in business, they would go after our personal net worth growing within my husband's farming operation. The reality was that I would be working for some time solely to repay this huge debt with no hope of retrieving any of my losses."

Thankfully, the SBA took the peculiar nature of Deb's situation into consideration and, working with her local bank, restructured her debt into payments she could handle. Today, Deb is focusing on developing her wholesale print line, "From the Hand of Hannah," and has set up a Web page to increase business. "A friend gave me space behind her beauty shop, rent-free, in return for my helping with the utilities," she says, "so I now have my own door for UPS and enough space for my framing and packing, desk, and drawing area."

Deb is doing craft shows again with the help of her fourteen- and eleven-year-old son and daughter says getting back out on the craft show circuit was good medicine for her. "I ventured out to three large craft fairs in Iowa and found the kind souls there a refreshing experience after the backbiting politics of downtown. What would this world be without crafters helping crafters?"

Deb offers these tips for other small craft businesses who may be hiring employees:

- Make sure you do a thorough background check on employees. If they don't have good references, don't hire them.
- Check business insurance policies thoroughly in terms of employee consequences, not just outsider problems of theft and liability.
- Find a temporary trustworthy person or spouse to authorize expenditures if you do leave your business for any length of time.
- Check inventory monthly to spot potential shortages.

A Production Reminder List

Working longer hours to make more products is one way to increase income, but greater profits may more easily be generated simply by working *smarter*. Remember:

- Stand back from your business and look more closely at how you actually make products to see where improvements might be made.
- To learn your true production capabilities, keep accurate records on the time you spend making individual products for sale.
- To stay on schedule, develop and use production plans.
- Consider ways to standardize your product line.
- Look for design embellishments that might be eliminated. (You may love them, but will your buyers really care whether they are there or not?)
- Identify production tasks that might be more efficiently done in larger batch sizes. Even one-of-a-kind artisans can employ production-line techniques by working on half a dozen pieces at a time, doing work of a similar nature on each.
- For repetitive production jobs, buy or invent a tool or device that will improve your production capabilities.
- Reread Chapter Eight to remind yourself of the connection between organization and productivity, then work at becoming even more organized than you already are.
- If you decide you need help to produce more product, carefully analyze the various types of outside help available and discuss with your accountant or financial adviser which type is best for

your business from a legal and tax standpoint. Do not hire independent contractors without careful consideration of the related tax and legal implications.

▶▶ If you use employees, contact OSHA to get information on how to keep your workplace safe and in compliance with OSHA regulations.

HELPFUL RESOURCES

Fine Art Reproduction

Producing and Marketing Prints—The Artist's Complete Guide to Publishing and Selling Reproductions, Sue Viders (ColorQ Inc.).

ColorQ Inc., The Art Education Div. of ColorQ, Inc., 2710 Dryden Road, Dayton, OH 45439. (One of the nation's leading printers in fine-art reproductions.)

Sheltered Workshop Contacts

The ARC (1,200 offices nationwide) 1-800-433-5255.

United Cerebral Palsy Association 1-800-872-5827.

Easter Seal Society, Goodwill Industries, and Veterans Administration (Veterans Industries Program); contact your nearest local office for information.

Commercial Equipment and Tools

Check the *Thomas Register of American Manufacturers* in your library. It lists suppliers by company name, brand names, trademarked names, and product categories.

Chapter Eleven

The Problem of Pricing

||||||||||||||||||||||||||||||||||||||||||||||||

Pricing is a continuous balancing act between subjective and objective data. Relying totally on one exclusive of the other is probably not appropriate. We use the objective as a baseline from which to determine the retail price, then, depending upon feedback from the marketplace, we adjust the price. The marketplace is a good teacher."
— CHRIS NOAH, PAPERWAYS

Pricing is secondary to actually having a product someone wants to buy.
— HOWARD BROMAN, REAL ROSE JEWELRY

Pricing is a problem that never goes away, no matter how long you're in business. If you're selling only for extra income, pricing may not be of much concern to you. Something either sells or it doesn't. But if you want to make a living from your art or craft, you have to give a lot of thought to this topic. "When it comes to pricing, few artists think about hard numbers," says Jacqueline Janes, "but we all need to ask ourselves how much money we need or want to make per month. If you don't know this, how are you going to be sure that you make it?"

This chapter isn't likely to answer all your pricing questions—it would take a whole book to do that, and I've listed some of them at the end of this chapter—but it does offer valuable insight on how my book contributors:

▶▶ use pricing formulas;

▶▶ justify/rationalize the cost of their labor;

▶▶ trim overhead costs; and

▶▶ increase sales through special pricing strategies.

Although the emphasis in this chapter is on the pricing of crafts and artwork, the information about labor and overhead costs apply to service businesses as well.

NETWORKING SESSION #12:
PRICING IS EVERYBODY'S PROBLEM

Here is what experience has taught several sellers about pricing, with information on how they actually set prices and use pricing formulas. Notice that I've referenced each individual's art or craft as well as the number of years of selling experience they have so you can take this into consideration as you weigh the value of their pricing advice.

Do you use a pricing formula? If so, would you share it?

Howard Broman (real rose jewelry, 18 years): "I used to use various formulas to set prices until I learned that pricing is secondary to actually having a product someone wants to buy. To me, the most important part of pricing is to sell the item as cheaply as possible while still making a profit."

Nancy Jaekel (dough art, 22 years): "I don't use a pricing formula because the material in my product is so low-cost. I simply price what the market will bear, striving for at least a $3 profit on each item. (That may not sound like a lot, but I sell in volume, and $3 on 500 items makes a good profit for me.)"

Tabitha Haggie (professional crafter, 2 years): "I've never found a pricing formula I like, but I've developed my own system and it works well. Before the start of my show season, I meet individually with the members of my 'pricing committee.' It's a group of friends who enjoys crafts and has varying attitudes about the value of things. I show each of my creations and ask what they would pay for it. (I don't ask family members, because they are not honest like friends.) I compare my prices to what my friends say they would pay for each of my items and settle on the final selling price. Since I con-

How to Get Higher Prices for Your Products

The type and quality of the materials you use in your work automatically determine your market and the prices you can charge. When you elect to work with ordinary or common materials, buyers may expect your prices to be common as well. When you use luxurious or exotic materials, however, you automatically attract more affluent buyers.

▶ What you call a product and where you try to sell it has everything to do with the price you can command for it. A "handmade patchwork vest" is likely to appeal to the type of buyer who might pay from $25 to $45 for the item at a crafts fair or small shop. However, if you were to create a line of unique vests bearing a fancy designer label, you might be able to sell them in exclusive outlets for ten times that amount.

▶ When you realize that people will pay a great deal more for certain things nostalgic, whimsical, or collectible, you will have discovered an important pricing secret related to human nature. People will always pay more for products that satisfy their inner longings.

▶ Products with hang tags tend to command higher prices because they look professional and make items more suitable for gift-giving. Tags that strike a nostalgic or humorous chord can actually clinch a sale and lead to reorders.

▶ If you can't sell something at a certain price, try reverse psychology. Don't lower the price—raise it! Yes, you may lose some customers, but your higher price will automatically attract a totally new audience of buyers. An artist who found this advice in one of my earlier books later reported he had a painting that wouldn't sell at $325. After increasing the price to $750, he said, the painting sold after being on display only a few hours.

tinually sell out my booth, have a high profit margin, and a tremendous repeat business, I figure I'm doing something right."

Jacqueline Janes (beadmaker, 7 years): "I make jewelry using my own handmade beads. In the beginning, my prices were way too low. Now I have two pricing formulas that are working well—one for retail, one for wholesale. They both start the same. First, I make the 'cane' (the design in clay) and the beads. I figure my time at $35 per hour for wholesale and $50 to $60 an hour for retail. Then I make the jewelry or other piece from the clay, figuring my time with the same figures above. I then calculate the cost of jewelry findings and double it for wholesale and triple it for retail. When I get the price, I try to find a comparable product on the market and adjust the price if necessary. This last step is one that many people don't do, but I find it the most important. If I realize the item is overpriced, I go back to the drawing board and find a way to make it less expensive. I used to just lower the price, but after many years of giving my items away, I realized I was the one losing out."

Chris Noah (printmaker, 15 years): "Here's the basic pricing formula Tom and I use for our Paperways business. To determine a cost-per-item, we punch in several numbers, including total overhead, manufacturing costs, how much salary we need, and our desired profit (usually 10 percent). Once we've determined our cost-per-item, we have a basis for setting the wholesale price, which can then be doubled or tripled, depending on what the market will bear. I also tend to group prints by size and, to a secondary degree, by complexity. I price everything in one group the same or very close. One may have taken longer to make and another less, but it all averages out within that category. Hourly wage? Ballpark, $10/hour. That's actual, hands-on, decorative work. Basing, varnishing, and other chores have to be figured in, but not at the same rate."

Derek Andrews (woodturner, 4 years):
Material + Labor + Overhead x 2 = Retail.
"I figure out the material cost, add labor costs and overhead, then double it and round up or down to whatever I think is a good price.

If, after awhile, I find that a particular product is not making me much profit, or is a hassle to make, I push the price up."

Bill Mason (gemstone jewelry, 15 years):
Materials x 2 + Labor + (Profit 0% to 100%) = Wholesale.
"Profit is where I adjust the price, as the materials and labor are fixed costs. If these aren't covered, then the business is out of business. If I am not making a profit over and above materials and labor, then I am probably missing an important element of the market (cheaper materials, labor, or more effective marketing) I am trying to mine. Since I actually design and fabricate my jewelry, labor cost is very important to meeting my income needs. Materials are doubled because every time I handle and move a material, it costs me time and money. Doubling the cost allows me to cover this hidden expense and to upgrade to better quality materials or buy larger quantity for a better price, if a surplus actually appears in the materials column."

Susie Little (spinner/cottage industry owner, 6 years):
All costs/expenses + 20% to 30% of Costs = Wholesale.
"My costs include raw wool, washing and carding expenses, shipping costs, and labor to turn the wool into yarn, and the yarn into fabrics."

Linda Beattie Inlow (soapmaker, 6 years):
Cost of materials + Labor divided by # of bars = Wholesale.
"When I was making and selling soap, I broke down the cost of each bar by adding an hourly rate of $10 to the cost of materials. I divided that figure by the approximate number of bars of soap in a batch to arrive at a price. Because the cost of materials varied dramatically on each kind of soap, I then took a general median price for all bars. I would lose a few cents on one particular kind of soap, but make it up on another."

Dodie Eisenhauer (manufacturer of screenwire gifts, 28 years):
Labor x 4 = Wholesale.
"This is simple, but it works for me. Of the wholesale price, I gen-

erally figure that 25 percent covers marketing costs (show fees, commissions, ads); 25 percent is for materials/supplies cost; 25 percent for labor; and 25 percent for profit and certain fixed costs. To determine the cost of an item, I carefully clock the time it takes to produce several pieces and assign a labor cost. On my products, the labor is higher than the materials. When I have the labor cost figured, I can usually multiply it four times to get the wholesale price. Occasionally I vary this depending on perceived value of the item. I like to make about 20-percent profit, but that falls when volume is down or a bad show with high expenses crashes down on me. This also allows me to give a 20-to 25-percent discount to certain companies that market my things under their umbrella."

Michael Noyes (calligrapher, 8 years):
Production costs x 2 = Wholesale; x 4 = Retail.
"I generally set prices according to this formula, which enables me to wholesale and still make a profit. It's true that the market ultimately dictates the selling price, but I cannot afford, necessarily, to sell only based on the market. If the public will not purchase my calligraphy priced at four times my production costs, I must sacrifice some profit. However, I can go only so low, at which point I'll have to get a 'real' job."

Jan McClellan (jewelry, 9 years):
Cost of goods x 2½ + Labor = Retail.
"I make hand-fabricated jewelry using silver, gold, and semi-precious gemstones or beads. I sell at fairs and do some special orders. For my silver pieces, I take my cost of materials plus $10 to $20 an hour (depending on the perceived value of the piece) shop time for each piece, more or less. Lately, I've been charging more. This usually brings the product price to $40 to $350, which means they are hard to sell. I make more money on my one-of-a-kind pieces than on my lower-end things. This means I need to be really careful which fairs I do. I like to have professional people or those with enough income to be able to spend more than $40 for a piece of jewelry. Many times I think I need to charge more because I'm not figuring in enough for overhead, but there seems to be a cap on

what people will spend. As a result, I may never be sure how to do my pricing. The market has everything to do with pricing; obviously, it doesn't do any good to set a price that no one will pay."

Sue Cloutman (stuffed toy kits, 19 years):

Manufacturing cost + Profit (25% of manufacturing cost) = Wholesale x 2 = Retail.

(If selling through reps, increase wholesale price by 15%.)

"I do all my cost calculations on computer using a spreadsheet program. Each product I make has a Built Item List (see below) that describes and calculates the price of all materials and supplies used in that product. Incorporated into my cost of manufacturing are all costs for materials, supplies, labor, and packaging. When I was selling through sales reps, I added a figure of 15 percent of my manufacturing costs to the wholesale price, and then doubled that to get retail."

Sue Cloutman's "Built Item List," generated by spreadsheet software. It breaks down the cost of all supplies, materials, labor, and packaging costs of every product in her line.

Color Me Creations
Built Item List
as of 5/4/99

Item Code	Description 1	Description 2			
101	Tippy Tyrannosaurus	3 Markers			

Item Code	Description 1/Description 2	Qty	Cost	Ext. Cost
302	Story Tag/	1	.025	.02
303	Fabric/	.16	2.95	.47
PF10	Fiberfill/	5	.09	.45
306	Window Box/	1	1	1.00
312	Care tag/	1		.00
1038	Broadtip markers/red, blue, green, yellow	3	.3	.90
400	Packaging cost Box/	1	.5	.50
401	cutting/	1	.2	.20
402A	stuffing/	1	1	1.00
403	sewing, clipping, turnin/	1	.8	.80
			Total Cost	**5.34**

Item Code	Description 1	Description 2			
102	Wally Stegosaurus	3 Markers			

Item Code	Description 1/Description 2	Qty	Cost	Ext. Cost
302	Story Tag/	1	.025	.02
403	sewing, clipping, turnin/	1	.8	.80
402A	stuffing/	1	1	1.00
401	cutting/	1	.2	.20
400	Packaging cost Box/	1	.5	.50
1038	Broadtip markers/red, blue, green, yellow	3	.3	.90
312	Care tag/	1		.00
306	Window Box/	1	1	1.00
PF10	Fiberfill/	4	.09	.36
303	Fabric/	.13	2.95	.38
			Total Cost	**5.16**

Do you set retail prices and stick to them, no matter where you sell, or are you always raising them or lowering them in an attempt to find the "right" price? And do you ever lower prices at the end of a show?

Jacqueline Janes: "I've been known to adjust my bead and jewelry prices. When I was in fourteen craft malls, my perception was that the people patronizing these places were looking for lower-priced items. This is true to a point, but I sold more items over $20 than I imagined I would. I have been slowing raising my prices the last couple of years. It is so difficult to sell a product when people don't understand the process or the material."

Susie Little: "I have a set price for all the items in my wholesale line of handmade wool products (yarn, teddy bear fabric, baby diapers, soakers, and blankets), but I will waver if a customer buys a large amount or if I want to get rid of what I have in stock in favor of new materials. (I don't like to keep wool around for too long.)"

Liz Murad (calligrapher, 15 years): "In my first couple of years in business, I switched prices a lot, trying to be competitive at each show. Then I switched from year to year, trying to find a comfortable level. I am now comfortable with my pricing and reason that those who have a problem with it won't buy my calligraphy, while those who truly appreciate it will buy lots."

Steve Appel (bolt people sculptures, 13 years): "I stick to my prices. A pet peeve of mine is people who walk into my booth asking, 'If I buy two, do I get a discount?' No! If my work doesn't sell today, it will sell tomorrow. However, if someone buys several pieces and says nothing about the price, I may give them a discount."

Bob Gerdts (decorated eggs, 13 years): "I refuse to cut my prices at a show. If I want to get rid of something, I'll mark it down at home before taking it to the next show. Same way with refusing to dicker over prices; as soon as you start, there will be no end to it. Everything you sell will be negotiable. I think you should tag a piece with the price that it's worth. I've heard of some people who over-price their stuff so they can offer 10 percent off, but in my opinion, people who do that belong in the flea markets."

Wendy Van Camp (bead jewelry artist, 7 years): "When I first have an item on the table, I might either raise or lower the price based on the sales I get until I find a price that seems to work for it. I absolutely never will lower a price if a customer asks me to do it. To me, this indicates a swap-meet atmosphere, and that is cheapening my goods. I do a regular schedule of shows, so anything that does-n't sell at one fair more than likely will sell at the next one. There is no reason to lower my prices to bargain with customers."

Rochelle Beach (professional crafter, 9 years): "I've learned the importance of maintaining the retail prices of my Cinna-Minnies dolls. Here in Michigan, I keep my prices the same no matter what area I happen to set up in, even though I know I can get higher prices at shows in the Detroit area. I believe my customers respect this because I've heard some of them complain about other crafters they've seen at shows up north who have raised their prices for Detroit shows. I never reduce or change prices during a show. If you do this, you'll soon get a reputation for lowering your prices and customers will either delay their purchase until you lower your prices or lose respect for you and the product you're selling."

Derek Andrews: "I try as much as possible to maintain the same retail price at all locations, but this may change as I try my hand at Internet marketing."

Liz Murad: "I think we're all going to be experimenting with prices on the Internet. I get $10 for a 5 x 5 calligraphy at craft shows, but on the Internet, this price will include the cost of postage to the forty-eight contiguous states. I figure lower profits here will be off-set by the goodwill and customer ease I'm creating."

Ultimately, as you adjust your final retail/wholesale price for a product, do you find yourself setting prices according to what

others are charging for similar merchandise, or do you set prices based strictly on what you believe your products are truly worth?

Jacqueline Janes: "Looking at the market price is an important factor in pricing. With higher end pieces, you should not settle for a lower price, but there is more competition than ever in this business. People do price-check, and tend to buy what they consider a 'value.'"

Cheryl Eaton (artist, 20 years): "In the end, pricing is a combination of what you feel something is worth and what you think the market will bear. I have some things people tell me (after they have bought them) I should sell for twice the amount. But would they actually have bought them at that price is the question."

Nancy Jaekel: "I check out the competition to see what they are charging and also pay close attention to what my customers are buying from me. If they really like an item and then hedge about buying it, that usually means it is priced too high. Sometimes I can lower the price, and other times I decide to scrap the design as it would not be worth making for a lower price. Otherwise, I pretty much stick to the same prices. If I'm not sure about what to charge, I start low because it's easier to raise a price than lower it. (If you sell an item for $10 to one party and then $8 to another, you'd better hope the first party doesn't find out.)"

Chris Noah: "You're right about pricing lower to begin with. It never looks good to start high and have to lower prices. Customers have long memories. If they bought it a year ago for $90 and it's now $95, they're very pleased with themselves; however, if it's now $90 instead of $95, they would be justifiably irritated."

Tabitha Haggie: "When I nervously raised prices on two of my most sought-after pieces from $60 to $80 and $80 to $115, I was sure I wouldn't sell one. But I sold just as many as the year before at the lower prices. I also ventured into accepting credit cards and believe this paid for itself. People often try to decide whether to buy this one or that one, and I'm now finding that when indecisive people learn they can charge their purchase, they often buy the higher-priced item—and sometimes both."

Craftspeople are so reluctant to raise their prices. Some don't want to appear to be greedy while others are fearful things won't sell at a higher price. Those who have the courage to do this, however, often report to me that their higher prices did not deter sales at all. I believe you raise your prices when (1) your production, selling, or overhead costs increase; (2) you notice that others are selling similar products at a higher cost; and 3) you can't keep up with the demand for a particular product.

Derek Andrews: "In general, I find that sales are not that price-sensitive. If someone really wants to buy something from you, they are probably willing to pay a fair price. Try not to pay attention to the moaning minnies who think your prices are too high; many are just looking for an excuse not to buy anything, and most have no idea about the work that goes into handcrafted items. The bottom line is that you have to price for profit, and if the product doesn't sell at that price, then drop it."

Kim Marie (potter, 7 years): "I've got to rid myself of the ambivalence I have towards money. I've always felt that money means too much to most people and I was going to be different. Reality is, however, that I'll never be able to get a loaf of bread by trading a pot for it. I have to live in the society I'm in. If I want to survive, I need to make money. Money is okay—it's not an evil thing. Money will allow us to keep the house we live in and get a good credit rating. I'll keep repeating this to myself."

What is the most important/surprising/unusual thing you've learned about pricing (either retail or wholesale) in all your years of selling?

Derek Andrews: "The most surprising thing about pricing, and the thing that makes it difficult for me to set prices, is the wide variation in customers' perception of the value of my work. For every customer who tells me my prices are too low, there are ten who whisper to one another that everything is so expensive."

Wendy Van Camp: "I've learned to not set the price too low. A low price indicates poor quality in the minds of the buyer. However, there are certain ceilings you can't cross. Generally, I like to price my items inexpensively enough so they are good impulse buys; in other words, under $20."

Liz Murad: "I've learned that formulas are only a starting point. It's good to find a way to break down all your jobs and assign worth to them, but pricing goes much deeper than that."

Rochelle Beach: "The most important thing I have learned about pricing is that it all depends on what you are selling, where it is being sold, the time of year it is for sale, and to whom you are selling."

Cheryl Eaton: "I've learned that price doesn't matter . . . and price is *all* that matters. It depends on demand and desire."

Susie Little: "I've learned that people always want it cheaper!"

Michael Noyes: "Right. Consumers have become incredibly price-conscious and savvy. In a booming economy, cash abounds, but choice abounds all the more. Just a few pennies' difference in price is all it seems to take to lose out to the competition. Gas prices offer a good example. If there are two stations on a corner, I will typically go to the one that sells for a penny below the other. A penny! That's ridiculous . . . but true."

Figuring Labor Costs

Why do the same handmade items sell for one price here, another price there? Because no two people place the same value on their time. How much is your time worth to you? Do you price on this

Let Your Spouse Do the Pricing

Maria Nerius may have the perfect solution to pricing problems. In her book, *Soapmaking for Fun and Profit* (Prima) she says she stopped pricing her work a few years ago when she grew frustrated with customers' comments:

"Some said my prices were way too expensive while others snatched up my work telling me how reasonable my items were to purchase. So I asked my husband, Ken, to take over the pricing. I gave him all the information he needed concerning material costs, and labor time, and I let him set the overhead percentage. In some cases, he doubled my prices. And guess what? Most of my customers didn't blink an eye."

basis, or do you figure (like so many sellers) that you can never get what you're really worth so you'll have to settle for something less? Here is what some of my book contributors told me in response to these questions.

"Pricing my product is one of the hardest areas for me," says potter Kim Marie, who has been selling fine pottery at craft shows for seven years. "Occasional time studies are crucial. If I don't know what kind of time goes into making a product, there's no way I can accurately price it. Once I become relatively proficient at making a product, I'll do some time studies—how long on average it takes me to throw the item, how long to alter or put handles on the item, etc. Once I gather that information, I have a better sense of how much the item should cost."

Few craftspeople ever bother to track the time it takes them to make a product, but that's a mistake. In pricing, production time is everything. Hobby sellers often set prices simply by doubling or tripling the cost of materials, but that simple formula works only in some cases. For example, if a small crafts item costs you $2 to make and you can make six per hour and get $4 each, that would give you a gross profit of $12 for an hour's worth of your time. But if each item has $2 in materials and takes *an hour* to make, doubling the cost of materials would give you a pitiful profit of just $2 an hour for your labor.

Many professional artisans do base their prices on cost of materials, however, believing they cannot charge for the labor they put into their products. As bead jewelry artist Wendy Van Camp explains, "My jewelry is priced by doubling the cost of the item for wholesale and quadrupling it for retail. I don't factor in labor costs at all. If I did, my work would be priced so high I could not sell it. There is little way I can compete with the low labor costs in Hong Kong or other third world nations."

Calligrapher Michael Noyes has a similar problem. "My labor costs are based on a $10/hour rate," he says, adding that in the Washington, D.C. area, this is basically minimum wage. "It's hard to compete with Chinese labor at $1 a day. Like it or not, import prices profoundly affect customer's attitudes and buying habits."

"Labor costs are difficult to figure," says woodturner Derek Andrews. ""I don't think the real cost of making a retail sale can be stressed enough, and this must be considered when setting retail prices. Even when I sell direct from my shop at home, it costs me a considerable amount of time and expense, attending to customers, setting up and maintaining displays, lighting, wrapping and packing, credit card charges, losses, tours of the workshop—all these things take time and cash. Although I have a pretty good idea of how much time I spend at the lathe for each item I make, all the other workshop and management tasks are really difficult to quantify. I figure on $10 an hour, which includes overhead. I wish it were higher, but I don't believe my present market can stand anything more. If, at the end of the year, I haven't made enough money, I look for ways to do things better."

Jacqueline Janes works in polymer clay, which is very labor-intensive. "I not only calculate my labor," she says, "but I figure it out over a period of time, not just piece by piece. There are so many steps involved in turning the bricks of clay into the finished piece, so I have to break it down. I've learned that it takes me less time per piece to make 100 beads than it does to make ten, and I don't think this concept is exclusive of polymer clay."

"My labor works out to about $20/hour," says calligrapher Liz

Murad, "but if I rented a studio or had lots of overhead, the reality would be $10/hour. A 5 x 7 calligraphy takes about fifteen minutes and I sell it for $10, which yields a good profit for me."

"I set my prices on what I think my products are worth," says silk artist Phillippa Lack. "I put a value of $20 on my labor, which is way too low, I know, but it's the best I can do now."

In figuring labor costs, few sellers ever take into account the time they spend doing craft fairs. Steve Appel, who constructs bolt people sculptures, has thought about this, however. "I figure I'm worth about $15 an hour, and I figure that into my costs," he says. "But when I travel, I like to make at least $500 a day including travel days. So if it takes me two days to get there and two days back, with a two-day show I figure I need to make $3,000 at the show to justify returning."

As a production artisan who has five part-time employees, Nancy Jaekel knows the importance of getting serious about labor costs. "My hourly rate for dough art creations is figured at between $35 and $60 an hour," she says. "This is not to say that I set my prices using these hourly rates in a formula, only that this is what the sale of my products must yield on average if my business is to be profitable. If I can't make at least $35 an hour for my labor on a particular product, I'll drop that product from my line. The way it usually works out is that some days we produce a low-cost item very quickly and I might average $60 an hour; whereas on another day, a more time-consuming ornament might average out to only $40 an hour."

Charging for Design Time. "If someone really wants my personal time set aside to design just for them, I charge $20 to $25 an hour for my time," says Cheryl Eaton. "In creating pins and jewelry, I have not found the hourly rate figure workable as some things come quicker than others, but value is the same. The same is true of painting. I just did two bluebirds on a decorative bird house. How do you figure that? I really completed it in about two hours, but if I figured the mental time laying it out, looking at pictures, getting ready to paint, let alone the time learning the skill . . . it's really hard to figure."

Cheryl's comments reminded me of something I read in Susan Young's book, *Decorative Painting for Fun and Profit*. In it, she tells the story of how a crafts fair shopper watched her demonstrate her art by painting an apple design on a kitchen accessory. The woman picked up a finished item with the same apple design on it and in a loud voice in front of the crowd asked, "How can you charge this much? I just saw you paint an apple in three minutes!"

Susan said she gritted her teeth, put a smile on her face, and said, "You're right about the three minutes. But it took me three years to perfect the technique." I'll bet many of you have "been there, done that," haven't you?

An artist who has sold her work for twenty-one years, Susan has given considerable thought to pricing and the time it takes to design products. "I've figured out my studio time has to gross a minimum of $12 per hour, whether it's painting or time on the computer. Otherwise, I do not do the project. I don't feel an average of $12 an hour for contracted crafting or artist's work is excessive. However, I don't tell any client, '$12 an hour' as the client has no concept of how many hours it takes to produce anything. Hourly rates scare people, especially when it has to do with crafts. Failing to grasp the production concept, they assume crafting is child's play, or worse, you are just in it for a hobby. Once, when I was asked to do twenty custom-crafted items and offer a bid for the project, it took me an hour to come up with the design itself. Once I had the concept of execution in mind, thanks to past experience, I felt twenty projects would take twenty hours to complete, plus I estimated I would need two hours to shop and to assemble supplies, and that the client would expect delivery, another hour. Total studio time: twenty-four hours. Very easy to figure my labor costs. Another thing I always do is tally my material/inventory costs and triple them, adding this cost to labor figure."

Pricing Patterns. "The most important thing I've learned about pricing patterns over the past fourteen years," says Elizabeth Bishop, "is that, after all the calculating and tracking of costs, I wind up pricing according to what the market will bear-roughly what other similar products cost. The meticulous bookkeeping lets me know that I am covering all my expenses, but my hourly wage is pretty much limited to that market ceiling. People expect patterns to stay within a certain range, and mine are always at the top of that range. I raise prices minimally only to offset postal-rate increases or other changes."

Jacquelyn Fox, a needlework designer with ten years' experience in this field, confirms the market ceiling for patterns. "In the needlework pattern industry, prices for patterns are generally consistent among designer offerings," she says. "I have found that I have to keep my prices in line with other similar designs or the shop owners won't buy. That means I have to set my prices lower than I'd like. I really can't factor in an hourly wage, increased costs of printing, photo developing, etc., or my pattern prices would be out of line

Keeping Better Records

The only way to know if you're really making a profit in your business is to set up a good record-keeping system and study your financial figures at the end of each year. Nancy Jaekel has the right idea. "I keep track of all costs, labor, materials, overhead, etc., and my hours," she says. "At the end of the year, I add up the costs and subtract from the profits. I take that total and divide it by my hours and decide whether or not I'm working too hard for the money I make."

"Setting a price point that makes a profit while garnering the most sales is a tricky thing," says Susan Gearing. "The key is keeping supplies and overhead costs low enough. Make sure you know your bottom-line profit, and build your pricing structure from there. If you don't, you may be in the position of selling more and making less with each increase in sales."

"Pricing is refined by experience in the market," says Chris Noah. "After a show, we do a statistical analysis of the show—what sold, what didn't. From that we can determine whether we can raise our prices in that show the next time. We do only shows in our region where I have a following. It's practically an operational definition of success when they call me to find out if I'm going to be at a certain show."

continued on following page

continued from prevvious page

In earlier chapters, you have learned how some overhead costs can be lowered through better business management and the use of computer technology. Here's another example. In reviewing her previous year's business records, potter Kim Marie saw that her lack of business acumen had led to some hard lessons. "Although my gross income was more than I expected, the profit was less than I had hoped. This proved that I have a product the public will spend money on and brought my pricing problem to light. I saw that I had underestimated a few of my overhead costs, particularly my glazing and firing costs. Electricity is my biggest expense since I have two electric kilns. I'm on commercial rates, which is a nightmare, but a reality and a constant. So I did some research and talked to my electric company. I found out that since all my electricity is used in product, it is tax exempt. This has saved me between $11 to $20 per month. I also enrolled and was accepted for the electric company's Small Business Growth Incentive program, which may save me a small amount in the future as my electric needs grow."

with the competition. This bites into my profit margin, because unlike other designers who have been in the business longer and have greater working capital at their disposal (and who have access to the cheaper printing/developing services of the larger cities), I can't yet print in huge quantities to get a super-cheap per-item cost. I'm not a big enough name to sell a thousand of a given design in a year's time, so I'm forced to print in smaller quantities or risk having a basement full of merchandise gathering dust. Right now, factoring in my actual production costs, not including time, utilities, etc. (about $.50 per printed pattern with no extras), if I sell it wholesale at $2.50 directly to the shops, the profit margin is about $2 per pattern. But I've found that most shops like to buy through distributors and so I must pay them an addition 25 to 30 percent (sometimes 40 percent), which cuts my profits per item to $1.38 or $1. I could complain on and on about this, but I guess it's something I have to deal with until my business grows large enough to take advantage of the larger print runs."

Trimming Overhead Costs

Are you careful to keep close track of your overhead costs, so you can incorporate them into your pricing formula? "For craftspeople, overhead costs are the first place to look for budget cuts," says Wendy Rosen in her book, *Crafting as a Business.* "Keeping overhead down, and production and sales up, is the key to adding to your own income."

Overhead costs are all expenses not directly related to the production of your products (raw materials and labor). They include:

▸▸ selling costs—show fees, related travel and meals, sales commissions, samples, displays, photography, printing and promotional mailings, packaging, advertising, credit card processing fees, web site development/maintenance;

▸▸ general office expenses—telephone, fax, e-mail and Internet service provider fees, office and computer supplies, stationery and other business printing, postage and postal fees, bank charges, legal and professional expenses, subscriptions, memberships and conference fees, etc.;

▸▸ other expenses—general travel and auto expenses, equipment purchases, maintenance and depreciation, employee or independent contractor expense and "home office expenses" (a percentage of your rent or mortgage expense, taxes, insurance, and utilities).

If you have been in business for at least a year, it should be easy for you to pull all your overhead figures together to determine your average monthly overhead cost. If you're just getting started in business, however, start with a figure that is 10 percent of anticipated gross sales and adjust it at year's end when you've made a study of annual expenses. This may be too low for your particular business, but it's a good place to start.

"At the end of each year when I am totaling expenses in order to file my income tax, I get a general idea of overhead," says Jan McClellan. "I think 10 percent is low, especially with all the expense of doing shows, but I find I can't seem to figure much more into my pricing structure and still sell the jewelry."

"I keep track of overhead and materials on a computer spreadsheet," says Linda Beattie Inlow. "This allows me to do an inventory check at the beginning and end of the year for taxes."

Two Insider Pricing Tips

Howard Broman and his wife, Ruthann, operate Real Rose Jewelry, a business that has been their livelihood since 1981. Howard is a savvy marketer with a keen understanding of today's quickly changing crafts marketplace, and he generously shares his advice with hundreds of professional artisans on the Arts-n-CraftsBiz Mailing List he moderates on the Internet. The following pricing strategies offer a good example of the kind of inside information you would get if you became an active participant on this list. To many readers, these two tips alone will be worth the price of the book.

The Two-Digit Pricing Secret. Howard has a great pricing trick that enables him to know at any moment during a craft show exactly how much he has sold of everything he's taken to the show. He sells dried roses and rose jewelry-necklaces, earrings, and pins-at a variety of prices, but the last two digits of any price automatically identifies the item. That is, all pins are priced with an ending of $.95 ($7.95, $12.95, etc.); all necklaces end in a price of $.90; all earrings in $.85.

"We have a form we take to a show on a clipboard," Howard explains. "It's divided into columns the width of the removable Avery price labels we use, with headings of $.95, $.90, and $.85. When we sell an item—say, a necklace at $12.95—we remove the label from the item and stick it under the $.95 column heading, and do this throughout the day. At a glance, we know exactly how much business we've done at any time of day. I even do this by hours to gauge how a show does during the morning, over the lunch hour, mid-afternoon, and evening, placing the stickers in columns based upon time."

Moving into Wholesaling

Selling at wholesale doesn't necessarily mean producing more; it only means having the right prices to make a profit on items you're offering at wholesale.

Most craftspeople say they can't afford to give 50 percent off on wholesale orders, but if you don't have enough profit built in it to give this discount, how can you afford to do a crafts show, particularly one away from home where you have show fees, perhaps a jury fee, a motel bill, food, gas, and incidental expenses? You can't just wave all these costs away. In truth, they are coming directly out of the money you make at a crafts fair, and by the time you deduct all these fees from your total income, you may have even less than 50 percent remaining. So you might as well wholesale and save all that time, wear and tear on your body, the aggravation, etc.

"You should never approach the pricing of your product from the retail end," says Howard Broman. "Instead, think of the retail price as a bonus (what the market will bear) and set wholesale prices to begin with, simply doubling them for retail shows. Then, if a rep gets excited about your product and you decide to give wholesaling a try, you won't be standing there with your mouth open trying to figure out a decent wholesale price in which you actually make a profit."

Most craftspeople are selling at discounted prices to begin with. True retail prices are not the retail prices at most of the craft shows, but rather what one finds in stores. "When I was challenged to compare my pottery prices to those in stores, I realized they were too low," says Emily Pearlman, "and this realization motivated me to move into wholesaling."

Many sellers who once thought they couldn't wholesale because of pricing problems have learned otherwise. Sometimes moving from craft fair selling to wholesaling is as simple as changing the heading on your price list, from "Retail" to "Wholesale."

(No two shows are ever alike, but this kind of record would become increasingly valuable if you return to the same shows year after year. You would have a much better idea of how much inventory to take the second or third time around, and you'd also have some clues as to when the heaviest selling periods are likely to be.)

Now here is Howard's greatest and most profitable pricing secret, a theory he tested for a whole year. "I've found that it doesn't make a bit of difference whether a product is priced at $5 or $5.85; $10 or $10.90; $12 or $12.95. People bought the items with no consideration to the *last two digits*. It's as if they don't exist in buyers' minds. It's only the first part of the price they're concerned about. So we never set round-number prices anymore, but always tack on the extra 85, 90, or 95 cents (our 'coded prices') and consider it *pure profit*."

State-Fair Pricing Strategy. In talking with a thirty-year veteran of selling at state fairs, Howard learned that the impulse purchase price has moved up in the last five years to $19.95, the amount of money people will throw away on almost anything. "And, in fact, that was the upper limit on most gadgets being sold at the fair I participated in," he says. "Gene, the veteran, also pointed out that my pricing strategy was wrong for the fair. I was offering a necklace at 50 percent off (regular $10, fair special $5). Gene commented that most people would not know what that meant. He asked me if I wanted to make $5 per purchase, or $10. The answer was obvious, so he suggested this pricing scheme which he says worked "fantastically well': **regular price $10, discounted to $7— 2 for $10, your choice.**

"I actually had customers convincing their friends that they really wanted to buy a necklace too because, that way, they could each save $2 on their purchase. I had to sit back and smile. Gene really knew his business. It worked, and the vast majority of my "widget" sales were $10. If they wanted just one, I picked up an extra $2."

Things Are Changing

As you learned in the second chapter of this book, businesses must always be ready to make changes of one kind or another to adjust to changing times and marketplace situations. Howard Broman says there has been tremendous resistance in the crafts community to recognize that price perceptions of customers are changing.

"Many in our industry feel that products are inordinately more desirable simply because they are handmade," he says. "But that type of thinking will put us out of business. The primary emphasis in purchasing a product is perceived value. The first consideration is given to the cheapest price or what is thought to be the cheapest price. It's a head game, an illusion, a trick, like my state fair pricing strategy. We can curse Madison Avenue all we want to, but it's a real-

She Sells Service!

In the previous chapter, you read about Rita O'Hara, who designs and die-cuts her own gift boxes to stimulate sales. In addition to the packaging she offers her buyers, Rita also gives them free prepricing and barcoding services.

"I don't give quantity discounts, but I offer service," she says. "I've found that service gets more attention than a discount. I love to do private labeling and my shops love it, too. I offer to put any label they want on the products they buy from me. I'll put their logo on the tag at no charge, but I make it clear that my name goes on the back. For example, a chain of fourteen Hallmark stores ordered products with matching box, tags, and tissue paper."

Rita got into barcoding when she began to sell to a much larger group (300) of Hallmark stores because she knew this kind of service would not only encourage reorders, but would get her products on the shelf quicker. "It takes retail buyers time to price your product, so they appreciate it when I offer to do this for them for nothing. This is also advantageous to me because it gives me control over what my tag looks like, and it keeps the store from putting a sticky label on my product that the customer may not be able to get off. It's so easy to do this now; I see no reason for all artisans not to do this."

continued on following page

continued from previous page

To bar code, Rita advises registering with the Bar Code Council ($350/year) to receive your own unique barcode number and prevent others from using the same number (which would be a problem if you both ended up selling in the same store). "You must buy barcode software which then

enables you to assign product code numbers to all products and create a unique barcode for each of them," she explains. "The first six numbers on my price tag is my unique Stonewares barcode number; the next five are the code numbers I've assigned to my product. The last number is picked by the software.

Rita cuts, perforates, and punches holes in her hang tags and price tags using different inexpensive tools from Fiskars. "The advantage of using a perforated price tab is that the craft mall or retail gift shop can keep one part for their records and the customer goes home with the label that bears your name and address," Rita explains. "Otherwise, the customer walks out without a tag on the product they've just bought."

(Fiskars' products are readily available in craft shops and office supply stores. Check out their Portable Paper Trimmer, Perforating Blade, and decorative punches in a variety of shapes. Web site: www.fiskars.com.)

ity. The most obvious example of this change is the shift of holiday discounting away from the first of January to the first of December. Do you realize what a massive shift in thinking that has been? Even within the wholesale market, the traditional Christmas shows in July and August have fallen flat on their face, and store owners are waiting, even into November, looking for 'distressed merchandise' (overruns, specially manufactured discounted items, etc.). I even experimented successfully with newly manufactured discounted items and was quite successful in my Christmas kiosk. The customers loved it, and they knew they were getting a good deal."

Yes, things are changing, and it's important that you pay attention to what's happening in your particular field and respond to those changes with changes of your own. Let this chapter serve as your reminder to reconsider your pricing methods and ask yourself if you need to make some adjustments to ensure a fair profit for all the time and effort you're putting into your business.

HELPFUL RESOURCES

Books that offer pricing and wholesaling guidelines:
The Crafter's Guide to Pricing Your Work, Dan Ramsey (Betterway Books).
Crafting as a Business, 2nd ed., Wendy Rosen (The Rosen Group).
The Crafts Business Answer Book, Barbara Brabec (M. Evans).
Creative Cash, 6th ed, Barbara Brabec (Prima).
Handmade for Profit, Barbara Brabec (M. Evans).
Homemade Money, 5th ed., rev, Barbara Brabec (Betterway Books).
How to Survive & Prosper as an Artist, Caroll Michels (Owl Books).
The Official Guide to Pricing Your Crafts, Sylvia Landman (Prima).

Discussion group on the Internet
The Arts-n-CraftsBiz Mailing List, moderated by Howard Broman, is strictly for professional craftspeople who are interested in exchanging ideas and information that will help advance one another's businesses. The author and many of this book's contributors are active on this list. To see if you qualify for admission, go to www.onelist.com and click first on the "Arts" category, then on "Crafts."

Chapter Twelve

Supplies and Shipping

||||||||||||||||||||||||||||||||||||||||||

I never rely on just one supplier for my raw materials because I don't want to get stuck if the company goes out of business or stops making a product I need. And I save money on shipping and packaging supplies by getting them free from the post office.

—GAIL PLATTS, INCALICO

This chapter is sort of a P.S. to the preceding chapter on pricing. Clearly, the prices paid for raw materials, supplies, and shipping charges are an important part of the pricing formula, but the following material was just too lengthy to tack onto the end of the pricing chapter. What follows, then, is a collection of tips and ideas on how to:

- ▸▸ save money on craft supplies and materials,
- ▸▸ monitor supply costs,
- ▸▸ save money on shipping charges,
- ▸▸ get some craft supplies and equipment free of charge,
- ▸▸ figure shipping and handling costs, and
- ▸▸ get free shipping supplies and materials.

How to Save Money on Craft Supplies and Equipment

Buying supplies is directly related to the production of crafts. If supply costs are too high, you end up with pricing problems. If your source of supply is cut off, you lose everything. Here are a few helpful tips on finding and working with suppliers and buying equipment at lower prices.

Shop Around. Many companies who once sold only by mail now have online catalogs, so you can simply use a search engine to find their Web sites. This makes it easy to compare the prices of several suppliers before you place an order. Buying from suppliers close to you will cut shipping costs, but check the policies of all companies to see if free shipping is offered on orders of a certain size. Some of the craft professionals featured in this book are buying computers, scanners, and other high-tech equipment online because prices there are often a couple hundred dollars lower than the same equipment in retail stores. This may soon be a trend, given the fact that online bookstores are now offering a 50 percent discount on hardcover books. (This kind of pricing policy is great for consumers with online access, but it will eventually put more retailers and independent bookstores out of business.)

Don't Rely on Just One Supplier. In Chapter Nine, in the section on design considerations, you may recall my warning about having reliable supply sources when you design a new product and introduce it to the marketplace. As I stated there, "Companies go out of business, get overworked, or have their own supply problems." As needlework chart designer Jacquelyn Fox has learned, this is not a problem to take lightly.

"Custom beads and embellishments are big in the cross-stitch design market right now, and many designers are incorporating these handmade embellishments into their new designs," she explains. "I recently featured in several of my releases the embellishments of a talented button creator who has been in business for several years. But her business has become so successful so quickly that she has become overwhelmed with work and cannot fill the hundreds of orders pouring in for her buttons. The shops that are buying my charts can't get the buttons that go with the design, and so my charts aren't selling as quickly as they should be. I empathize with this craftswoman, but I hope she gets her act together soon because it's costing me sales."

Gift wholesaler Pat Endicott ran into a similar problem when she designed a new Oak Note Keeper. "It was a great seller at the January/February trade shows, but by February I was having trouble getting the wood cut from my supplier," she says. "Since I normally ship the next day, this frustrated both me and my customers. In trying to find a new supplier, bids were a dollar more per unit, and I couldn't raise the price a month after bringing out a new item, so I just had to wait for my supplier to deliver."

Ask for Discounts. If you can't buy at full wholesale, look for suppliers who will sell at bulk or discounted prices. When artist Susan Young can't get art or craft supplies free of charge (see next section on this topic), she lowers her costs by asking for discounts. "The mail order companies I deal with don't advertise bulk prices," she says, "but as a regular customer, I never hesitate to ask for a better price. The last time I ordered from one supplier I asked if he would give me a 20 percent discount if I doubled the order, and without a moment's hesitation, he said yes."

To get a better deal on prices with local businesses (printing, etc.), Jacquelyn Fox suggests bringing up the fact that you'd like to keep your business dollars in town. "This loyalty to local businesses usually results in a pretty fair price quote," she says.

Look for Sales. Pat Endicott uses a lot of fabric in her products and says cotton calico fabrics have almost doubled in price in less than ten years. "Buying fabric wholesale in many situations is more expensive than buying at retail, due to sales by desperate retailers who have bought in volume and can't get rid of their inventory."

"I find auctions and I buy in bulk," says Steve Appel, who makes bolt people sculpture. "The best Christmas I ever had was when someone in town bought out a hardware store and was trying to get rid of stuff. I walked away with *a lot* of nuts and bolts! I also have a friend who owns a scrap yard, and he's always calling to ask if I need anything. Bartering in the crafts business is a wonderful tool."

Like Steve, Nancy Jaekel also buys at auctions. "Anyone who needs heavy-duty equipment of any kind should check out auctions for restaurants, bakeries, and other stores that are going out of business," she says. "At one auction or another, I've purchased a food processor, pasta machine, pizza oven, and other kitchen equipment used in my dough art business, plus shelving, bags, and cash register tapes."

Network with Other Crafters. "Go the extra mile when looking for materials," says Jacqueline Janes. "Networking with other crafters really helps. I've found many of my sources for materials by talking to others. We are all out there buying materials, and we tend to run into things we don't use, but know about. I found my source for clay from a painter who lives in the same city as the company that sells the clay."

Check Library Directories. When trying to locate raw material suppliers and wholesale supply sources, don't overlook the tried-and-true library reference, the *Thomas Register of American Manufacturers*. This multi-volume directory lists products by category as well as by trade and brand names. Manufacturers who won't sell to you direct will be happy to refer you to distributors who will.

How to Get Free Supplies and Equipment

If you teach your art or craft, write how-to articles, or are otherwise in a position to influence buyers in their decision as to what supplies, materials, and equipment to purchase, you may be able to get a lot of "stuff" free.

In *Creative Cash*, I wrote about how Charlene Anderson-Shea got a thousand dollars' worth of knitting needles to play with when she contacted every manufacturer of knitting needles and told them she and two of her friends would review their needles in a leading magazine for knitters.

Professional craft designers who regularly write how-to articles for craft magazines never have to buy their own supplies and materials. They simply contact manufacturers of products they want to use in their how-to projects and sit back and wait for free boxes of materials to arrive. "As a published writer who uses certain product lines consistently, I no longer have to buy some of my favorite supplies and materials because manufacturers keep me well-supplied," says craft designer Susan Young. "Some of them have a special mailing list of designers who automatically receive boxes of supplies and materials, particularly new items a company wants publicity for. Getting on their list will be well worth your time."

Quilt designer Karen Combs has made a name for herself by selling her quilts, writing books and articles on the craft, teaching, and making television appearances. In interviewing her for this book, I learned that fabric and sewing machine companies have given her considerable supplies of fabric, batting, and thread, not to mention a $5,000 sewing machine. So how can *you* get all this free stuff? First you have to be able to prove to the manufacturer that you are visible to a large segment of the market it is trying to reach, and in a position to influence their prospective buyers. Having a good portfolio or presentation package will be essential. Then you simply contact companies whose products you like.

"I first approached a batting manufacturer, telling them I was writing a book and making some quilts for illustration," Karen explains. "I said I loved their product and needed batting for my quilt projects and would they be interested in sending me some to work with. They called to ask how much I needed, and soon afterwards I received several boxes of batting. Now in my writing and teaching, I always recommend my favorite batting product, giving the company free publicity."

Karen did the same thing for the fabric and thread manufacturers whose products she used regularly. Then she reached higher by contacting Viking to see if they might give her a sewing machine. "I had used a Viking for years and really liked it, so I contacted them, told them I was an author and speaker who regularly saw thousands of people a year, etc., but I never heard a word from them. When a friend told me how much she liked the Pfaff machine, I decided to try the same strategy with this company. I said I'd always used a Viking, but would love to be able to use a Pfaff, and could they put me on their consignment program. It took about eight months, but I finally got a call and, before long, I had one of Pfaff's top-of-the-line sewing machines complete with all the software and accessory items."

Writer, teacher, and designer Mary Mulari, who has six sewing machines in her studio now, says sewing machine companies have special policies and quotas for loan-out or consignment machines. "They do recognize the value of placing their machines in the studios of influential designers and teachers," she explains, "but at times they also have more requests for loaner machines than they can fill. It would be important for someone who wants a loaner to contact the person at the sewing machine company who has direct responsibility for assigning the machines. Be prepared to present a resume and examples of sewing, a listing of future commitments in teaching/designing/writing, and then, wait patiently. By keeping in touch and updating the company person about your ongoing work in sewing, there will be a good chance to receive a sewing machine or serger on loan."

Why loan out free machines in the first place? Because manufacturers realize that free-lance writers and teachers have the ability to reach and influence the purchasing decisions of countless buyers. There is nothing to sign in these arrangements. Companies simply ask that you mention their product by name whenever you write, teach, or lecture, and that you'll return the machine when you're through using it. Whenever a newer model becomes available, you simply trade in the older one.

I'm talking about sewing machines here, but I don't see why this idea wouldn't work for a whole lot of other machinery and equipment used in craft production, from wood lathes and carving tools to potter's wheels and quilting frames. The point is, you'll never know if you can get such things without charge unless you *ask*. As a writer who regularly publicizes books, I haven't had to buy an art, craft, or business book for the past twenty years; publishers are delighted to furnish me with review copies. So what is it you'd love

Price Labeling Tip

"I use a pricing gun with preprinted stickers that have my business name, ornament care, and copyright symbol on them," says Nancy Jaekel. "I can sticker so many more ornaments that way, over the peel-and-stick (very expensive) stickers. I get them from Kenco Label Sales in Wisconsin, and the cost is so much less than getting them through a printer."

to have but can't afford to buy? Think of a way to publicize that product for the manufacturer (or publisher), and maybe you can get it free . . . just by asking.

Monitoring Supply Costs

Many crafters buy supplies whenever they see something they might like to work with, without any regard for how they are actually going to use them. While you may need a stock of basic supplies, much like a good cook always has a well-stocked pantry, you need a much better handle on your supply situation than this if you're serious about making a profit from your business. Since it is impossible to set a profitable price on a product if you don't know what your raw materials cost, you need to devise a way to monitor your purchases and inventory of such materials.

Tabitha Haggie says one reason she has a high profit margin on her products is because she pays attention to what she pays for supplies. By planning supply needs ahead of time, she not only gets the best price, but never finds herself in the uncomfortable position of being without essential supplies when she's preparing for a show. She uses spreadsheet software (Excel) to keep track of her inventory. "Some may think I waste too much time keeping records when I could be producing more crafts instead, but if I'm not organized, I tend to get a lot of nothing done," she reasons. "At times I do feel I should be away from the computer, painting in the basement. But then I would be stressed, feeling like I was driving at night without the lights on—trying to get there, but not quite seeing the way. Having a good working list of what I will be producing affords me the opportunity to know very early in the year what supplies I will need. It also helps me save money. I list all needed supplies on a spreadsheet with columns for my various suppliers. Then I pull out all my catalogs, go down my list, and look at each catalog for the best price and enter that company's item number in the corresponding column."

The primary benefit of keeping records, as Tabitha and other professional crafters have learned, is that they enable one to identify areas where money can be saved, or profits can be increased. "I keep a chart that shows the quantity of each item I make, and make sure I have materials on hand to do so," says Derek Andrews. "This is particularly important since 90 percent of my sales occur in six months of the year, and I really have to work hard during the other six months to ensure that I have product ready to ship when it's needed."

Soapmaker Linda Beattie Inlow uses Microsoft Excel to keep track of inventory, as well as ascertain the actual cost of each bar of soap. "Since essential oils vary in cost, production cost can be dramatically different from one bar of soap to another."

Needlework business owner Meg Sullivan uses Microsoft Excel (part of the Microsoft Office package software) to manage her inventory of raw materials and finished goods. "At the time the worksheets are set up, the calculation formulas can be built into the program," she says. (See illustration of Materials Inventory Worksheet.) "The categories can easily be adapted for other businesses. I assign each raw material or supply item a stock number. I created special tags that list the stock number, amount, unit cost, and what I intended it for (sometimes the most valuable info on the tag). As I use fabric, for example, I mark off how much is left on the tag and make the same note in the computer. At a glance, I can tell how much I have and the value of my inventories (which could be vital in case of a disaster such as a flood or fire and getting the insurance company to pay off)."

To create tags, Meg purchases 2 x 4-inch adhesive labels that can be printed on her inkjet printer. Once printed, the labels are attached to 4 x 6-inch index cards, three labels per card, then cut apart. "I then punch a hole in the corner of each tag so I can pin one to each fabric in my inventory," Meg explains. "As I purchase fabric, I log it into my materials inventory using a system of letter/number codes. I log the inventory number on the tag along with other pertinent information. When I use the fabric, I mark the tag so I know how much I have left and log usage in the computer. Finished items are also assigned an inventory number. My worksheet includes a description, creation's cost, asking price, selling price, and date sold. (For various reasons, asking price and sell-

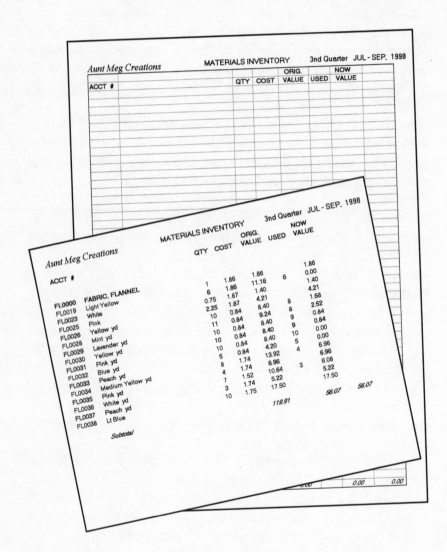

Aunt Meg Creations		MATERIALS INVENTORY			3nd Quarter JUL-SEP. 1998	
		QTY	COST	ORIG. VALUE	USED	NOW VALUE
ACCT #						

Aunt Meg Creations		MATERIALS INVENTORY	QTY	COST	ORIG. VALUE	USED	NOW VALUE
ACCT #							
FL0000	FABRIC, FLANNEL				1.86		1.86
FL0019	Light Yellow		1	1.86	1.86	6	0.00
FL0023	White		6	1.86	11.16		1.40
FL0025	Pink		0.75	1.87	1.40		4.21
FL0026	Yellow yd		2.25	1.87	4.21		1.68
FL0028	Mint yd		10	0.84	8.40	8	2.52
FL0029	Lavender yd		11	0.84	9.24	8	0.84
FL0030	Yellow yd		10	0.84	8.40	9	0.84
FL0031	Pink yd		10	0.84	8.40	9	0.00
FL0032	Blue yd		10	0.84	8.40	10	0.00
FL0033	Peach yd		10	0.84	4.20	5	6.96
FL0034	Medium Yellow yd		5	1.74	13.92	4	6.96
FL0035	Pink yd		8	1.74	6.96		6.08
FL0036	White yd		4	1.52	10.64	3	5.22
FL0037	Peach yd		7	1.74	5.22		17.50
FL0038	Lt Blue		3	1.74	17.50		
			10	1.75			56.07 56.07
	Subtotal				119.91		
					0.00		0.00 0.00

Materials Inventory Worksheet

Meg Sullivan's method for keeping track of her inventory of raw materials. "At a glance," she says, "I can tell how much I have, how much I've used, and how much it's worth."

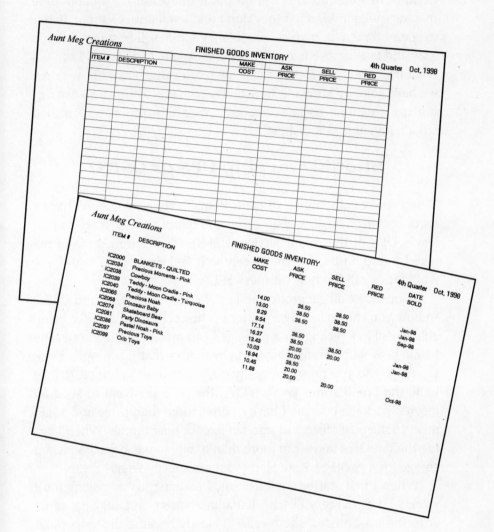

The first worksheet (blank):

Aunt Meg Creations

FINISHED GOODS INVENTORY

4th Quarter   Oct. 1998

ITEM #	DESCRIPTION	MAKE COST	ASK PRICE	SELL PRICE	RED PRICE

The second worksheet:

Aunt Meg Creations

FINISHED GOODS INVENTORY

4th Quarter   Oct. 1998

ITEM #	DESCRIPTION	MAKE COST	ASK PRICE	SELL PRICE	RED PRICE	DATE SOLD
IC2000	BLANKETS - QUILTED					
IC2034	Precious Moments - Pink					
IC2038	Cowboy	14.00	38.50			
IC2039	Teddy - Moon Cradle - Pink	13.00	38.50	38.50		
IC2040	Teddy - Moon Cradle - Turquoise	9.29	38.50	38.50		Jan-98
IC2065	Precious Noah	9.54		38.50		Jan-98
IC2068	Dinosaur Baby	17.14	38.50			Sep-98
IC2074	Skateboard Bear	16.37	38.50	38.50		
IC2081	Party Dinosaurs	13.43	20.00	20.00		Jan-98
IC2086	Pastel Noah - Pink	10.03	20.00			Jan-98
IC2097	Precious Toys	18.94	38.50			
IC2099	Crib Toys	10.45	20.00	20.00		Oct-98
		11.88				

Finished Goods Inventory Worksheet

Meg Sullivan's method for keeping track of her inventory of finished goods. "Once we use the raw materials, we assign a Finished Goods Inventory number to the finished product and attach a perforated price tag," she explains. "When we sell a product, we pull the bottom half of the tag, which becomes our record of sales, and the part that's left is another form of ongoing advertising for us."

ing price can be different.) I track when items are sold, looking for trends. For example, there is no point in spending valuable time making quilts in March if they don't really sell until October. Better to spend time making receiving blankets that sell best in April and May and take a nosedive in November. Again, at a glance, I can tell what my inventory cost is, what my retail value is, and how much we have sold. By knowing how much each piece cost me, I can figure my creations costs accurately." (See illustration of Finished Goods Inventory Worksheet.)

Should You Ship UPS or USPS?

When you're shipping art or crafts items to shops, you don't have a lot of options. The cost of air express is out of the question, so that leaves UPS or the postal service (USPS). (That reminds me of the joke I found on the Internet recently: If Fed Ex merged with UPS, would they call the new business FED UP?)

Seriously, we all get pretty good service from both UPS and USPS, so how you ship is largely a matter of choice. Personally, I like being able to call in a pickup for a package I can insure on the phone. The hassle now with sending anything by mail is that if it weighs more than a pound you must physically carry it to the post office, thanks to all the bomb scares we've had in the past. If I want to send an insured package by mail, I have to drive more than three and a half miles to the post office and stand in line for ten minutes. When I figure the time this takes, I'm more than happy to pay the UPS pickup charge for a package. Kate Harper knows exactly what I mean.

"When I first started my business, I couldn't justify paying for a weekly UPS charge, so I wheeled all my orders on a luggage carrier to the post office," she recalls. "I slowly became the 'unpopular customer' and no one wanted to stand behind me because I held up the line, mailing off twenty boxes or more. So then I thought I would be considerate and come early, right when the post office opened up, before it got too busy. Over time, however, the postal workers would see me coming and say, 'Let us just take this one lady before you since she just has a small request and then we'll do your boxes.' One day, the clerks kept asking to serve other customers first, even though I was first in line. This went on for about fifteen minutes, with them serving about ten people. I finally said to the clerk, 'Look, you've got to cut the cord somewhere; I did come early and waited in line like everyone else.' It was that day I knew I had to go with UPS, whatever the cost."

UPS Residential Pickup and Delivery Policies. UPS will pick up packages from any residential address, but the company has some special policies regarding pickups and deliveries to residences and businesses that you might want to check out on your end. For example, if you live in a remote area and normally order supplies that are shipped by UPS, it may take longer for you to receive them this way than if you used USPS. That's because it is the policy of UPS to hold parcels for up to three days after they have been scanned in at the carrier's pickup site if the recipient is twenty miles outside the normal delivery route. They say it's not economical to deliver to "remote addresses" until they have enough packages going to the same general vicinity.

UPS does guarantee that deliveries to *businesses* will be made anywhere in the U.S. within three days, but their definition of "business" excludes all home-based businesses, covering only those businesses operated outside of a home. Thus, to UPS, all home-based businesses, farms, and ranches are residential addresses, and they charge a dollar more for shipments to residences than to businesses. You can ship a parcel to a business name, but if the place looks like a residence to the UPS driver, you will get a charge-back on that delivery. This happens to Dodie Eisenhauer all the time. "Theoretically, I wholesale only to shops and stores," she says, "but I frequently find UPS charge-backs on my bill, so some of the 'shops' I'm shipping to aren't retail stores at all." Bob Gerdts ships everything by UPS and he has a sign in the window that says YES or NO, depending on whether he wants the truck to stop that day for a pickup (like the old days when the iceman came and the sign in the window told him how much ice to carry in).

Using Drop-Off Services. You pay much less when you set up an account for UPS to pick up at your home than when you drop off packages at an outside service. There is a weekly fee for UPS pickup service, of course, but the more packages you send in a week, the more economical the fee becomes. I've always hated to pay that fee for just one package, so recently when I had to ship a small package by UPS, I took it to our local Mail Boxes Etc. outlet, thinking I could save some money this way. Ha! The price seemed high, so I asked how much was shipping and how much was their service charge. "I don't know," the clerk replied, "it's all done automatically in the computer." Later at home, with my UPS chart in hand, I called and asked what it would cost to ship a three pound box to a particular zip code and compared the figure they gave me with the one on my chart. I found I could have saved a dollar by having UPS pick up the package at home. Remember: We *always* pay for "service": the question is *how much*? To save money, always ask.

Priority Mail. Shipping orders by Priority Mail is certainly an economical way to go if you don't mind taking packages to the post office. (The post office will also pick up packages at your door, but their pickup fee is higher than that of UPS.) In many cases, Priority Mail only costs a few pennies more than parcel post, yet it gets preferential treatment with delivery anywhere in the country usually within two or three days.

One big reason to ship Priority Mail is all the free tape, labels, cartons, tubes, and boxes USPS now provides. (See sidebar, "Free Shipping Cartons, Tape, and Labels.") Currently, you can ship up to two pounds for $3.20. For 35 cents extra, you can buy a green tracking label so you have proof of delivery (especially helpful to anyone who works on a drop-basis and never actually handles the products). The tracking label has a barcode number, and once you register that number on your shipping label, tracking can be done online at http://www.usps.gov or through the Post Office's toll-free number, 1-800-222-1811.

Determining correct postage for Priority Mail is easy because the rates for packages weighing up to five pounds do not vary by zone (distance). For greater weights, you can get a rate chart from your postal center or print out the charts on the USPS Web site. "Priority Mail is fine for uninsured lightweight packages," says Bob Gerdts, "but check the rates for an insured six-pound package, which will probably cost more than UPS."

Joann Haglund shipped by UPS for eleven years but now uses

Priority Mail exclusively. "Unless a package weighs over eight pounds, UPS costs are two to three times higher than Priority Mail rates," she says. "I ship a lot of packages to individual buyers that weigh less than two pounds, so I simply charge a flat fee of $5 shipping and handling for all these packages. For just $4.40, I can send that package by Priority Mail, insure it, and get a confirmation of delivery—with 60 cents left over to cover my labor in packing it."

Shipping Boxes

Craftspeople who are into recycling, or who simply lack funds to buy custom-designed boxes, often get boxes from local stores. Nancy Jaekel, for instance, ships everything using recycled packing materials she gets from a gift shop down the road, and a grocery store saves all their heavy-duty cardboard wine boxes for her. "Stores are only too glad to get rid of these materials," she says, "because it costs them time and money to break down boxes and have this 'trash' hauled away."

If you do a lot of shipping, sooner or later you may want to upgrade your professional image by shipping in boxes made to order. (Box manufacturers are everywhere; check your Yellow Pages or the Internet or the *Thomas Register* for contact info.) Dodie Eisenhauer orders a variety of boxes from Southeast Missouri Box Company, which makes them to her particular specs (size and weight of cardboard) and prints her name and address on them. "Since my items are lightweight, I sometimes double-box shipments when I'm sending samples to market or an order with a high dollar value. To do this, I ordered some boxes one-inch smaller all around so they would fit inside one another to give me a double-weight box."

To save money on boxes, Dodie says you should always ask the manufacturer if he has any overruns or boxes with minor flaws. "My oversize boxes cost two or three dollars each, but I have often bought a supply of miscellaneous smaller boxes for as little as thirty-five cents a box," she says.

Free Shipping Cartons, Tape, and Labels

"Shipping supplies and packaging materials are a major expense for me, so if I can cut corners on boxes, I will," says Gail Platts. "The Post Office's site on the Internet is a mailer's mecca for supplies, and all are free. (Now we know where our stamp money is going.) You wouldn't believe the shipping boxes I now have 'in stock.' Not to mention free address labels, envelopes, stickers, and tape."

Gail particularly likes the 200-pound weight Priority Mail boxes. "They're fabulous for shipping," she says. If you can't get them from your local post office, you can order them online or from the toll-free number mentioned earlier. Except for video boxes, which are shipped in quantities of fifty, boxes are packed twenty-five to a carton. Here are the different-sized boxes currently available:

Large Priority Mail box, 12¼ x 15½ x 3"
Medium Priority Mail Box: 11¼ x 14 x 2¼"
Box #4, 7 x 7 x 6¼"
Box #7, 12 x 8 x 12"

Chris Gustin's shipping supplies closet. "The post office gets 99% of my business because of Priority Mail and the great supplies it provides," says Chris. "Boxes of several sizes, packing labels, Tyvex and padded envelopes, tape and tubs are all free on request."

Figuring Shipping and Handling Costs

"The buyer always pay shipping," says Joann Hagland, "and shipping always includes packing and related supplies—plus the cost of your time to pack the order. It's how you quote the cost that makes the difference. You can quote shipping and handling as a percentage of the order, depending on actual costs by distance and weight, or build them into your wholesale prices and offer free shipping."

"According to an article in a trade magazine," says potter Emily Pearlman, "many retailers prefer that packing and shipping charges be built into the wholesale price. Recently when I got a request from one of my customers for prices that included shipping and handling charges, I simply added 10 percent to all the prices on my wholesale list and sent it to her."

Some sellers build all their shipping and handling charges into their wholesale prices and offer free shipping. Of course the shipping isn't "free" and retailers know it, but when everyone else is charging for shipping and you aren't, that gives you an edge on the competition. It's an idea worth considering.

Handling Charges. It's a mistake to not charge for handling. "Handling charges" include not only boxes, tape, labels, bubble wrap, popcorn, corrugated paper, etc., but the time it takes you, or one of your employees, to pack an order. Although some sellers charge only 5 percent for shipping and handling, Joann Haglund says that's not nearly enough. "I charge between 9 and 11 percent," she says, "using 9 percent for lighter shipments and 11 percent for heavier ones."

Emily Pearlman came up with her 10-percent figure for shipping and handling by first figuring where she routinely shipped orders, and what an average box weighed. "Most of my shipping is within fairly close zones and an average box weighs 20 pounds, so it was easy to come up with a figure that covered my costs. If I ship a package to the West Coast, I may lose a dollar, but I make it up on a package sent to Connecticut."

For her shipping and handling figure, Rita O'Hara charges an average of just 5 percent of the wholesale order, but each order is figured individually and adjustments are made where necessary. "You have to take into account the weight of the product," she says. "The weight of my Stonewares products to dollar value is very small, so I might be able to ship an order valued at $100 for a UPS charge of $4. Five percent ($5) wouldn't cover the cost of the boxes and bubble wrap I use, so I would probably adjust the shipping charges to $8 total. Recently when I had to ship a $500 order by 2nd-day air, the actual shipping cost was $28, but I charged them $40 for shipping because the order took time to pack, went out in six boxes, and used a lot of bubble wrap."

Dodie Eisenhauer considers her handling costs as part of her overhead and works them into her wholesale prices accordingly. But because there is some room for error here, she also tacks on a dollar or two to the actual shipping charge (depending on whether the box is regular or oversized). She has keyed in all the UPS rates for different sizes and weights of boxes, so she just punches in a preassigned code number to get the right shipping charge to add to the invoice as it is being prepared.

Dodie points out that UPS has a Hundred-Weight option for multiple box shipments to the same address. "You have to ship at least 200 pounds to the same address, and they charge you so much per hundred pounds," she says, adding that her customers appreciate the fact that she ships orders in oversize boxes. "They are easier for us to pack and the rates are more economical for the customer, who doesn't have to pay the extra cost of receiving several small boxes."

Remember: UPS has a minimum charge per package and, for boxes over a certain size, you must pay their 30-pound rate. "UPS also has a diabolical dimensional charge," says Phillippa Lack. "If your package is a bolt of fabric that is fifty-five inches long, they will charge you $5 to ship, plus $5.60 for the 'dimension.'" Thus, to save money on shipping, you need to take all these different rates into consideration since they could affect the way you pack and ship your products. Back in Chapter Six, you may recall my mention of how Emily Pearlman used her Quicken software to categorize and graph her pottery-making expenses. By doing a computer

COD Shipments

Shipping COD (collect, or cash, on delivery) to first-time buyers has become standard policy in the crafts industry. While this can be a great solution for how to deal with customers you feel uncomfortable about invoicing, it is not without problems. Some crafters have a policy that first orders from all new accounts must be shipped COD, but others specify "No CODs" on their order form because they don't want the hassles involved with such orders.

"Sometimes you ship COD and get the package back, which means you're out the shipping charges," explains a professional crafter who often ships COD to questionable wholesale buyers. To avoid problems, she always calls the customer before shipping an order COD. "I tell them it's ready, give them the amount they need to have on hand, and ask them if it's okay to ship today."

This is a good idea for accounts you know, but this method leaves you at risk if you're dealing with a new customer whose check might bounce, or one of the con artists that are currently running COD scams at craft fairs. Here, the only way to protect yourself is to check the box on the COD form that says you will accept "Cash or Money Order Only." (Both UPS and the Postal Service will accept cash, but the post office won't handle any COD package valued at more than $600.) Your customer, not you, should pay the extra amount involved in sending the order COD, and some sellers add a note to this effect on their price list and order form. (Note: UPS will collect these charges for you, but if you ship by mail, the post office will collect only for the value of the goods in the box, not for postage or COD charges.)

Bernard Kamoroff, CPA, is the author and publisher of *Small Time Operator* (Bell Springs Publishing). Stung by COD con artists in the past, he offers this advice to others: "Be suspicious of large orders from unknown businesses,

continued on following page

continued from previous page

from businesses that don't have preprinted letterheads and purchase orders, and from businesses that don't list phone numbers. We always call Directory Assistance to see if a business is listed. And, like the old gambler's warning, we never ship more books than we can afford to lose. When you are dealing with hustlers, collection threats and demanding letters never work. Those people just laugh at you."

Special Tip: If a customer asks you to send a shipment COD and it is packed in more than one carton or box, be sure to put a COD tag on each carton. A reader reported that a customer who ordered five cases of products returned the one case bearing her COD tag marked "delivery refused" but kept the other four cases and never paid for them.

from The Crafts Business Answer Book & Resource Guide, Barbara Brabec, (M. Evans).

analysis of her shipping expenses, she learned it would cost her less to ship two items in a larger box and pay for shipping at the 30-pound rate (even though the package weighed only 2 to 25 pounds), than it would to ship the same merchandise in two smaller boxes.

Insurance. UPS automatically offers $100 worth of insurance, but in talking to several craftspeople, I find that few of them ever insure a shipment beyond that amount. "I've had so little damage through the years that I can't justify this extra expense," says Dodie Eisenhauer. "And besides, it has been my experience that UPS is hesitant to pay claims, frequently claiming the package was not packed properly to begin with."

Dodie's products are lightweight, but what about heavy items? Potter Emily Pearlman told me she doesn't insure her UPS shipments either. "First, I get very little breakage to begin with, and it's unlikely that a whole box of items would ever be destroyed because

I pack everything so carefully. Items are wrapped in bubble wrap (small bubbles) with corrugated cardboard around that; then they are placed in a large box with a lot of 'popcorn.' The trick is to make sure what you pack stays away from the sides of the box. Things that touch in the middle aren't a problem, however."

COD Shipments. A crafter asks: "When a customer requests an order be sent COD, do you add the COD charges on top of the regular cost of postage?" Whereas the cost of insurance on an order is for the shipper's protection, COD charges are the result of special service given to a customer, and should be included in the total shipping costs for the order. (See sidebar, "COD Shipments," for more information on this topic.)

This chapter isn't exactly a definitive guide to buying supplies and figuring shipping and handling costs, but I think you'll agree it contains some valuable tips—any one of which could save you a bundle and immediately put you on the road to greater profits.

HELPFUL RESOURCES

UPS: 1-800-PICK-UPS. Web site: www.ups.com
USPS: 1-800-222-1811. Web site: www.usps.gov

Trade Magazines

Craft Supply Magazine. Krause Publications, Inc., 700 East State Street, Iola, WI 54990-0001. 1-800-258-0929. Web site: www.krause.com. Subscription includes annual directory issue of hundreds of sources for wholesale craft supplies.

Craftrends/Sew Business, Primedia Special Interest Publications, Inc., 2 News Plaza, Box 1790, Peoria, IL 61656. 770-497-1500. Web site: www.craftrends.com. Subscription includes valuable annual directory of suppliers.

The Gift & Decorative Accessory Buyer's Guide. Gifts & Decorative Accessories, 51 Madison Avenue, New York, NY 10010. Annual directory that lists some 30,000 manufacturers, importers, and distributors serving the gift industry; with sources for manufacturing and assembling materials.

Label Suppliers

The Drawing Board (laser/ink jet, mailing, and advertising labels) 1-800-527-9530.

Desktop Labels (for laser, ink jet, and copier machines) 1-800 241-9730.

Kenco Label Sales, 6655 North Sidney Pl. Milwaukee, WI 53209. 1-800-236-1021 (in Wisconsin); 1-800-537-3336 (national).

Chapter Thirteen

Sharpening Your Marketing Skills

||||||||||||||||||||||||||||||||||||||||||||||||||||||

A small business cannot afford to take the shotgun approach to marketing today. We must narrow our focus, define our target market and our customer, and center our marketing efforts on a specific niche or market segment.

—BARBARA ARENA, MANAGING DIRECTOR,
NATIONAL CRAFT ASSOCIATION

To survive in business, you must stay current with your industry and the people in it, know what's new, what's changing, what's working, what isn't, and why. You may have an edge on the competition now, but the picture could change at any moment. What do you do when you find yourself swimming upstream in the face of increasing competition and greater sales resistance on the part of buyers? The answer is simple: you have to become a better marketer.

Since this is a business management book and not a marketing guide, I can't begin to discuss the specifics of selling products and services in this book; I do, however, want to give you some general marketing advice that is closely related to both the design process and the overall management of your business. *Without spending a dime for advertising,* you can dramatically increase both sales and profits simply by learning how to

▸▸ do simple market research,
▸▸ identify consumer benefits that sell products,
▸▸ compete with imports,
▸▸ sell more products in hard economic times, and
▸▸ generate more interest in your products.

How To Do Market Research

Do you have a great idea for a new product? Will anyone buy it? How should you price it? The best way to get answers to these questions before you lay out a lot of time and money making products that might not sell is to do some market research.

Few craftspeople do any market research before venturing out to sell their wares. Most beginners, and many longtime craft show sellers as well, simply make things they want to make, offer them for sale, and hope people will buy. That may be okay if your instinct about what's likely to sell is finely tuned; if not, you could lose a substantial investment of time and materials if you create a large inventory of products you can't sell. Most sellers get a handle on the market for their work simply by browsing shows and networking with other sellers, but here are several other things you can do to get market research information:

Wear it and Check Response. Joyce Birchler makes a whimsical line of stained glass jewelry. She test-markets all her new designs simply by wearing them, a strategy that would work for anyone who makes any kind of wearable item. "Every time I design a new piece, I wear it everywhere—to the bank, the grocery store, the post office—and I count how many people (if any) mention it. If someone says, 'I like your pin,' I count that as a maybe. But if more than one person asks me where I got the pin, it's a 'go' and I add it to my line."

Ask Friends, Family or Customers for Comments. "Because I sell and teach locally, I often use my friends and students as guinea pigs for new products," says crafter/teacher Jana Gallagher. "When I make something new, I put it on display in my classroom for everyone to see. It's a good indicator to me when folks ask if I'm going to teach a class for that particular item."

"I test-market new pieces with my old and established customers to see if they like it," says Joyce Roark, who makes gold-filled jewelry with semiprecious stones. "I also have my relatives wear the jewelry where they live and get reactions from their friends. I usually make only a few pieces to try out. If it looks like a piece will do well, I go into production with it. Otherwise I drop it."

"Having a thirteen-year-old daughter to ask what her age group is interested in helps a bunch," adds potter Kim Marie.

Check Price and Functionality. It's easier to set prices if you know what "the going prices" are for items similar to yours, so start a pricing reference file or scrapbook. Check newsstand magazines that showcase American handcrafts and clip ads for products similar to yours. Add descriptive listings from mail-order gift catalogs. Record what others are charging for your type of products at fairs, malls, and gift shops.

Dodie Eisenhauer produces a unique line of gifts made from screen wire. Several years ago when she introduced her wire mesh bows (door ornaments, now one of her most popular items), she began her market research by first figuring out how long it would take to produce bows of varying sizes (three to twenty inches) and how they would have to be priced to generate a good profit. "Then I checked my prices against the price range people normally pay for products with this kind of function," she says. "People hang fairly expensive wreaths on a door, so when I knew my prices were right for my market, I introduced the item at a trade show."

If you can't get the price you need on a particular product, don't stop making it, just look for a new market for it. The same item offered at different fairs or shops across the country might sell at a much higher price, depending on the economy of the area, the sophistication of buyers, and the way the product is presented to them.

Test It at Market. "If your new product is a totally original idea—nothing like it anywhere—you just have to take it to market and see what kind of reaction you get," Dodie adds. "At a wholesale market, you only need one or two samples, so I'm never out much by  introducing a new product. If a new product sells at a show, it's a success. If it gets only interest, I figure it has potential and may keep it in my line for a couple of years. Sometimes you have to look for a while to find the right market for a particular product."

Bob Gerdts, an egg-art artisan, says he usually takes one or two pieces to a show to see whether they sell or not. To test her new jewelry pieces, Joyce Birchler makes at least a dozen pieces for a retail show. "If I sell more than half, I go into full production with the piece," she says. "Since location and time of year have a lot to do with sales, I'll sometimes give a piece a few shows to see if it creates any interest."

Patricia Kutza, a fashion and home-dec designer of one-of-a-kind and limited-edition neckwear, says trade and craft shows are good divining rods for gauging market appeal, but relying on this type of marketing is tricky since what sells at one type of show—especially Christmas-focused shows—may not sell that well any other time of year. "People buy stuff at Christmas time that they might not take a second look at another time of year," she notes.

American tole artist Joann Haglund tries new items on eBay, an Internet auction site. "If a new item sells well over a certain period of time, it goes into limited production for the two regional shows I do each year," she explains. "And it also stays on eBay as a recurring item."

Woodturner Derek Andrews simply offers new products in his shop during the summer tourist season and at shows in November. "I generally find that everything I make sells eventually, so nothing is lost," he says.

Talk to Your Buyers or Sales Reps. Greeting card manufacturer Kate Harper works with more than sixty sales reps, whom she relies on for advice on new products. "First I run an idea by a few sales reps to see if I'm out-to-lunch (artist temporary insanity)," she says. "Then I manufacture a small quantity and test-market them with a few reps. If they sell through and there are reorders in a reasonable time, that's a good sign. It's also good to test it out on just a few reps because you may find manufacturing the item just isn't the cup of tea you thought it would be. There are always snags that have to be worked out. Better to goof with a couple of reps, rather than all of them."

Listen and Observe. You can get instant feedback on consumer preferences simply by listening to people who browse your booth at a show and noticing when they make statements such as, "I wish you had this in a different color." When a prospective buyer walks into Dodie Eisenhauer's wholesale booth, she walks around with them, asking questions about their shop and the kind of merchandise they carry. "I get a lot of marketing insight in these conversations," she says.

"Most of my product lines have evolved from customer feedback," says Patricia Kutza. "For example, a Victorian-style brooch of mine was seen by a customer in a Victorian-era store. The customer remarked that it would look great enlarged as a decorative accessory. The store owners then took that idea a step further and suggested I try making it in the style of a Victorian picture hanger. And that's how my line of picture hangers, Hanging by a Thread, was born."

"I present new products in a small number at a show," says printmaker Chris Noah. "If they are snapped up, I'll try some more in another show. I also listen very intently to what customers say, especially criticism. I learn much more from good criticism than anything else. When the person is right, it can be very humbling, but you get over it, then look back and see how much you've grown."

Do Online Research. "Craftspeople need to be 'Net-savvy,' Patricia Kutza emphasizes. "I've gained a lot of marketing insight simply by typing in certain words on a search engine and visiting the sites that come up on the list."

Once you have a Web site of your own, doing market research is both easy and profitable, says Sue Johnson. She diversified her Gramma's Graphics, Inc., business by writing and publishing *Grandloving: Making*

Grandloving:
Making Memories with Your Grandchildren

Welcome to grandparenting!

Grandloving will help you grow closer to your grandchildren with...

200 inexpensive, fun activities

Reminders about child development

Ideas from 300 families worldwide

Sue Johnson's book flyer, which she designed on computer and prints in color as needed.

Memories with Your Grandchildren and giving it publicity on the Internet. "We've gained invaluable market research information simply by encouraging Web visitors to sign in and fill out a brief questionnaire. Their responses have shown us that the market for our book is much broader than we originally thought. We assumed that grandparents would be our primary buyers, and we have confirmation that they are buying the book not only for themselves but as gifts for other grandparent friends. But we've also learned that young parents are just as eager to buy the book as a gift for their parents and in-laws. A surprising market has been day care, nursery school, and elementary school teachers who are finding the activities in the book very helpful."

Read Trade Magazines. Illustrator-artist Pamela Spinazzola spent two years doing market research before introducing her line of baby and wedding commemorative gifts to the wholesale marketplace in 1986. "I went to stores and shows, talked to buyers and sales reps at merchandise marts, and read trade magazines to gain an understanding of the giftwares industry," she says. "Two of the best trade magazines are *Giftware News* and *Gifts & Decorative Accessories.* In both magazines every month there is feedback from retailers as to what they're looking for and how things are selling in their shops. Particularly helpful is their coverage of trends (what store buyers are looking for), along with colors that will be in style in the coming year. "

As you can see, there are many ways to gather market research information, and the time you spend doing this work is likely to make all the difference in your ability to compete in today's ever-changing marketplace.

Identifying and Marketing Product Benefits

Long before that new product of yours is ready for the marketplace, you should be planning how you're going to package it, promote, advertise, and sell it—always with customer benefits in mind.

For example, when I began the research for this book, I asked my book contributors how many years' experience they had in business

Watch the Marketplace and the Competition

Sometimes you can market till you're blue in the face, and the results just aren't there because of changes in the marketplace. Sue Brown has had a successful rubber stamp business (selling her own designs and making her own stamps) for several years, but business declined steadily in 1998.

"Initially, I was under the false impression that maybe it was our fault," she says. "I tried so many times to come up with marketing plans to boost sales and found they weren't working. Previously, when I'd offered the same specials to customers, I had gotten a good response. But now they aren't working. My regular customers aren't even ordering like they used to. This tells me that our so-called good economy isn't so great after all. Stores have made fewer purchases, too, which tells me the stores aren't doing so well, either.

"One thing that has directly affected our business is the increase in competition. When I first started my business in 1986, there were few rubber stamp companies. Whereas there used to be forty or fifty advertisers advertising in the rubber stamp magazines, now there are more than 200."

Note: This is important marketing insight for those of you who have been thinking about selling your designs in the form of rubber stamps. Sue told me about one of her former customers who used to order $10,000 worth of stamps a year. She decided to go into the business herself but, after a year or so, stopped advertising because she wasn't getting sufficient response anymore."

because I knew I could use the answer to this question as a marketing benefit when promoting my book. That is, I could tell readers that I wasn't just offering them a book containing my advice, but a book filled with the business and marketing wisdom of many individuals who, collectively, have more than *twelve hundred years of business experience!*

In commenting on this point, publisher Betty Chypre said, "Of course you need this info! I really have to learn to look beyond the obvious to see the promotional and marketing value behind it all. Facts are facts, but it's what you make of them, isn't it? I believe this is a learned skill—this awareness of the value of facts and how to use them to benefit a project—and you can learn it simply by being more aware."

She's right. The essence of marketing or selling anything you make, or any service you provide, is to offer both product and service in such a way that prospective buyers see you as the answer to one or more of their special needs or problems. The more benefits you offer, the higher the price you can get. Remember this: people don't buy products, per se; they buy solutions to a problem or some other thing they need. As one astute marketer put it, people don't buy electric drills because they want a drill; they buy drills because they want *holes*. They don't buy a mousetrap because they want a trap; they buy a mousetrap because they *don't* want mice.

With so many handcrafted products on the market today, you

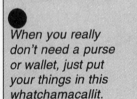

● *When you really don't need a purse or wallet, just put your things in this whatchamacallit.* *Made in the USA, One at a Time* **HOUSE OF THREADS & WOOD INC.**	●*Cell Phone Holder* • Protects portable, two-way or cellular phones • Use inside car or briefcase, outside when gardening, biking, golfing • Top strap prevents phone from falling out • Removable webbed belt for waist or shoulder use • Also for bottled water *Made in the USA, One at a Time* **HOUSE OF THREADS & WOOD INC.**	● **Memo Book** • More reliable than your memory • Privacy cover keeps your notes clean (and secret) • Room to store a pen or business cards • Small enough for purse, briefcase, pocket HOUSE OF THREADS & WOOD

These hang tags, used by Pat Endicott on her House of Threads & Wood products, tell buyers how to use her products. (Notice her emphasis on the consumer benefits of each product.) "I make no mention of city, state, or my geographical area (the Ozarks) on my tags because my buyers have told me they want their customers to think all their products are locally made. They have also confirmed that they like my simple tags (black ink on white or colored paper) better than the fancy and more expensive two-color tags I used to use."

have to give your prospective buyers a *reason* to buy your products. While some people buy art for art's sake alone, few buy handcrafts just because they are handmade. Regardless of whether you sell art, crafts, or other handmade products, you will always sell *more* of what you make if you identify and market the benefits in your products. They need to be emphasized in all your advertising and printed materials, especially on hang tags. (See illustration.)

Product benefits can also be conveyed in conversations with retailers and craft fair shoppers alike. Since buyers cannot see the intangible benefits of your products, you must identify them and bring them to buyers' attention. Here's how Howard and Ruthann Broman of Real Rose Jewelry do this at a show. As they draw people into their booth, they begin to chat, saying something like, "These are real roses we grow in Oregon." At that point, Howard says, people either walk on or say, "Oh, really?" And then he emphasizes a product benefit, such as, "These dried flowers will never ever fall apart."

By then, the buyer is hooked, he says. "You've got to tell prospective buyers why your product is great and why they can't live another day without it. But selling is the last thing most artisans want to do because they see it as being pushy or bragging."

If a prospective buyer were to look at your work and ask, "Why should I buy this? How can I use it? What does it cost so much?" what would you say in response?

"My small bolt people sculptures look great on a desk," says Steve Appel, "and some items are functional as well (cardholders, paperweights, etc.). "My advertising material states that 'Bolt People make perfect gifts that people will go nuts (and bolts) over.' Sometimes I mention that my soccer players make a good present for the soccer coach because moms buy that kind of stuff all the time. I think my product sells because people have

APPEL'S BOLT PEOPLE
www.boltpeople.com

605 Flora St.
Prescott, AZ. 86301

Phone: (520) • 445•3373
Fax: (520)•776•7704
boltpeople@yahoo.com

Steve Appel

never seen anything like it before, and because it can be carried away right then and there."

"The benefits of my greeting cards are a moment of sanity in a crazy world," says Kate Harper. "People hang my quotes up in their offices as a meditative reminder. They buy the product because either it makes them laugh, they know someone who would use it, or they are deeply touched by a truism. Many people buy my cards for themselves."

Craftspeople must continually contend with competition from imports, so always point out benefits in your product that are missing in cheap imports. "Many people look at my bottle stoppers and think they will break with the first use because cheap imports are usually made by gluing a cork to a piece of ceramic," says Derek Andrews. "I explain to these customers that the cork on my stopper is connected to the body by a dowel, and they are extremely strong-a benefit that often sells the product."

"What sells my line of art prints is its individuality," says Deb Otto. "In developing it, I looked within my own interests in painting, decorating, and my love for history, then tried to use my own unique style as I painted each original. From my teapot painting to my stretched-out snowman, my style unites the line and suggests to the buyer that if they like my style, they can get it only from me."

If your products are truly unique, be sure to emphasize this in all your promotions. "I strive to make items buyers can't find anywhere else," says Tabitha Haggie. "If I make a particular snowman and find that other crafters at a show are making one similar to mine, I eliminate that item from my line. As a result, many of my customers tell me.'I should buy this because I'm not likely to find it elsewhere.'"

"The most important aspect of my work is the signature on the base," says Joann Haglund. "I personally paint and sign everything that goes out the door. Even the under-$10 items carry my signature, and customers are looking for that. They know it's not an import (or a buy-sell item, as it is now commonly called)."

Art often sends its own message. Chris Noah realizes that two of her prints, titled 'The Fifth Day' and 'The Farm,' communicate love of nature, the earth, a simpler way of life and daily spiritual reflection. "There is also a whimsical quality people respond to," she says. "The biggest appeal, reported to me by customers, is that my pictures make them feel good. A simple answer, but an important one."

How to Compete with Imports

Earlier I mentioned the necessity of sometimes having to change the kind of products you make and sell. One thing that is prompting many to do this is the problem of imports, something that has been a problem since the '60s and is getting worse now that foreign imports are of a higher quality.

"Crafters rack their brains to come up with original products only to see something similar at Wal-Mart months later after it has been cheaply mass-produced and imported," says Pat Endicott. "Only a small percentage of shoppers understand and are willing to pay for handcrafted USA-made goods. We have to continue to educate them. In the fabric media, the public has been tricked by handcrafted hang tags on imported cheap goods. Shows, advertising, travel, the cost of raw materials—all seem to be increasing, and the crafter-manufacturer can't afford to pass these costs on."

A discouraging trend in craft fairs is that many show promoters are letting in exhibitors who do not make all the products they sell, or even offer handmade products by others. In fact, many are importing items and reselling them at craft fairs while some are simply buying or taking on consignment the handcrafts of other sellers and offering them in their booths at a show. This "buy-sell" problem is causing a lot of problems in the craft fair community, but it is not something most sellers can do anything about. As Nancy Jaekel puts it, "The promoters know the products are imported. They just don't want that fact acknowledged. I think most craft shows today should simply be billed as retail shows. Actually, there is nothing wrong with buying and selling—I've been tempted to buy and sell some products myself. The bottom line is *profit*. Shows just need to be billed or promoted right."

In other words, if a show bills itself as selling nothing but handcrafts made by exhibitors, that should be what is offered. If it's not, what are you going to do about it? Sue? No, most likely, you just won't enter that show again . . . unless you actually made good money there—and, if you did, then perhaps you shouldn't complain. Often, the craftspeople who are making the most noise about this problem are the ones who aren't selling well and are jealous of the business others are doing.

"The economics in our profession are changing, and the primary reason is imported arts and crafts," Howard Broman stated in his discussion list on the Internet. "Once of very low quality, many imports are now well-made from excellent designs worked out in this country. Importers of offshore arts and crafts are becoming very knowledgeable about the American market and are demanding that the independent artisans with whom they trade raise the general quality of their work."

As Howard illustrates, this is serious competition. To compete, he believes craftspeople must:

» develop a fantastic widget to pay the bills,
» subcontract large portions of work that can be more efficiently done by another artisan,
» offer to do work for other artisans,
» investigate mass-production techniques,
» lower overhead costs, and
» be more careful to purchase quality materials at the best price.

"Competition is what makes this country great," Howard adds. "Onezys and twozys are out for production artisans. Deal with it. It's simply how it is. Instead of worrying whether something was imported or made in this country, dig deeper into the making of a trend."

Adds Susan Gearing: "As our profession matures, the audience for our products becomes more sophisticated, resulting in increased competition. Formerly, nearly anything handmade sold; currently, you have to have an innovative, useful product to capture a large market. The public is becoming more careful regarding its spending—we boomers already have lots of goods and are putting kids through college and saving for retirement. If we can provide certain gift/personal/home-decorating needs that give good value, then sales will continue to climb."

On Finding Your Niche

"The circuit is always in a state of change," says Bill Mason, a contemporary jewelry artist. "The savvy craftsperson who wants to make money must observe what is selling and at what price and if the venue will support their particular creation; *or*, whether they need to adjust what they are marketing to suit the audience and their expectations, needs, desires, whims, and wants."

Bill says juried fairs in his area (Semmes, Alabama) are considered very good if one does $1,000 in a three-day weekend show, but he knows some people who do that much per day, consistently, at the local flea market with a booth fee of $30 for two days.

"No, they don't create or make what they sell, they merely sell what sells," he says. "What so many craftspeople don't seem to realize is that they are competing with a global economy. We are all enjoying the fruits of the cheap world labor that is supplying us with raw materials, parts, finishes, tools, clothes, foods, etc. And we all have to find our own niche and then cultivate it if we are to succeed in business."

Show promoter Anita Means believes her business is growing because she has found a niche that needed to be filled with high-quality craft shows in outdoor park settings. "My commitment to quality craftspeople, plus the extras like live music and decorations, make my shows different from most shows in my area (Monmouth County, New Jersey). My reputation as a promoter is good, so I have started to get word-of-mouth advertising among craftspeople and customers for presenting a fun, quality craft event. The process of getting to this point has been mixed with major setbacks and challenges, but throughout it all, I maintained my focus and conviction that I knew it could work."

Selling in Hard Times

Historically, crafts have fared rather well in recessionary times, the logic being that consumers who can't afford new houses, cars, furs, and the like can at least indulge themselves with moderately expensive art and craft works. But in times when too many people are struggling to meet daily living expenses—people who may also be worried about job loss or already unemployed—artists and craftspeople are going to lose sales, no question about it.

If people buy crafts at all in hard economic times, they are usually looking for something small and inexpensive. The next recession may be just around the corner, so now is a good time to reflect on the marketing strategies that have worked for professional artists and craftspeople in previous recessions. To survive, they had to make changes of one kind or another. New markets had to be explored along with ways to lower the costs of reaching new buyers. Cutting raw material costs and creating different products for sale were strategies used by many.

When the marketplace becomes sluggish, put your emphasis on products in the following categories, which seem to sell consistently in both good and bad economic times:

- ➤➤ functional items people can use in their daily lives,
- ➤➤ gift items that answer specific needs,
- ➤➤ decorative accessories and furnishings,
- ➤➤ collectibles and other nostalgic items,
- ➤➤ garments, jewelry, and other fashion accessories, and
- ➤➤ personalized items.

Now look at this list of products in a different way, remembering earlier discussions about focusing on consumer benefits. To sell more of what you make:

1. Make It Practical. When money is tight, buyers may be looking for crafts that offer both beauty and practicality. Handcrafted products with a functional use will sell even better if they also (1) offer a timesaving or organizational benefit; (2) make a dreary job more fun; (3) elicit feelings of nostalgia; or (4) make one smile.

2. Make It a Gift. Even when there is little money for luxuries, people need gift items, and they will buy art or crafts that solve specific gift-giving needs for such occasions as birthdays, anniversaries, graduation, a housewarming or baby shower, Valentine's Day, Mother's Day, Father's Day, Christmas, and so on. When such products can also be personalized in some way, their value increases.

3. Make It Decorative. Some people derive great satisfaction from buying inexpensive art or decorative accessories when they don't have money for larger purchases. They may not be able to afford that $150 painting or piece of furniture, but they can still go home from a crafts fair feeling good because they bought something they liked "for just $20" (which, by the way, is now the amount of money most people will throw away on almost anything).

4. Make It Collectible. Buyers tend to buy on impulse whenever they find something that strikes a nostalgic chord or satisfies a longing of the heart. And make no mistake about it, these are marketable benefits.

5. Make It Wearable. Rich or poor, we all need clothing, and we all want to look as good as possible. Sellers who offer handmade garments, designer jewelry, and related accessories need to emphasize how their products make people *feel*. People naturally want to feel more attractive, and they enjoy wearing clothing and accessories that make them stand out in a crowd (the benefit). Even today's work-at-homers buy designer jeans, humorous sweatshirts, and handmade sandals both for comfort and because they want to look good in their private environment.

6. Make It Personal. Creature comforts must be filled even when there is less money. We must all eat, clothe ourselves, take care of the children, manage our homes, buy occasional gifts, etc. Therefore, products that meet such practical needs *while also satisfying an inner personal need* will sell with regularity in both good and bad economic times.

"If we run into problems selling, we need to analyze the market closely," says woodturner Derek Andrews. "Then we must use our creative talents to make our current product more marketable (what the customer wants, or can be persuaded to want), or simply design new products. It's also a good idea to have a range of products that appeal to a wide clientele, so if the market trend shifts, you can cope. I have products that would suit gardeners, cooks, animal lovers, home decorators, wine drinkers, flower arrangers, left-handed people, lovers of wood, corporate buyers, young people, old people, etc. I didn't set out to do this initially; it just happened, and has paid off. It is much easier to find customers if you don't have to search out a very specialized customer niche."

"When you come right down to it, arts and crafts are something people can live without," adds Cheryl Eaton. "Often, what we are really selling are things that touch people's fancy, get into their memory banks, call up fond memories or hopes for the future,

Bundle Your Products!

In helping sewing machine dealers plan for the seminars she gives, Mary Mulari has observed how bundling merchandise makes a bigger price-point sale and also makes it easier for customers to pick up one of everything.

"Take my ten sewing books, for example," she says. "They're sold individually at my seminars, but they're also bundled together, tied with a pretty ribbon, and sold as a set, often at a discounted price. I'm always amazed by the number of students who pick up the whole bundle, which usually sells for $100 and over. We've done bundling also with a variety of stabilizers for sewing and also fusible products. They can simply be grouped together in a plastic Ziplock bag. If I talk about the products, they'll generally sell and a bundle of them is attractive and easy to buy. This technique can work with all kinds of items, I think, as long as there's some relationship between the items."

Craftspeople could apply this concept to items in their line that have a natural "go-together" appeal. Put a couple of them in an appropriate container and perhaps add one or two inexpensive commercial items that relate to your products-and suddenly you've got an impressive gift basket.

touch the imaginary, or take us to 'a Calgon moment.' In times of high stress, problems, or depressions, people often look backward to a time they remember as being safer, more fun, more comfortable, like the styles of the '60s and '70s—old-timey stuff, old shows, cast iron skillets. In short, we can either think and grow rich, or complain and go bankrupt." (See Sidebar, "What You Have in Common with Wal-Mart.)

Ways to Generate More Interest in Your Products

The following things are so easy to do and cost only pennies to implement, yet few artists and craftspeople bother to do them. So if you want to get ahead of your competition, simply:

Name Your Products. A name gives a product personality, which in turn increases its salability. In developing new products, give both your individual products and product lines names of their own. Have fun with words, and use humor whenever possible or appropriate. Neckwear designer Patricia Kutza has garnered considerably media attention for her Whatknots, a line of fabric apparel and accessories. Her products bear such names such as PickPockets, Hanging by a Thread, and Pressing Matters, while her press releases have titles such as "The Way We Wear" (playing, of course, on a familiar movie) and "Fit to be Tied."

"For maximum success," Patricia emphasizes, "follow the 3 Cs: *Concentrate* on the aspect of your business you feel most passionate about; *Communicate* this passion to your customers; and *Cultivate* these customers, for they will spread that passion and help you build your client base."

Sign Your Products and Use Hang Tags. What's the sales value of a hang tag? Shortly after she began attaching hang tags to her seashell music boxes, a crafter reported that she received over $2,000 worth of business from shop owners who had spotted her boxes in other shops.

"My handpainted work is always signed and dated," says Pamela Spinazzola. "Each item comes with matching gift and product tag, usually with matching ribbons. Buyers love this kind of attention to details and product presentation."

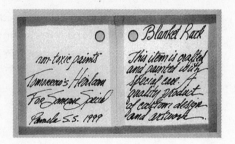

(Pamela says she always uses a liberal amount of ribbon on her tags because it is attention-getting and pleasing to customers.)

"You create a wonderful product—finish it with a tag," says Rita O'Hara, who creates a line of artful and fragrant clay bisque products called Stoneware. "My name stays with my product, and that builds name recognition in buyer's eyes. That's where I get most of my new customers nowadays; a retailer shops a store, sees my name, and tracks me down from the product info on the back of the tag."

Many sellers complain that shops remove the part of their hang tag that has their name and address, making it impossible for shoppers or other retailers to contact them directly. But Rita has cleverly solved this problem, and her "secret" could be worth thousands of dollars to you.

"First," she says, "you must put pertinent information on your tag so shops won't be tempted to remove it, such as care instructions or a comment about different ways to use the product. Second, position your name and address info on the other side of the tag *directly behind your pertinent information* so they can't remove one without removing

Notice the placement of Rita O'Hara's address information on this sample tag. It's deliberately positioned so shop owners can't remove it without losing the tag's sales-boosting copy.

(front)   (back)

These small flyers offer copywriting examples of the kind of information that helps sell products. They are normally included with products sold at fairs or by mail.

phillippa k. lack
2923 Pioneer Avenue
Cheyenne, WY 82001
307 • 635 • 4657 (phone)   307 • 632 • 3453 (fax)
Internet www.silkbyphil.com email phil@silkbyphil.com

About the Artist . . .

I began painting, on paper, at an early age, and received certificates from the Royal Academy of Art in London for my efforts. Drawing was always a favorite hobby, and I did many pen-and-ink studies of Jamaican flowers and plants. I find that my painting enables me to cope with the stresses of everyday life; it is my meditation. My work and the colors I use vary with my moods, so it is wise to be in a positive frame of mind when beginning work! I draw inspiration from Nature: bright, calypso colors from Jamaica; moody blues from the Pacific; rich, russet tones from the Southwest.

A truly international entity, I was born and raised in Jamaica of English, Scots, Portuguese, Jewish, and Creole ancestry. My family and I have lived all over America, coming to Wyoming via Texas, Arkansas, North Dakota, and California.

I was introduced to the delightful medium of silk painting by a good friend, Madame Marie Therese Piquart, whom I met in France some 12 years ago. I was so intrigued by the beautiful scarves she painted that I asked for more information--this was a bit difficult, as she spoke almost no English, and I, no French!

Mainly self-taught in the art of silk painting, I have thoroughly enjoyed the process . . . Examples of my work are featured in the book *The Best of Silk Painting*, by Diane Tuckman and Jan Janus; apaintings were juried into *CrossCurrents*, an exhibition of contemporary art at the Walter Anderson Museum of Art in Ocean Springs, Mississippi., and also into *Women's Work*, the 11th Annual Exhibit of Fine Art by Women in Woodstock, Illinois. Showings include the San Francisco Women's Artists Gallery, the Alameda Bank, and the 595 Market Street Lobby Gallery and the Cheyenne Civic Center.

My pictures, scarves, wall hangings, greeting cards and garments are individually crafted from 100% pure silk with professional dyes.

Custom commissions are welcomed.

Art from Egg Shells

The earliest recorded instance of a decorated egg happened about 722 B.C. in China, where decorated eggs are still used as temple offerings in some places. Early Persians and Egyptians are also known to have dyed and gilded eggs. In thirteenth century England, Edward I gave eggs decorated with gold leaf, and in sixteenth century France, hinged eggs and ones cut away to reveal miniature scenes were in evidence. King Louis XV gave a gilded egg containing a Cupid to Madame du Barry. Lacquered eggs have been a tradition in Russia and Eastern Europe for 600 years.

Perhaps the most famous decorated eggs were created by the House of Faberge for the Russian Court. They began with the First Imperial Egg (which was probably inspired by a French 18th century egg) and ended only with the Russian revolution. While none were made from real egg shells, all were modeled of ivory, gold, and precious jewels to resemble real eggs.

Carrying on this tradition is Bob & Carol's Egg-Art, Limited. Bob is a retired Army officer who retired for the second time after becoming "burned-out" as a Data Processing Manager. Carol, a long time needle worker who had collected egg art for several years, asked him to take lessons in egg artistry with her from an artist 85 miles from their home who had been fashioning art objects from eggs for close to 20 years. From a desire to create beautiful and useful objects from all types of egg shells came an inclination to make them for sale to others.

Now a full time business, their work has gained them awards at art shows in five states as widely separated as Florida and New Mexico. They have been included in a hard-cover book featuring artists from across the United States commemorating the Year of American Craft, 1993. Always utilizing a real egg shell, they continue to stretch their imaginations to create designs they refer to as "simple but elegant". Each handcrafted egg is unique and no two are exactly alike. Some of their creations incorporate precious stones, thus continuing the opulent tradition of the Russian Imperial Court.

Examples of their work may be seen by visiting their web site:

http://www.egg-art.com

Bob & Carol's Egg-Art, Ltd.   (812) 527-2997
1604 N Cayuse Trail   Orders: (800) 292-0609
Greensburg, IN 47240   E-Mail:EggArtMan@msn.com

House of Threads & Wood
Specializing in String Quilted Creations

Each House of Threads & Wood product is created one at a time using a century-old technique called "string" or "strip" quilting. A patchwork method originated by Florida's Seminole Indians, the process calls for narrow strips of fabric to be sewn onto a foundation. By sewing and flipping each strip row by row, a design is formed. String quilted items are more time consuming to construct than quilted whole cloth items.

At House of Threads & Wood, each base piece is quilted in this fashion, then re-cut to size for a particular item. Hundreds of calico prints and cotton solids are rotated, creating unique one-of-a-kind products. Machine stitching is utilized for both durability and quality consistency.

True to the definition of *handmade*, House of Threads & Wood products blend or coordinate rather than match. They are designed and crafted in the USA one at a time, not mass produced.

Our truly specialized gift items are made by cottage workers—stay at home Mom's who prefer a lifestyle which allows them to work flexibly. These HTW "elves" span a three state area and most have been with us for a long time. We are family to one another, sharing ideas and suggestions, collaborating to fine tune our product line while offering functional items for home, personal and decorative use.

Most of our customers are women. The natural timestamp of fabric patterns and colors links us with the past, invoking strong, warm memories—a trip to Grandma's or the old quilt you carried around as a child. We treasure these pieces of yesteryear and pass them on.

Affordable quilted accessories are the backbone of House of Threads & Wood. Single family owned and operated since 1981, our products are made to help you every day or to give as cherished collectibles.

Thank you for your interest in our items and we hope you enjoy your purchase.

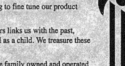

the other. Smart retailers know that hang tags help sell products, and they won't remove a good sales-boosting tag even if it means they have to leave address information on it." (See illustration).

Create an "Artist Card." To convey your professionalism, design an "artist card" that speaks of your experience or shares the story behind your art, craft, or business. Such cards (which can be printed either on card stock or paper) will make your products seem more valuable to customers and enable you to get higher prices for everything you sell, whether you're selling at a local crafts fair or wholesaling to stores across the country. (See illustrations.)

Ask for Testimonials from Satisfied Customers. After a customer has made a purchase at a crafts fair, tell them you are doing market research and would like to know why they selected that particular piece. See if they will comment on the quality of your work, the materials you've used, the colors, or how the product has touched their heart or nostalgic button, etc. In asking this question, I predict you'll often be astounded by the simplicity of their answers and the reasons for their purchase. If you like the comment you've received, jot it down and ask if you can use it in your brochure. When you get home from the show, send them a form with the quote you want to use (write it to your advantage; they won't remember exactly what they've said), and have them sign and return it. Use their full name, city and state, but no address. (Never use testimonials like "J.C., Chicago," which are useless.)

How to Get Repeat Business

"An existing customer should be recognized as a valuable asset," says Barbara Arena. "You must cultivate an ongoing rapport with your customers, a system of communicating with them at least four times a year. NCA does this by sending its members a free monthly newsletter by first-class mail. It allows us to provide them with news they can use, but it's also a vehicle for us to offer new products or services. As a result, we benefit from additional sales to existing customers while maintaining an open rapport with them. It allows the customer to feel connected to us."

Many sellers who have computerized their buyer lists don't use those mailing lists for marketing purposes. What a mistake! Every product or service seller can benefit from periodic mailings to their list of buyers, and many would also profit from mailings to their prospect list as well. Here are examples of how to stay connected to your customers and increase sales through regular mailings to them. Craft fair sellers, in particular, should pay attention to this advice.

Send an Announcement. Meg Sullivan started with a promotional newsletter that quickly became cost-prohibitive. Now she sends only postcards, making mailings eight to ten times a year to

What You Have in Common with Wal-Mart

As time goes on, there is more competition in the art/crafts world. That means you have to be more creative to get your market share. When times are tight, most businesses back down and try to cut corners. But that means fewer customers, which means less income, which means more backing down and cutting more corners. Research has shown that when times are tight, the person or company that is more creative and offers more instead of less has a big advantage. In fact, a creative person or business can do really well in tight times because the competition is less.

At a time when other retailers were raising prices and tightening return policies to compensate for a sinking profit margin, Sam Walton of Wal-Mart offered more in his field with lower prices and a liberal return policy. Then he promoted his image of a store that puts the customer first. To reinforce this image, he used employees and their families in advertising. In his daily visits to his many stores, Walton had contact with both customers and employees. He found out what the public wanted most, provided it, and then advertised it to the max. The reason Walton is a success is not that he provided extra services, but that he let the public *know* he provided them.

continued on following page

continued from previous page

A one-person business may not seem to have much in common with a huge company like Wal-Mart, but the difference is mainly in size. A small business still has to handle accounting, manufacturing, distribution, payroll, taxes, etc. Sam Walton found out what the customer wanted, provided it, then let everyone know he provided it. *Too many artists/crafters do everything right but don't advertise.* In the art/crafts field, advertising is mostly what is said to the prospective customer by the artist/crafter. Too many times creative people are reluctant to blow their own horn. But this is selling the customer short (or not selling at all) because the customer is not being made aware of the great product that is before him.

My advice is to tell your customers about the extra care you have taken to produce your work. Give them a special story to tell friends about how the quality was obtained. That's why 'imported,' 'handmade,' 'one-of-a-kind' and other adjectives are used so often to describe products. Never is the image of specialness more important than in arts and crafts. As publishers of a show guide, we have increased our business by advertising that we give special care to our subscribers, promoters, and advertisers. As an artist or craftsperson, you can also increase your business by advertising (talking about) the specialness of your work. Take a tip from Sam Walton: it isn't enough to offer something special—you must let your potential buyers know it is special.

by LaVerne Herren, reprinted by permission from Arts & Crafts Show Business.

about 400 of her prior customers. She gathers addresses from people who fill out little cards to get on her list or takes addresses off checks (after getting permission to do so).

"Our postcard mailings announce upcoming shows, may include a blurb about new items, promote the craft malls we're in, and publicize our Web site address," she says. "Sometimes we'll tell people they should bring in the postcard for a 10-percent discount on a purchase, or we'll ask them to mention the mailing to get a free keychain with any purchase."

Meg doesn't know exactly how many people come to each show because they got a postcard, only that the postcard mailings are working. "Customers who have been on our list for awhile always tells us when they come to our booth that they got our card. At times when I've tracked postcard response closely, I've found that as much as 25 percent of our sales at a show are from people who got a postcard."

Send a Thank-You Card. "It just makes good sense to stay in touch with your buyers," says Tabitha Haggie of Bunny Hutch Handcrafts, who sends regular postcards and thank-you cards to all her customers. "It's amazing the response this has generated. To everyone who buys, I send thank-you cards that match my business cards and hangtags, and people really seem to appreciate this ges-

Notice how Tabitha Haggie has designed all of her printed materials to match one another. She prints them in black ink on a rustic brown card stock.

ture. I preprint the inside message, but hand write the date, their name, and my signature. I also mail an itinerary at the beginning of the season to everyone on my database. I see this as a good customer-relations strategy."

Offer a Special Discount. One way to promote to your customer list is to offer a 10-percent discount when you invite previous buyers to a show. Joyce Birchler's business, A Glass Act, features a whimsical line of stained glass jewelry. She sends mailings to her customer list whenever a show provides her with free postcards to promote it. "I put stickers on the back of the card that read 'A Glass Act will be at this show. Bring this postcard back for a 10-percent discount on purchases.' I have been getting back anywhere from two to seventeen cards per show. Every person that brings back a card spends money, and most spend a great deal more than they would have spent if I hadn't offered a discount."

Promote to Buyers in a Particular Area Only. Jacqueline Janes of Eggplant has a database file of all customer names captured from individual shows where she has sold her handmade beads and jewelry. "Whenever I plan to return to a particular area or show, I send everyone on my list a postcard announcing the show," she says. "Such mailings may be anywhere between fifty and one hundred names. I always offer a discount to people who bring the card with them, but almost no one ever does. Yet many who visit my booth mention that they received my mailing, so I know mailings are profitable for me."

Whether shoppers bring cards back isn't important so long as the mailing brings them to the event. After Jacqueline sent her flyer and forty-five free-admission passes to a show she was doing, half a dozen people visited her booth to thank her for the pass, and they all bought something. This sounds like a successful strategy you might try if you are able to get free admission passes.

Offer a Deal. Vicky Stozich sells patterns and clothing for cement geese and bears. "Something I've done for years is send a mailing out once a year when new patterns are released," she says. "I go through my files, and everyone who has ordered from me at least once during the year (since the last mailing) gets a coupon they can return for free patterns. It is a 'Buy Two-Get-One-Free' deal

Ten Tips for Financial Success

Good marketing involves much more than just selling a product or service; you must develop special strategies for growth and greater financial success. Here is the ten-point list I developed one year when I found myself in a tough marketing situation. These things worked for me; they'll work for you, too.

1. Remain consistent in the quality of your products and services.
2. Further develop your own special style of doing business. In the end, people do business with people, not "companies" or "businesses."
3. Size up your competition. Find their weak points and capitalize on them. Fight back with appropriate marketing strategies and sales pitches.
4. More sharply identify your special industry niche and your special customer prospects; then intensify your sales/marketing activities in this direction.
5. Enlist the aid of those who believe in you and what you are doing. Figure out ways to work with others on a commission basis. Let them help you grow.
6. Get serious about managing your business. Make things happen by first making plans, then implementing them.
7. Add to your overall profits by adding new products or services.
8. Keep looking for new ways to sell everything. The possibilities are enormous and often overlooked.
9. Study the financial figures of your business to pinpoint your strongest, most profitable products and services. At the same time, look for ways to cut costs and increase profits.
10. If you do not always meet your financial goals, remember that you're doing fine when you can simply hold your position in the face of increasing competition. Longevity in one's business is an important success factor.

good for up to three free patterns (good only on older patterns, not the newly released ones.) This is my way of thanking people who have purchased from me, and I get many thank-you's from customers as a result. If your product isn't one that you could offer this kind of deal, consider sending a "Free Shipping" coupon as a thank-you. Good customer relations is the key to a successful business."

It costs very little to do a small mailing to your buyer list and, as these comments prove, this is simply "smart marketing."

RECOMMENDED TRADE MAGAZINES

The Crafts Report—The Business Journal for the Crafts Industry, Box 1992, Wilmington, DE 19899, 1-800-777-7098; On the Internet at www.craftsreport.com.

Gifts & Decorative Accessories (see resources, previous chapter).

Giftware News, Talcott Comm. Corp., 20 North Wacker, Suite 1865, Chicago, IL 60606, 312-849-2220; Web site: www.giftware-news.net.

Ornament, Ornament, Inc., Box 2349, San Marcos, CA 92079, 760-599-0222. (of special interest to anyone who makes clothing or jewelry).

Chapter Fourteen

Keeping Everything in Perspective

||||||||||||||||||||||||||||||||||||||||||

Success in business takes perseverance and courage, a positive mindset, strength of purpose, untiring discipline and determination-along with so much more in attitudes and attributes-to keep up the pace, to meet goals and set new ones, and to keep the entrepreneurial spirit alive. Faith, and believing in yourself, your uniqueness, your talents, is Number One.

—PAMELA SPINAZZOLA, PAMELA'S STUDIO ONE

Once again I find myself writing the closing chapter of another book. I'm always frustrated when I get to this point because I usually have at least 50,000 words of copy I'd like to include but can't. Publishers do have their limits as to the length of book they want to publish, and I've pushed my luck by making this one more than 25,000 words longer than requested. In this final chapter, I must therefore limit my discussion to just three topics:

➤➤ the realities of running a business at home (what you must give up to do this),
➤➤ the stress a business at home will cause (and what you can do to reduce it), and
➤➤ the importance of keeping your sense of humor (with some stories to make you smile).

NETWORKING SESSION #13: THE PERSONAL COST
OF A HOME-BASED BUSINESS

A business of your own is going to cost you something. The question is whether you're willing to pay the price. If you're just getting started in a home-based business, the following networking session will be like a dipper of cold water in your face. If you're an "old pro," you may be surprised to know how many others have made a decision similar to yours.

Home-business beginners rarely have a clue as to what's really involved in running a business at home until they actually get started. So tell me what you've given up for the sake of your business.

Dodie Eisenhauer: "What I gave up when I went into business was keeping the house clean. This in turn stops all social life because the task of cleaning looms as a huge job that I would rather die than tackle. It's one of the things that cripples me. I'm embarrassed when someone comes and would like to hang out a quarantine sign."

Pat Endicott: "I have lost most of my decorating pride in my home. It must be clean, but I no longer want all the extra 'stuff.' A woman comes every two weeks to clean, a small luxury I allow myself for something I don't have time to do."

Myra Hopkins: "Do housework? Absolutely not! Since my husband found out that my project is helping others, and I do have something special to sell, I've had a housecleaner once or twice a month, which is all it needs now that the children are grown and gone."

Joyce Roark: "I wish I could eliminate housework, but so far I haven't found anyone who wants to clean my house for the thrill of it. Paying someone to do it cuts into my profits, so I still do it when I can—just not as often as I used to."

Dodie Eisenhauer: "I would love to hire a person to clean, but I'd have to clean before she could even start. I'm certain she would never know what to do with my stuff. She might complain about cat hair. Catbert would have to conform to sleeping on a towel or live on the outside of my screen door."

I, too, have let my housecleaning "slide" (to put it mildly), but I don't have any guilty feelings about it so long as the house is picked up. (My husband doesn't share my viewpoint on this topic, but he finally realized that complaining would only lead to my insistence that he help me with the work.) Besides housecleaning, what other things have you eliminated from your life?

Deb Otto: "I've eliminated a lot of local socializing and replaced it with network socializing with other artists and crafters. I never know the local gossip, but I know who to call to get updated if necessary."

Eileen Heifner: "We, too, were forced to eliminate a personal life. Starting a new business is a backbreaking job, especially if you don't have a template of what you are doing and no help or money."

Pat Endicott: "You do lose friends when you run a business at home, but we make acquaintances along the way. Since my husband's stroke, I have made it a priority to put my church and its members and our children at the top of the list."

Kathy Wirth: "I've been forced to eliminate painting from my life. I used to enjoy painting in watercolors or acrylics, but that takes so much of the same type of creative energy that I use in my design business, that there isn't enough left over. I try to pursue hobbies that don't relate to designing, such as working puzzles, or golf. Basically, I have turned all my hobbies from the past into my business."

Annie Lang: "I've given up afternoon shopping, luncheons, and phone chit-chats to have more time for my work. No regrets, though, as I don't spend as much, keep my weight in check, and have lower phone bills than most of my friends."

What do you miss most, or regret about the things you've given up?

Chris Noah: "I miss piano-playing times. And sometimes I miss time just to sit and do nothing."

Jana Gallagher: "I regret that I do not have as much time for craft sessions with my friends. We have always enjoyed painting together and chatting, but in the past year my business has taken over so much of my life that the social aspect has almost disappeared."

Nancy Jaekel: "I gave up country dancing because business grew too fast and I didn't have the time. I do regret doing that (I gained forty pounds because of lack of exercise), but probably would have regretted not growing my business more. Life has a lot of give-and-takes. You just can't do everything."

Susan Gearing: "I regret having to give up some of the pleasure reading I used to do. But I try hard not to give up a social life or friendships outside the business, as they are important for both mental and physical health reasons. I've found that outside contacts and activities often spark my creativity in ways that are surprising. It's important for all of us not to get tunnel vision about our art or craft."

Meg Sullivan: "I miss reading, too. I used to read several books a week plus newspapers and magazines. Now, if I get the paper read a couple times a week, I feel I've accomplished something."

A business at home often creates special problems for other family members, who may feel shortchanged when the business owner doesn't have time for them. What do you do to prevent this kind of problem?

Jana Gallagher: "I do my craft production work during the day before my children get home from school, then I stop around four o'clock to spend time with the family. However, I often go back to the studio after nine and work until well after midnight during the busiest times of the year."

Jacqueline Janes: "I like to travel to shows in areas where I have family, not because I'm looking for free accommodations, but because I have so little time for social life. Being able to have breakfast or dinner with them makes me feel I am not neglecting them."

Elizabeth Bishop: "At the risk of sounding unprofessional, I have to admit that I've been forced to skimp on some of my business activities for my people priorities. I do not regret the many times I have put friends and family first; the older I get, the more this is reinforced for me. I once read that life is like juggling several glass balls; if you drop the business ball it can be mended, but relationship balls cannot. In retrospect, this approach cannot be done without the strong support of one's spouse. I want to have it all, of course, so I maneuver in that direction. For example, if my sister wants to come visit and talk about problems, I tell her I have a deadline, and if she'll chip in with filling orders or filing, we'll hurry through and then have concentrated time together. It's surprising how well this works out. People love to trade small jobs for attention, and my work is interesting to those who know me. The creative design process intrigues them. I still get friend's comments like, 'I remember when you did those quilted paintings. I got to stretch the muslin for you, then I went to a movie while you painted, and later we visited in the porch swing while the paints dried.' When work won't allow this kind of distraction, my spouse, children, family, and friends understand. I call this having it all."

Dodie Eisenhauer: "I agree with Elizabeth where family is concerned. I always stop everything and talk to my dad when he comes down in the afternoon. I can live with delays but I can never get back the visits I would miss if I don't take the time to talk to Dad."

Vicky Stozich: "The day my business takes over my personal life is the day I'll quit. Family is more important than business. I'm not trying to make a million dollars and I am not supporting a family on my income, which is basically for extra things we may need, or just to save for retirement."

It's easy to say this when you're working part-time only. But it's different when your business is your only means of support. The full-time business owner may yearn to put his or her spouse or children's needs before those of the business, but the demands of business must always be met or the bills don't get paid. And that's the worst stress of all.

Oh, the Stress of It All!

There are different kinds of stress—some good, some bad. One that is seldom discussed, especially in books like this, is the way life has forced lifestyle changes never imagined by earlier generations. Today, a growing number of men are working at home, taking care of the kids, and doing work that only women used to do. Sometimes a woman is more career-oriented or more capable of being the breadwinner, but often she falls into the position of breadwinner because her husband has lost his job due to company downsizing, a trend that seems likely to continue for some time to come. Sometimes, especially in the case of artists and craftspeople, men are staying home because they're building a home-based business that may in time support the family.

These men experience a special kind of stress, as evidenced by one letter I received from a fellow who prefers anonymity. "When I first started working full-time at home," he said, "I about drove my wife and daughter nuts. Every evening I would give a blow-by-blow description of everything I had done that day. Housework, telephone calls, my artwork, everything. I later realized that I unconsciously felt a need to justify my staying at home all day. I feel guilty, I guess. And it doesn't help that much of the time I can work a whole day on my art without others being able to see the progress I've made. The average person who gets up every morning and goes to a job that has benefits and brings in a regular paycheck doesn't need to prove himself. Our culture says they are a worthy person. I work twelve to sixteen hours a day, and sometimes wake up in my chair when a tool falls out of my hand and hits the floor, or I'm still at the bench working when my wife gets up to go to work in the morning. So how come I feel this way? I'm not as preoccupied with this now as I was in the past, but I must admit I still sometimes feel the need to justify my existence."

In a situation like this, a lot of the resulting stress could be relieved by honest discussion between the couple or whole family. The kind of overwork this artist describes often leads to burnout, a problem that seems to hit all full-time business owners sooner or later. It can be brought on by any number of things—a year of too much work and too little income, family problems, a move to a new location, illness, or simply doing the same thing for too long a time. As one business owner told me, "I let the gray-spirit get me last year, which is something I can usually overcome, being a positive person. But after a stressful year with low sales and being overly tired, I found it difficult to get excited about my new products and almost impossible to set up my dry-run version for the trade show booth. If the 'boss' has this attitude, it passes down to the workers, reflects on the phone, and keeps on going. I think most of us have a tendency to beat up on ourselves for awhile, but we must also remember that we all have a wonderful talent even if our self-image drags sometimes. I say some prayers, call some friends, and do some networking. It also helps me to take all the positive comments I've received about my products and booth layout and crow about them by writing them down so I can refer to them on gray days."

You can't just ignore this problem; you must take some kind of positive action to correct the situation. The following tips will help.

HOW TO "GEAR DOWN" AND LOWER YOUR STRESS LEVEL

One of the best ways to reduce your stress level is simply to gear down a bit. But this is easier said than done. As discussed in an earlier chapter, work does become addictive to most self-employed people, and it will be a constant struggle for you to find ways to build in some down time to relieve stress and just have a life. Kim Marie told me that she had recently confessed to her husband that she didn't know how to gear down. "Instead," she said, "I end up trying to find the motivation to gear up higher. Even when a sinus cold knocked me for a loop, I just kept working at a slower pace, feeling my body had betrayed me."

Renee Chase tells about the time she finally gave up and went to bed for a day after feeling ill for several weeks. She later learned she had an abscessed tooth; the dentist told her she had probably been running a low-grade fever for at least a month. Her experience is typical of people who work for themselves. They just keep pushing and pushing until they wear themselves down to the nubbins. As Renee told me later, "You realize you're dragging, but you just keep on going, never stopping unless you're in severe pain or seeing blood."

If we self-employed folks actually have to stop and have surgery, we simply plan a week's worth of work we can do in bed while recuperating. A few years ago when I learned I had breast cancer, my primary concern was not whether I was going to lose a breast or perhaps *die* . . . but whether the surgery could be postponed until I finished writing the newsletter I was working on. That, and whether I'd lose my hair from the radiation treatments and have to give my next keynote wearing a wig. It's funny how our sense of what's important changes when we're running a business of our own. In most cases, we tend to put our business ahead of our own health.

When I asked my book contributors what they did to gear down or lower their stress level, many commented on the rewards of reconnecting with nature by walking, sitting outdoors, feeding the ducks on the lake, sitting on a pier, going to a park, or watching the birds. To me, all of these things suggest our natural need to reconnect with God and everything He has made.

"After a marathon run on the computer, phone, copy machine, scanner, or a tedious stretch at the painting table, when I think I've 'had it,' I go sit in the backyard deck with binoculars and a cup of tea or a flute of champagne," says Susan Young. "We feed hundreds of birds, and there are a couple of families of muskrats that live down by the tiny creek that runs behind our yard. To listen to the sounds and observe these animals in their simple and often comical routines is literally a breath of fresh air. If the feeders are low, I walk out to the little barn and replenish the birdseed, always sprinkling some on the ground for the muskrats. After half an hour or so, I'm refreshed and ready to get back to work. Something in that simplicity takes away a lot of stress."

"Nature has incredible healing effects," says Chris Noah. "So does music. I play the piano. When stress levels are really high, I prefer Bach. It's total involvement, total focus. You may note that both of these activities involve all of you all the time that you're doing them. The degree of 'presentness' is as much or more than the art or craft activity done the rest of the time. They're also both very different from art or crafts work. I think this is particularly important. Many times I've found it curious that this shift in modality can be quite conducive to creativity. To ward off really high stress levels and the health hazards they may pose, it's important to monitor our inner states continuously. Being attentive to even the smallest harbingers of overstress is a learned skill. It takes only one or two panic attacks to convince a person that vigilance is a good idea. It can also save your life."

"I know about panic attacks," says Gail Platts. "I work long hours—sometimes as much as eighty-four hours a week during holiday seasons. I have learned, although slowly, that working all the time is not healthy. I was having anxiety attacks, and what I did to get them under control was get better with time-management. I got angry when the counselor said I was doing too much and had to cut some stuff, but I learned he was right."

"The best antidote of all to high stress is good planning," confirms Chris Noah. "Most of my worst stress moments have come about because I don't know exactly what I have to do in the time allotted, or even if I can do it. Solution: find out."

Like many other businesses mentioned in this book, Dodie Eisenhauer's Village Designs business has been built on faith. After a particularly stressful year of changing market conditions and heavy stress, Dodie decided to pull back a bit and "float" for awhile. "I'm like a little sail boat in a big ocean. I have my sail up, ready to go if God sends a breeze. If everything is still and quiet, I will be content to wait and pray, but I'll be alert, not sleeping. If God sends a wind, I'm off for the races!"

TEN GREAT STRESS-BUSTING ACTIVITIES

▸▸ **Take several little breaks during the day.** "My busy days are full of five-minute breaks here and there. It's the little breaks in the day instead of one big one that relieves my stress before it reaches the boiling point. When I've really overdone it, I light an aromatherapy candle, sit down in a big easy chair in a darkened room, hang a Do Not Disturb sign around my neck (handpainted, of course), and thirty minutes later, out pops a human being again." —Joann Haglund

▸▸ **Work in your garden or go fishing.** "I don't get a lot of exercise making rubber stamps or drawing, but I get some exercise caring for my big vegetable garden and flower beds. I freeze lots of sweet corn and can tons of tomatoes and pickles. My husband and I also love to fish, and our freezer is always loaded with catfish." —Sue Brown

▸▸ **Do a jigsaw puzzle.** "As an avid mystery fan, I love to do the mystery jigsaw puzzles in the "Bits and Pieces" catalog. Each is a mystery that can be solved only by putting the puzzle together. Great fun, and very relaxing." —Linda Beattie Inlow

▸▸ **Do aerobic exercise.** "After hearing about the benefits of aerobics, I finally decided to try it, meeting three times a week with a group of women at our local church. This has been the best non-business decision I have ever made because it relieves stress wonderfully (and it has also done wonders for my middle-aged body). I now have much more stamina, which has made my job and life easier. This activity has also provided me with a social outlet of women from all walks of life that I probably would not have come in contact with otherwise." —Eileen Heifner

▸▸ **Go swimming.** "I swim at least twice a week. After my workout, I lay flat on my back in the pool and float—not only do I feel like I'm being rocked in this 'water cradle,' but I can also focus on not controlling, letting go, and simply letting the water take me where it wants to go. I find this a very calming experience. Of course, this works best when the pool is vacant!" —Patricia Kutza

▸ **Schedule a "Play Day."** "Life in the 'crafting lane' is stressful; you know stress is coming, so you need to prepare to cope with it in advance. I try to schedule at least one Play Day a month. This day can include a trip to the mall, lunch with a friend, or just taking a day to work on pet projects for myself. I post my 'Play Day Possibilities' on a bulletin board near my work area in clear view where I'll notice it every day. I recently came off a strenuous three-week project. To help me get through it mentally, I could look at my posted possibilities and choose my reward when the project was completed." —Annie Lang

▸ **Treat yourself to a picnic** (or a massage). "I like to take a nature hike, packing a picnic basket with all my favorite foods/drinks/munchies. I find a comfortable spot with a gorgeous view of a river, lake, or other majestic scene and then reward myself with a short but wonderful snooze under some shade trees. Totally therapeutic! If the weather is too ugly or cold and I need a break, a total body massage is usually the perfect remedy to wipe away tense muscles, aches, and pains associated with long tedious hours of endless crafting, stitching, and designing." —Eleena Danielson

▸ **Shut everything down.** "When I'm at my wit's end, I shut down completely. Everything that can wait gets pushed aside. ('What do you mean, no clean laundry? It looks clean to me. Stand downwind!'). I just 'cocoon' with cups of tea and magazines and let the answering machine do its thing. I do not make any to-do lists, I don't say yes to anything except 'Want to order out tonight?' and I might even (gasp) keep my kids home from their after-school activities." —Liz Murad

▸ **Take a bubble bath.** "During our busiest season, my guaranteed stress-reliever is a hot bubble bath. I turn off the phone and the computer, put on soft music, and grab a romance novel and read till the water is cold." —Meg Sullivan

▸ **Leave home.** "I find it difficult to leave the worries of work behind when I am home, so I travel a fair amount for pleasure. After a day or two away from work, I can forget the stresses involved and concentrate on relaxing." —Charlene Anderson-Shea

By *Gil Gordon, from* The Complete, Unedited and Totally Hilarious Collection of "Homer" Cartoons *that originally appeared in Gordon's Telecommuting Review newsletter from 1985 to 1988. © 1991 Gil Gordon Associates. Reprinted by permission.*

Take Time to Laugh

Humor is a proven therapeutic tool—a valuable business tool that can diffuse potentially explosive situations, and a helpful tool for facilitating camaraderie. If you don't have a sense of humor at the time you start your business, you'll acquire it quickly or suffer the consequences.

"You have to roll with the punches and laugh as much as possible—the only attitude I can control is my own," says Bill Mason, who shares his least-favorite comment of all, made by a shopper who visited his art gallery. "'Man, that is some fine furniture,' he told me, obviously meaning it as a compliment. 'You made it . . . wow . . . it looks just like the stuff from the factory . . . all of it does.' Accepting the nature of all potential clients is a tool as important as any other; maybe more so, if enjoying one's work is an important aspect of doing the work and sales."

"Some people lose their sense of humor when they work alone, but mine rarely quits," says Phillippa Lack. "I figure things can only get better after you've knocked over your water container and spilled black dye all over the floor, which the cat immediately walks through."

Susan Young will identify with this story. In her book, *Decorative Painting for Fun and Profit* (Prima), she tells of the time when her cat jumped up on the washer and dryer where she had oil paintings drying. "I came home from shopping to find red paw prints leading away from the laundry room into the living room where kitty was cowering in a corner. While the ice cream melted, I worked to get the red paint off its paws. Since you can't put turpentine on a cat's paws, I tried peanut butter (simple logic, I thought at the time) and it worked. Afterwards, kitty had a good time licking the remains of the peanut butter off while I worked to remove the paint from the floor." (Have you ever noticed how the farther removed you get from a situation like this, the funnier it becomes?)

"It's always good to laugh at our mistakes," says Sue Cloutman. "I have an angel with wings and yarn hair that I make on a small scale. On one of them last Christmas, I sewed the hair on backwards so her wings ended up on her chest. I've left her hanging where I do my packaging as a reminder to laugh when I get stressed out."

"Laughing is the best thing anyone can do for themselves," says Kate Harper. "There's no time I feel more alive and at peace with the world than when I am laughing."

The Benefits of Networking

Networking with others who share your interests and ambitions may be the single most important thing you can do now and throughout the life of your business.

"I'm a one-person business with a wide support network," says Gail Platts, "and I have benefited greatly from attending monthly meetings with women business owners. We regularly share our frustrations, problem-solve, or just get a pat on the back for a job well done that, being your own boss, you never would get otherwise."

"I could never put a value on the many people I have met while being a business person, and how much they have enriched my life," says Pamela Spinazzola. "There is a lot of support and encouragement, enthusiasm, and energy within the business network community—besides what is learned and shared in talents and experiences."

Indeed, there is great healing power in laughter. It refreshes us, gives us hope, helps us overcome anger, release pent-up emotions, and softens the blows life sometimes deals. It benefits our body by reducing muscular tension and, thus, stress. A hearty laugh exercises the respiratory system (have you ever laughed so hard you could hardly catch your breath?). A hearty burst of laughter may also reduce physical pain because it releases endorphins, the body's natural painkiller. Without question, laughter provides important balance in our lives, and we can never get too much of it.

Craft Fair Humor

» **Fifteen Minutes of Fame.** "I had been featured on a public television show about artisans living in rural Maine. It won a few media awards and consequently got a lot of air time. One day while doing a summer show that was hot and slow, I took a break from my booth to sit under a nearby tree. A customer asked the person watching my booth where I was, and I was called back. The customer said, 'You're the one from the Public TV show?' I said yes, and she looked at me, smiling and nodding her head, sort of sizing me up and said, 'I just wanted to see you.' And left. I went back to my tree." —Gail Platts, InCalico

» **Always Maintain Your Demeanor.** "My husband's quips during shows nearly dissolve me in the aisle sometimes. But at all times we must be careful to maintain the proper exterior demeanor, which only makes things funnier. Tom is an astute observer of human nature, right down to the minutiae that women who peer at my art with a glasses stem in mouth never buy anything."
—Chris Noah Cooper, Paperways

» **That's One Way to Make a Sale!** At all of our craft shows, we feature cloth books for children, usually in a prominent position to attract attention. At one of these shows, as a young father was carrying his young son past our booth, the child reached out and grabbed one of these books and loudly declared, 'mine!' Despite urgent please from the father, the child would not relinquish his hold on the book. The red-faced father saved the day by writing a check

Are you old enough to know who Ish Kabibble was? He's gone now, but many years ago he was the humorous cornet player the Kay Kyser band, the one with the bangs who wrote crazy poems and added the words, "dittem, dottem whattem chu" to "The Three Little Fishies" song. You don't have to know who Ish Kabibble was to appreciate his poetry, however. Today's harried home-business owners can easily relate to this little ditty of his from an old television show:

"I've been very busy lately, going lickety-split *there*,
lickety-split *here*, lickety-split *there*.
Going to have to quit it—
I split my *lickety!*"

Keep Learning—Keep Growing

"Success doesn't come from spontaneous combustion.
You have to set your own fire!"

I like this anonymous quote, sent by Sue Cloutman. The thing that most often "lights my fire" and changes my life in some way is a new piece of information. I know, I know. We're all drowning in information—can't begin to keep up with all there is to read, to learn, to know. But as business magazine editor Jean Van Dyke once put it, "You owe it to yourself to browse, to read, to constantly seek new ideas. It keeps your mind sharp and adds to your self-worth and your value within the business community. The next idea or suggestion or technique you come across could be the one that pays off in increased quality, productivity, customer satisfaction, and, eventually, increased profits."

Clay artist Maureen Carlson was working on a book as this one was being written. She told me it was turning out to be a real education. "I thought I knew a lot until I started to learn again, then realized how much I still needed to learn." Life is like that. Just when we think we know it all, have it all under control, we learn something new that totally reshapes our thinking on a whole lot of other things; suddenly, we're off and running, learning even more, working even harder.

But be careful, folks. It's great to keep learning, to keep striving for new goals, to keep growing in your art or craft, but don't push yourself—or let others push you—beyond your limits, lest you collapse in the end with everyone losing in the bargain. Remember that *you* are in charge of maintaining your personal well-being. To succeed in both life and business, you must learn to balance the needs of those you are serving with the needs of yourself and your family.

"What should be taking priority in our lives today is not essentially any different than it was 200 years ago or even 2,000 years ago," says Laurence J. Pino, Esq., founder and president of The Open University. "Commitment to self, to family, to God, and to work must be in balance to achieve any success in life."

If you've taken the time to read this book from start to finish, I figure you've learned a lot in the process. It contains a lot of good advice, and you should pay attention to it . . . but also take it with a grain of salt. Never let others tell you how to run your life or your business. There is much to be said for following the dictates of your heart, trusting your intuition and gut instincts, and marching to the beat of a different drummer. After all, that's what being a creative person is all about.

Moving On

▸▸ "You grow most in knowledge when you are stretching yourself." —Eileen Heifner
▸▸ "Confidence has rarely been an easy commodity for me; knowledge builds it, however." —Chris Noah
▸▸ "Roadblocks? I never let them stand in my way. Whenever a door slams in my face, I find a new way to get into the building!" —Kathy Cisneros
▸▸ "The accumulation of experience and knowledge—the very building of a career—is by far the most exciting part of one's life. I needed to do things the hard way sometimes, as it takes a long time for some things to sink in." —Annie Lang
▸▸ "It took me too long to believe in myself. I bought into believing I could never make it as an artist or craftsman. For twenty years, I've lived how certain people thought I should live. Now time is on the short side, and I'm just beginning." —Kim Marie

Index